TROUBADOUR OF THE KINGDOM

TROUBADOUR OF THE KINGDOM

The Life and Times of J. Rufus Moseley, 1870–1954

GREGORY S. CAMP

Foreword by William L. De Arteaga

WIPF & STOCK · Eugene, Oregon

TROUBADOUR OF THE KINGDOM
The Life and Times of J. Rufus Moseley, 1870–1954

Copyright © 2019 Gregory S. Camp. All rights reserved. Except for brief quotations in critical publications or reviews, no part of this book may be reproduced in any manner without prior written permission from the publisher. Write: Permissions, Wipf and Stock Publishers, 199 W. 8th Ave., Suite 3, Eugene, OR 97401.

Wipf & Stock
An Imprint of Wipf and Stock Publishers
199 W. 8th Ave., Suite 3
Eugene, OR 97401

www.wipfandstock.com

PAPERBACK ISBN: 978-1-5326-7978-0
HARDCOVER ISBN: 978-1-5326-7979-7
EBOOK ISBN: 978-1-5326-7980-3

Manufactured in the U.S.A.   JULY 17, 2019

Photos courtesy of Middle Georgia Archives, Washington Memorial Library, Macon, Georgia

For Cinde:

Teacher and Example,

With Greatest Love and Gratitude

He drew a circle that shut me out—
Heretic, rebel, a thing to flout.
But love and I had the wit to win:
We drew a circle and took him in!

—Edward Markham,
　from the poem "Outwitted"

Contents

Foreword by William L. De Arteaga • ix
Acknowledgements • xi

    Introduction • 1
1   The Quest Begins • 12
2   Locusts and Wild Honey • 40
3   The Promised Land • 68
4   The Poor, the Downtrodden, and the Kingdom Response • 94
5   Approach of War • 124
6   Perfect Everything • 151
7   "I Have Run My Race" • 177

Recommended Reading • 201
Bibliography • 203
Index • 209

Foreword

Dr. Camp's biography of Rufus Moseley is both timely and necessary for our age. This work details the life and teachings of one of the holiest and most Spirit-filled persons ever to live in the United States. It shows that unfaltering Spirit-filled holiness is possible, as long as the Christian is willing to be obedient to the voice of the Spirit on all occasions.

Many Christians have been jaded by either the Catholic child abuse scandals or the scandals of the Evangelical Charismatic TV ministers. They have come to believe that great holiness is not possible in the secular world, and especially in America. As a Catholic boy attending parochial schools, I recall that several of my teachers thought America could never produce a saint as magnificent in holiness as Saint Teresa of Avila or Saint Francis of Assisi. The life and writings of Rufus Moseley proves that wrong. To boot, Moseley lived as a Pentecostal believer, and used many of the gifts of the Spirit in his life and ministry. That is something Catholic saints were often reluctant to do—think of Mother Teresa of Calcutta, who demonstrated the love of God in extravagant ways, but (so far as it is known) never the gifts of the Spirit, such as divine healing. My own work, *Agnes Sanford and Her Companions*, similarly showed the life and writings of another sanctified, Spirit-filled hero of the church who spent most of her life in Moorstown, New Jersey, as the wife of an Episcopal priest.[1]

As Dr. Camp so clearly shows us, Professor Moseley lived a life of simplicity (not to say poverty) and in extravagant, utter generosity to those in need. Dr. Camp rightly recalls similarities between his actions and those of the great saints and heroes of the Church Universal, especially Saint Francis. I am especially thankful of this aspect of Dr. Camp's writing.

Dr. Camp has researched the life and writings of Professor Moseley exhaustively. Just from a glance at his notes, one can see how intense his pursuit of the details of Moseley's life has been. Of course, other books on

---

1. De Arteaga, *Agnes Sanford*.

Moseley may stress different aspects of his life, but I do not think future books will be able to uncover much new data or documents on Brother Rufus. Dr. Camp took care to interview survivors who knew Professor Moseley in person, and that generation is fast passing.

In summary, this is a book that encourages holiness in the life of every believer. In our current moment, where we are demoralized by the uncivil discourse of our politics and the unceasing vulgarization of our culture, *Troubadour of the Kingdom* is an oasis and "pearl of great price" which I wholeheartedly commend to the reader.

WILLIAM L. DE ARTEAGA

Acknowledgements

As in the creation of any literary work, there are a great many people to thank. I begin doing so by thanking the administration and employees of the Washington Memorial Library of Macon, Georgia, where the Middle Georgia Archives is housed, for their assistance. Likewise, the many friends I made in Macon at High Point Church and the Covington House Church all provided guidance and sage advice throughout. Those who stand out in this regard are Pastor Trey Dickerson and his wife Shannon, Bobby and Joyce Covington, Caroline Harvey, Julie Dumas, Fred Remick, Patrick and Velvet Cramer, Don and Charlotte Van Hoosier, and Donna Nye.

In Bismarck, North Dakota, I have many to thank, beginning with my mother, Dolores Camp, as well as my late father, Harry. Both of them never doubted me and cheered me on when I sometimes wondered about the sagacity of the project. Pastor Kurt Chaffee and the congregation of New Song Church in Bismarck, North Dakota were from early on great sources of teaching and support. And of course, my children, Arlo, Aaron, and Abigail were sources of strength as well.

William De Arteaga and Jack Taylor were also sources of encouragement. From their lives as scholars and ministers came advice and suggestions that proved truly invaluable. Likewise, Vinson Synan was kind enough to read the manuscript when it was still in rough form and offered words of advice and encouragement. To Rufus Moseley's living relatives, in particular the Diana Vinson family of Byron, Georgia, their kindness and generosity in making "Uncle Ruf's" records available is greatly appreciated. Both for this biography of their eminent relative as well as the anthology of his writings, their assistance was invaluable.

Most of all, I owe a tremendous debt of gratitude to Cinde Mittuch, whose friendship, love, and example drawn from a life of humility and service provided me with needed encouragement and spiritual advice. On many occasions, when I could not see the end of the project, she was there with a kind word and uplifting spirit that invariably gave me strength to go on.

This Rufus Moseley project, as of this writing, is in its sixth year. It has included the collection and transcribing of some 1,300 of his articles and speeches, speaking with his family and others who knew him, and finding no small amount of amazement that he is not more widely known. It is been a journey of joy and hardship, but most of all one of spiritual growth as I learn of this singular Christian and the simplicity in which he lived.

Gregory S. Camp
February 22, 2019

Introduction

A Modern Francis Of Assisi

God, of your goodness, give me Yourself; You are enough for me, and anything less that I could ask for would not do You full honor. And if I ask anything that is less, I shall always lack something, but in You alone I have everything.

—Julian of Norwich

When Joel Rufus Moseley (1870–1954) set about to write his autobiography, *The Quest*, later entitled *Manifest Victory*, friends warned him that he would have to undergo suffering, crucifixion, and resurrection. In my own telling of Rufus's testimony, I have found the same to be true. Attempting to properly convey the story of this remarkable saint in a manner that captures his life and ministry is no easy task, at times bordering on the overwhelming. He was at once a very complex man, yet also lived a Christian life that was the very definition of simplicity and humility. While a spiritual giant, he was also an intellectual of the first order, taking undergraduate and graduate degrees at Peabody, University of Chicago, Harvard, and was a fellow at Heidelberg University in Germany.

Earlier in his life, he had been a university professor and scholar, journalist, and social activist. Yet he left a promising career in higher education to live in total abandonment to Christ, what he called "Life as Love," or what the apostle Paul called "faith that works by love." By this he meant a life that was drawn from a place of ineffable union in Christ. Far more than a mere mental assent to "union," he would not accept simple affirmation for belief in Christ to take the place of actual experience, something gained through yielding, obeying, and ever seeking God. His was a rare walk in the Spirit, taking Christ at his word and accepting nothing less than total surrender to His call.

Moseley's calling to give the love of Jesus to each and all also mandated that he fellowship and share with those with whom he might have theological differences. Earlier in his life, Rufus had been involved in some of the Mind Sciences, Christian Science in particular, a group he left when he received the baptism of the Holy Spirit in 1910. Throughout his life, he continued to minister among those of the Mind Science background, hoping to lead those receptive to a place of orthodox Christian belief. This outreach was something not always understood by his Pentecostal contemporaries, some of whom demanded he harshly denounce them. He refused to do this, not because he held to their metaphysical beliefs, but because he knew some of them were receptive to the wooing of the Holy Spirit. He defined his calling as:

> to abide in Jesus all the time and give his love to everybody and to report as best I can the light that he makes clearest. What I have to give fits in everywhere there is belief in and love for Jesus and for his love-way of life. So I go among all groups; seeking to bless everywhere. I belong everywhere there is an open door and freedom of the Spirit, and yet I belong nowhere in a sectarian and denominational sense.[1]

I know of few Christians over the course of the twentieth century who more successfully lived a life from that place of union with Christ than Rufus Moseley, yet part of the reason he is not more widely known today is because of those very qualities of humility that drew him on. It is thus with the utmost sense of honor and respect that I attempt to again introduce Rufus to a new generation of believers who have so much to learn from the simplicity and Life as Love, something he also referred to as "manifest victory." One who knew him well described Moseley as follows: "If you were to add to a small boy's joy in roaming fields and woodland with the adult sense of wonder and awe that sometimes attends our view of the starry heavens above, you might get a suggestion of Rufus'[sic] abiding appreciation and love of the external order."[2] His walk and revelation reveal missing elements in contemporary Evangelical and especially charismatic Christianity, namely pushing on to the Life as Love. Too often, at least in recent times, the primacy of the love walk has been overshadowed with programs, experiences, meetings, personalities or leaders, national politics, power, and money.

One will find that Moseley embodied what many other great Christian mystics and saints before him sought and lived: Francis of Assisi, Brother

---

1. Moseley, "Spirit of Jesus."
2. McLain, *Resurrection Encounter*, 182.

Lawrence, Catherine of Genoa, John Wesley, Charles Finney, Dwight Moody, and Henry Drummond, to name but a few. He greatly loved these great champions of the faith from days gone by, but was careful to make sure his walk with Christ was entirely, uniquely, his own. Rufus frequently warned that anyone following another teacher, however well-meaning, is faced with the real possibility of falling into a ditch when the teacher falls. Moseley knew this and resisted the temptation, and throughout his life encouraged all to believers with whom he spoke to seek union for themselves. As he often said, he could not be a disciple of a disciple, but must be a firsthand disciple of Christ for himself.

There was another Moseley biography, Wayne McLain's *A Resurrection Encounter* (1997), published some thirty-three years after Rufus's death. An excellent book, McLain's telling of Rufus's story stems from his personal knowledge of the man during his twilight years. While McLain sought to frame Moseley's life and teaching in terms of the theological and philosophical trends of the day, it is my hope that what I can provide will go beyond this. In an effort to explore his various and sundry experiences in the sometimes-rowdy days of early Pentecostalism to its maturing in the mid-twentieth century, I have included many of his interactions with leading members of that group as well as others. Mine is not a scholarly approach, but an honest effort to provide the reader with a more human view of the man and his ministry. His writings, public and private, and interviews with family members and others who knew and were influenced by him make up the overwhelming majority of source material, most of which has not been seen or heard in decades. It is my hope that the result is the framing of a life and ministry that begs to be told, especially in the times the American church finds itself today. This troubadour, this minister of the power of God's love, has a message that if listened to will show a simplicity and depth of Christianity that will at the same time awe and humble.

The reader will find that Rufus Moseley does not fit any neat categories in terms of his beliefs and teachings. He was a liberal holding some conservative beliefs; he was orthodox, yet also broke that mold; he was Pentecostal, yet did not adhere to all of its tenants. He belonged to no church or denomination, and believed that at least for himself and his calling, membership would throw up barriers to those he wanted to reach. Although humble and teachable, he would not be swayed by opposition, criticism, or praise. In his quest for God's best, he would not—in the words of Ralph Waldo Emerson—be swayed by the combined opinion of mankind.

The life of Rufus Moseley was one of those rare visitations God bestows upon the planet that both blesses and perplexes all who encountered such people. Even today, the few who know of him do not entirely know what to make of him, for his walk in Christ was quite different from many of his contemporaries. A kind and gentle man with steel-grey eyes, short and slight of physical stature, Rufus possessed and was possessed by a life in the Holy Spirit that both amazed and confounded. Moseley was a mystic in the best sense of the word. He did not like the term applied to himself because of negative connotations it might summon, but instead called himself a "first-hander," meaning he had a firsthand relationship with Christ.[3] As a contemporary of his, A. W. Tozer, was to describe this mysticism in his *Christian Book of Mystical Verse*:

> The word "mystic" refers to that personal spiritual experience common to the saints of Bible times and well known to multitudes of persons in the post-Biblical era . . . [the] evangelical mystic has been brought by the gospel into intimate fellowship with the Godhead . . . He differs from the ordinary orthodox Christian only because he experiences his faith down in the depths of his sentient being while the other does not. He exists in a world of spiritual reality. He is quietly, deeply, and sometimes almost ecstatically aware of the presence of God in his own nature and in the world around him. His religious experience is something elemental, as old as time and the creation. It is immediate acquaintance with God by union with the Eternal Son. It is to recognize that which transcends knowledge.[4]

But of all the mystics and saints in church history, perhaps Rufus's favorite was Francis of Assisi (1181–1226 AD).

Rufus Moseley and Francis of Assisi's lives, values, beliefs, and walk with Christ in many ways mirrored each other. Like Francis, Rufus was about simplicity itself, whether involving his relationship with Christ or his standard of living. After a coxcomb's life of revelry and opulence, Francis embraced what he called "Lady Poverty" and insisted that those who joined his brotherhood do the same.[5] The idea was to embrace an utter rejection of the pursuit of material things so as to place the believer into an all-or-nothing approach to being a disciple of Christ. For his part, in 1900 Rufus left a life of honor and privilege as a respected university professor as part of his spiritual quest, eventually coming to a place ten years later when he received the baptism of the Holy Spirit; he became, like Francis, "God's Fool."

---

3. McLain, *Resurrection Encounter*, 210.

4. Tozer, *Christian Book of Mystical Verse*, vi.

5. Chesterton, *Saint Francis of Assisi*, 81; see also Thompson, *Francis of Assisi*; and Vauchez, *Francis of Assisi*; Bonaventure, *Life of St. Francis*; Sabatier, *Road to Assisi* (edited version of the Sabatier classic biography of Francis); and Odo, *Journey and the Dream*, for fine accounts of the life and teachings of this remarkable saint.

In those early days, this once noted rising star in American higher education was looked upon by many as someone who had quite lost his mind. In the second decade of the twentieth century, he entered his own wilderness time, a period when he was widely considered a nobody as a result of his life and spiritual choices. Rufus understood Francis, who himself experienced rejection, very well.

As I pondered the approach to this biography, I frequently thought of Francis of Assisi, the positive influence he had on Rufus Moseley, and how very alike they were. Not that he followed the Umbrian mendicant in a doctrinaire fashion—Rufus never did anything in that frame of mind—but as one who like Moseley gave up everything to follow the Christ they both had come to love. Francis, being an obedient servant of the church, went so far as to seek the unusual permission of Pope Innocent III for the privilege of owning nothing; Rufus sought to have nothing material, be it money or possessions, have any hold on him. Francis said, "Above all the graces and all the gifts which the Holy Spirit gives to His friends, is the grace to conquer one's self, and willingly to suffer pain, outrages, disgraces, and evil treatment for the love of Christ."[6] Moseley responded with the simple necessity of seeking only to be in union with Christ and welcome the trials such a life was sure to summon. Rufus Moseley wrote of Francis:

> In the early part of his Christian life when he made the great resolve to be as poor as Jesus and so far as possible, be as loving, kind, and compassionate as he who received the worst indignities that a son could receive from his father, and that a gentle soul could receive from the rough and cruel who do not understand. So far as the records tell the story, there is no indication but that he failed to meet everything in the spirit of him who commanded us to turn the other cheek, and to love and bless those who attempt to do the worst to us.[7]

Neither Francis nor Rufus sought poverty for its own sake, but for the sake of living in perfect Christian love and the freedom. Both saw "that as long as one man gave himself to his acres, and another to his gold, the highest in man is crowded out,"[8] and "If we had any possessions, we should need weapons and laws to defend them."[9] Both men lived lives of remarkable simplicity and therefore free to follow the promptings of the Holy Spirit

---

6. Sabatier, *Life of Francis of Assisi*, 138–39.
7. Moseley, "St. Francis of Assisi," December 4, 1927.
8. Moseley, "St. Francis of Assisi," December 4, 1927.
9. Chesterton, *Saint Francis of Assisi*, 80.

wherever he may lead. They lived to serve others, and their lives had all the appearances of a grand spiritual adventure.[10]

A few words should perhaps be said about the troubadours of the thirteenth century, since I have seen fit to use the appellation to describe both Saint Francis and Rufus. During the Middle Ages, there were troupes of minstrels, usually traveling in pairs, who went the length and breadth of France and Italy entertaining the nobility with songs of love and heroism, and extolling values such as chivalry thought to be worthwhile. To be sure, bawdy songs lampooning institutions were also common, making them sometimes unpopular with the powers that be. Still others propagated teachings such as the Cathar heresy, something sure to draw Rome's ire. Some were even burned at the stake when they went too far. But on the whole, the nobility looked upon these traveling minstrels with favor and welcomed and sponsored them.

Rufus Moseley, though a deep spiritual seeker, was not an ascetic in the classical sense of the word. He loved life, enjoyed being with people, and saw ministry to the lowly as the highest of honors, undertaken with joy. Like Francis of Assisi, he was not called to a cloistered life wherein rules of a specific Order may be in place, sometimes blocking the very path it was meant to open up. Even in the Middle Ages, Francis saw this and sought to have his brotherhood free from such encumbrances. Francis's approach was radical in its time: teaching Christianity outside of the walls of a monastery or parish, on the level of the common man. So, too, did Moseley embrace the path of simplicity and gave himself to ministry to the commoner, mostly to those whom society had rejected. Because of this, Rufus would often be misunderstood. Although holding to many of its beliefs, Rufus was outside of Pentecostalism when it became doctrinaire or sought to control him. His view was that the spiritual life in Christ is one that is at once highly personal while at the same time inclusive of other brothers and sisters in the faith with whom he may have disagreements. The same holds true with regard to his view of the natural world.

Rufus loved nature and spent a great deal of time outdoors. He was an environmentalist before the term came into popular use, seeking to protect nature from the ravages of the human race and descrying it when he came aware of it. Like Francis, Moseley saw the natural world as something to be treasured. Francis went so far as to describe nature as being bound together in the Spirit, not in a pantheistic sense, but that God is evident in everything from humans to blades of grass. He would refer to Brother Sun, Brother Fire, Sister Moon, and Sister Water, and saw all things as being interconnected in God. Francis's "Canticle of the Creatures" speaks of this in most endearing

---

10. Spoto, *Reluctant Saint*, xviii.

terms. Moseley, too, highly valued the environment around him and spoke against the increased pillaging of the earth in the interests of industry and profit. Some of his loftiest spiritual moments were spent in the mountains, but as he came to travel further, he found a delight in all terrains.

There was one significant difference between these two saints: Francis was the happiest during the early days of his ministry, while Moseley found that his joy increased as the years passed. Francis suffered when he witnessed his brotherhood become an established order and the simplicity he sought to exemplify eroded. Rufus, too, suffered to see that much of Christianity, at least in the United States, was predominantly superficial, nominal, and the richness of a life hid with Christ in God largely rejected. Few across the span of Church history have lived in such rare simplicity, unselfishness, and love as did these two singular men. Both gave Christ's love to each and all without reservation, convinced it was the salvation of the world, and their example would be a beacon to others.

It is for that reason that I chose to entitle this biography *Troubadour of the Kingdom*, a phrase also once used to describe Francis. For both men were just that: Troubadours for the King and kingdom, seeking to impress upon all the joy of living in unimpeded pursuit of God, and of the Holy Spirit's providing to his seeking children the means to live it. Too much of Christianity, during both Francis's and Rufus's time, is bound up in a passive willingness to live in the borderlands of the kingdom when Christ provided the means to live in inward spiritual bounty. Although it is a rare portion these two lived and experienced, both were candidly clear that it was available to all; it is the life they both called to believers to again seek with all their heart. To a remarkable degree of similitude, Rufus Moseley and his thirteenth-century counterpart were traveling spiritual minstrels, and though separated by some eight hundred years, were generally welcomed by all as being genuine and well-meaning, even humorous. This is not to say that their audiences were always receptive, or that they never met with opposition. Both men found that to be a follower of Christ necessitates suffering and rejection. But on the whole, Francis and Rufus found that as they became better known, and the nature of their ministries clarified, they were welcomed and given opportunities to speak with some of the movers and shakers of their respective eras. But both men looked first to the poorest and neediest to bring their songs of joy.

Throughout the life and teachings of Rufus Moseley, there was a call for simplicity, of putting God first, and then believing Christ to keep his word. "Our only responsibility," he was fond of saying, "is the responsibility to remain in union with Him." That ineffable union with Christ of which he spoke was one in actuality and experience, a life of unfettered bliss, joy, and glory, regardless of life's maelstroms. Like anyone else, Moseley experienced setbacks in life, even being called to endure great physical suffering and emotional pain. He nonetheless embraced them as the means, the "cruciform" (to borrow a phrase Ann Voskamp used) of bringing him to an ever greater knowledge of God.[11] In that sense, he had been given heavenly kingdom keys. Not in the sense that he had some special revelation that was available to only the select few, nor that he would dole it out to only the "deserving" or those who considered themselves advanced in Christ's service. It was stark spiritual simplicity: there were no meetings to attend, no personalities to seek out, no money to give, no books and DVDs to purchase for step-by-step instructions; it was a free gift he had come to understand and experience, and was told to share with all who would listen. Like Francis, there was nothing at all of elitism about him.

What mystics have extolled as contemplation was what Moseley found and described as the perpetual seeking and then finding the realm of undisturbed rest. Just as one who, when submerged under the waves of a stormy sea, finds the water quite undisturbed, so too is that inward place free from the clamor and cacophonous noise around us. It is a matter of learning to stay there in good times or bad. Still, some who met Rufus thought him hopelessly optimistic, that his belief in this "Life as Love" was quite impossible in the here and now. One of his young protégés stated as much after his initial contacts with him, holding that Moseley's belief that love, as taught in the Sermon on the Mount (what Rufus called the Inauguration Address of the kingdom of God) was not possible in the actual world. His young friend thought Moseley lacked the realism and understanding of the harsh realities humans regularly encounter. Yet from both study and personal experience among the poorest of the poor, there have been few more aware of the true nature of the world than Rufus Moseley. Coupled with his honest and utterly sincere approach, he believed the worst things in the world could be overcome with Christ's love, because, as Paul tells us in 1 Corinthians 13, "Love never fails."

Several people who knew Rufus well said that he was the happiest man they had ever known. He often laughed, encouraged, and exhorted, and, like Francis of Assisi, was a messenger of joy. He inwardly burned with this joy and sought to pass it on to others, and did so even when he was met with rejection (and he encountered that often). One of Rufus's young friends said that when in Rufus's presence he never had the feeling of being with someone elderly, that Rufus never seemed bored and embodied a childlike joy. He was, his friend shared, "continuously in the quest for the highest" and

---

11. Voskamp, *Way of Brokenness*, 230–31.

constantly found it in his daily experience.[12] Although he had no known personal enemies, he had suffered from the slings and brickbats directed his way from believers who considered him to be unorthodox and therefore suspect; indeed, some Pentecostals had trepidation about him because of the great freedom in which he lived. This resistance extended to some in his family, too. Moseley lived with his younger brother Millard and family, and sometimes met with opposition there, as well. They did not always understand his spiritual life, nor did some other relatives. Despite the occasional calumny and ridicule from loved ones, something that doubtless was a source of pain for him, he spoke of familial tension only once that I have found, and then did not elaborate. Nonetheless, he constantly spoke well of his family and praised them, something he did throughout his life.

Although born and raised in the mountains of western North Carolina, Rufus lived the majority of his life in the central Georgia area, where he learned humility and performed some of the most menial tasks as part of his ministry: visiting prisoners, especially those on death row; the hospitalized or otherwise sick; the poor and destitute; and racial minorities who suffered from white bigotry and hate. These were all part of his daily experience. Although it was to be but a limited part of his life, he also became familiar with the world of pecan farming, and from this he drew a limited income. Besides travel and ministry to the poorest, one of his other callings was that of a writer.

Other than his weekly religion column for the *Macon Telegraph*, he authored two books: his autobiography, *Manifest Victory* (1941), and a work on the ministry of the Holy Spirit, *Perfect Everything* (1949). Although they receiving glowing reviews, the books were not widely known to the Christian reading public, then or now. Some theologians of the day from a variety of Christian traditions considered these two works to be superb modern embodiments of mystical Christianity, ranking them with the great historical works of the faith. Despite this, he is virtually unknown to the early twenty-first-century American believer.

By allowing the "Life as Love" to inform his walk in Christ, he took up writing for and against social and political positions in his day. Nowhere was this seen in a greater degree than in Moseley's opposition to capital punishment and Jim Crow laws in the South. He was a vocal champion against the dehumanizing effects of racial segregation, even when it meant being criticized for doing so, not infrequently from fellow Christians. Indeed, his willingness to speak at black churches cost him invitations from white houses of worship many times over the years. But whatever his outspoken

---

12. McLain, *Resurrection Encounter*, 50.

views for or against any position, he always tempered his opinions with the revelation of the Love of God and its availability for believers, and its power to change the worst of human behaviors.

If you are looking for a boisterous, bumptious, in-your-face Christian personality, Rufus Moseley will disappoint you. Besides, the world is already filled with such. Likewise, if in reading his essays you are looking for a didactic presentation of theology, you will likely find this lacking as well. For while Rufus Moseley had a first-rate mind and was educated at some of the finest schools in the Western world, his strength in speaking and writing was in his preternatural ability to sum up deep theological truth in a sentence or two. A stranger to circumlocution, his brief descriptions often leap off the page, causing one to laugh aloud at the depth of revelation before you. These truths were often shaped and presented in humor, and humor was one of the hallmarks of his character. Those who knew him best often stated that he always seemed in a jocular mood, offering homespun stories that delighted as much as instructed his readers/listeners. In 2016, I published an anthology of some of his newspaper columns between 1927 and 1937 entitled *Ineffable Union with Christ: Living in the Kingdom*, that captures some of his writings from the period. By no means a comprehensive list of his work, it nonetheless provides the reader with a sense of the man and his ministry.[13]

Rufus Moseley was a man born out of time, at once a throwback to an earlier period in Christianity and so unusual that that he garnered the attention of most everyone he met. Ever the peacemaker, he possessed a supernatural ability to bring people together, often those who might otherwise have harsh disagreements. While Rufus was friends with many Pentecostal leaders and laity, his circle of friends also included many other prominent Christian seekers of like mind and spirit outside of that circle, either knowing them personally or having kinship as a result of their writings, or both: E. Stanley Jones, Frank Laubach, Sadhu Sundar Singh, Toyohiko Kagawa, Frank Buchman, Henry Sloan Coffin, Harry Emerson Fosdick, Karl Barth, Glenn Clark, C. S. Lewis, Agnes Sanford, Evelyn Underhill, Edwin Poteat, Samuel L. Gordon, and numerous others are frequently mentioned in his writings. Near the end of his life, he spoke of hearing and in some cases meeting people like Oral Roberts and Billy Graham, and rejoiced in the ministry of these up and comers.

This is not to say that he always agreed with all of his friends, but Moseley was the sort who overlooked dissimilarities and sought to bring people together in love. The last ten years of his life, his influence on the

---

13. See Camp, *Ineffable Union with Christ*.

national level also increased, as he and some of his friends acted as advisors to Franklin Roosevelt, Harry Truman, and Dwight D. Eisenhower. He also periodically corresponded with India's Mahatmas Gandhi. All of this, however, was to come at a cost once the Cold War heated up and McCarthyism spread its pernicious fear. The reader will also find that I repeatedly refer to two of Rufus's young protégés, Tommy Tyson and Wayne McLain. Both of these Christians were privileged fellow-travelers with Moseley in his later years, and found their own lives and ministries enriched as a result. Tommy Tyson, in particular, would go on to have a profound impact on the Camps Farthest Out group, Oral Roberts University, and the charismatic movement in general.

To the end of his life, Rufus Moseley was a firm believer in and an example of the love of Christ. He personally demonstrated that a life lived in a place of love, joy, peace, mercy, and long-suffering was not only true, but available. His theology ripened and matured as the 1930s became the 1940s, and by his life's end, he had come to exemplify the Savior like few others. When he passed away in 1954, preachers nationwide who knew him felt ill-qualified to preach at the funeral. Yet this reaction was the very antithesis of what he was about, as any who knew him even briefly came away with a sense that he was among the humblest human beings they had ever met.

It is my profound hope that as you are introduced to Rufus Moseley and his way of life, you recognize in it a radical form of Christianity that is powered by the love of God unlike anything you are likely to have encountered. I also heartily encourage you to read his autobiography, *Manifest Victory*, recently back in print after being unavailable for decades. It is my hope that his work on the ministry of Holy Spirit, *Perfect Everything*, something of a sequel to *Manifest Victory*, will likewise again become available to the Christian reading public. Moseley will challenge you, call into question ideas you may hold dear, but always from a thoroughly scriptural point of view. That he seems different from his peers then and now is not so much a testament to his uniqueness as it is to how terribly far American Christianity has allowed itself to be taken over by the unnecessary, the superfluous, and even the dangerous. Like Francis of Assisi, J. Rufus Moseley was forgotten by a generation that followed him, or if remembered, in an often misinformed way. He was revolutionary in the best sense of the word, challenging assumptions, showing a better way of life in Christ, and joyfully laughing, always in delight at the world about him and Christ's willingness to bring his creation back to himself. He was truly a troubadour of the kingdom.

1

The Quest Begins

1870–1909

Let us begin, brothers, to serve the Lord God,
for up until now we have made little or no progress.

—Francis of Assisi

Joel Rufus Moseley was born in 1870 in the foothills of the Blue Ridge Mountains of western North Carolina near the village of Elkin. The fourth of eight children, Rufus entered the world at a time when Reconstruction was still in effect and the long and painful process of reuniting the nation after the Civil War was underway. During this period, federal troops occupied the defeated South, a harsh reminder of the failure of the Confederate cause. His father, James "Cubby" Moseley, had served in the Confederate Army with a North Carolina unit, and had his health compromised as a result of the war. Devout Christians, James and Theresa Moseley raised their children in a Primitive or "Hardshell" Baptist tradition. His parents were well-liked in the community, and many of their friends sought to help the Moseley children in any way they could. Indeed, community concern for all children in the area was common in a manner not often seen today, and Rufus was no exception to this. He liked to describe his youth and family life in this pastoral setting as ideal "seed, soil, and climate," and as preparation for his later ministry.[1]

---

1. Moseley, *Manifest Victory*, 39–40.

Rufus spoke with great love, respect, and pride that his father was the most honest man he had ever known. For instance, if selling produce at market, James Moseley would place the larger items below the smaller ones, and if selling a mule or piece of equipment, would set forth in great detail the faults of the item to be sold. He would then offer his own idea of what the livestock, produce, or equipment was worth. This even extended to periodic tax assessor visits, where he would review his property and give his honest opinion of what he thought the property was worth should he want to sell it. James's reputation as an honest man and a pillar of the mountain community was widespread. Often with his parents because he was a sickly child, Rufus also recalled his father's concerns in the morning that his children not overwork at their chores in the heat of the day. Often riding a mule, his father took Rufus with him on his various errands and told him of his hopes and dreams for the family and future. From this example, Rufus gained an appreciation for what he would later term "utter sincerity" in one's dealings with all people. When coupled with what he would later call "Life as Love," these early lessons were to provide the bedrock for a simplicity and honesty that is, by today's standards, startling in its purity.[2]

Rufus's mother, Theresa, was likewise a treasured memory, and he described her as a woman of great faith and a powerful prayer warrior. Early on, his mother made sacrifices for the Moseley children's education, and would often oversee their tending to their lessons while she went about her daily tasks. These chores ranged from such frontier fare as tending beehives and washing, mending, or making clothing to drying fruit and vegetables for family consumption. Moseley once shared how whenever there was any decision—seemingly large or small—that came before the family, his mother would disappear into the woods for quiet time in prayer and not return until she felt that she had heaven's answer. This even extended to what crops to plant. As a result of much prayer and specifically asking about her children, Theresa believed she heard from the Holy Spirit that one of her children would be used in a great way for the kingdom of God, and thought it might be her son Millard, one of Rufus's younger brothers.[3] Though she never revealed her conviction that it would be Millard until later in life, and then apparently only to Rufus, it doubtless provided Moseley with a framework and expectation that God could and would reveal himself on a personal level.[4]

---

2. Moseley, *Manifest Victory*, 40.
3. Moseley, *Manifest Victory*, 40–41; McLain, *Resurrection Encounter*, 32.
4. McLain, *Resurrection Encounter*, 33.

Moseley, his siblings, and the other nearby children attended the Old Rock Schoolhouse, a proverbial one-room school. It was a source of community pride, with parents and grandparents taking an active interest in the education of the young. Exceptional student work was discussed with a great sense of achievement, whether it was their own children who became accomplished or not. Of his school years, Moseley said:

> the neighborhood school, as crude as it was, was a far better school than are many city schools. It was full of aspiration; and the whole neighborhood was behind it. At one time a larger percentage of its students went to college than from any school that I know of. The neighborhood had many rare souls in it.[5]

As a child, Moseley dreamed of a life in public service and thought that going on to college and law school was a fine goal to that end. Interest in religion, other than as a backdrop, apparently did not enter his youthful mind; indeed, he considered Christianity to be something of a hindrance, and had difficulty understanding how it was possible to integrate secular with spiritual pursuits. He was of the mistaken opinion that the spiritual practices he had encountered up to then would be more of a hindrance to his future plans. Moseley reported plainly enough that he was afraid of what he thought religion was, and was disturbed by some of what he saw as a child among the Primitive and Missionary Baptists, as well as the Methodists, during their extended meetings or revivals.[6] Exactly what disturbed him, he did not say. To be sure, his parents provided a fine counterexample to this, but the young Moseley simply could not see a way beyond it, at least not then. Despite his reservations about religion, Rufus was naturally possessed of and raised in good humor; it was not until his adult years that he was to realize that the Holy Spirit was not in a bad mood, but had a sense of humor, and of course, unmatched joy.[7]

His early years in school, however, were most unremarkable, and by his own admission, he was a rather dull and unimaginative student. His later academic achievements would belie this inauspicious beginning. He seemed to have a particular aptitude for mathematics, but found it difficult to learn to read.[8] In fact, Rufus stated that he learned to read well simply so he could solve the math problems that were given in verbal terms. Not a great fan of his early matriculation (he was to learn his ABCs three times!), he reported that, on the way to his first day of school, he harbored the desire

---

5. Moseley, "Glory Hill."
6. Moseley, *Manifest Victory*, 45.
7. McLain, *Resurrection Encounter*, 33–34.
8. Moseley, *Manifest Victory*, 43–44.

of finding the school house burned to the ground. It is rather ironic, given that at age sixteen this reluctant learner would himself teach a few school terms for local children and later come to earn the respect of his professors during his college and graduate school days. But more than anything else, Rufus Moseley credits his family with providing an ideal foundation for his later life.[9]

On a warm summer day in 1876, a young Rufus Moseley and older brother Charles were near the Yadkin River, which ran through the family homestead. Charles read a portion of Scripture to his younger sibling that "Whosoever shall drinketh of this water shall thirst again; but whosoever shall drinketh of the water I shall give him shall never thirst; but the water I give him shall be in him a well of water springing up unto everlasting life" (John 4:14, KJV). Rufus, no more than five years old at the time, related there was in that Scripture something that made him inwardly leap for joy. Even at that tender age, he was to share—there is in the Holy Spirit power that no underdevelopment of mind can impede, that despite his youth he grasped a spiritual truth that "light that lighteth every man coming into the world."[10] Rufus was especially close to Charles, the eldest of the Moseley children, seven years his senior. He recalled with great love memories of his brother, who took something of a paternal approach to the rest of the children. Possessed of a great intellect at apparently an early age, Charles was remembered for his matter-of-fact approach to any number of things. When the great Charleston earthquake of 1886, which killed sixty people in that city, shaking the distant mountains of western North Carolina, Rufus remembers his brother commenting with great calmness "I don't see why we make all this disturbance. It is only an earthquake."[11]

Charles Moseley watched over Rufus in particular with what was described as a "kind domination." After Charles had witnessed his first water baptism, he sought to try it out on someone in his own family, and Rufus was the eager designate for the ritual. When he later complained of an ear ache, Charles feared that the baptism would be reported to his parents. No such tattling occurred, however, as the young boy highly valued any time spent with his older brother.[12] Rufus treasured his visits once or twice a year to the old homestead in North Carolina, and would, during these summer trips, stop in to see his brother in Greensboro or meet him near Elkin.

The Moseley family could trace their history to colonial times in Virginia and subsequent moves south and west across the frontier. The Moseley

---

9. Moseley, *Manifest Victory*, 44.
10. Moseley, *Manifest Victory*, 41–42.
11. Moseley, *Manifest Victory*; Moseley, "Kingdom of God Emphasis."
12. Moseley, *Manifest Victory*, 41–42.

and Hurt (Theresa's family) clans had moved to the foothills of the Blue Ridge Mountains sometime in the immediate post-Revolutionary War period. By the time of James and Theresa's marriage, they settled in what would become Surry County, North Carolina. The house in which Rufus was born was a humble single-room structure which, when considering that two adults and four children at one time lived in it, is something of a marvel. Sometime around 1875, a two-story home was built on their property for the growing Moseley family, which in time grew to eight children. Of his brothers and sisters, as well as his extended family, Rufus had the kindest of words, some of which are shared below.[13]

On his father James's side of the family, there was a younger brother, a widowed sister, and four unmarried sisters. Collectively, they had the most positive of effects on young Rufus. He described how they seemed to perpetually be thinking of each other over their own wants and needs, with any dissention being over who was more in need at any given time. "You are more tired than I am, let me finish the work," or "You need a new dress more than I do; I won't get another until you get yours," were typical, prompting Rufus to say "so great was their unselfishness."[14] His uncle, his mother's eldest brother, was a very tenderhearted individual as well, and encouraged the children away from any harm or cruelty they may be tempted to inflict upon animals. Rufus recalled his uncle teaching him in a practical way what Ralph Waldo Emerson would so poetically impress upon Moseley years later:

> Hast thou named all the birds without a gun?
> Loved the wood-rose, and left it on its stalk?
> At rich men's tables eaten bread and pulse?
> Unarmed, faced danger with a heart of trust?
> And loved so well a high behavior,
> In man or maid, that thou from speech refrained,
> Nobility more nobly to repay?
> O, be my friend, and teach me to be thine![15]

As with any of us who have been blessed with pleasant childhoods, we have specific memories of individuals whose personality and traits remain with us throughout our lives. In Moseley's case, one of these was a man named Ed Hampton, a physician, whom Rufus described as being a Quaker in every

---

13. Moseley, *Manifest Victory*, 41–42; See Moseley, *Search for West Mosely*.
14. Moseley, *Manifest Victory*, 41–42.
15. Emerson, "Forbearance"; Moseley, *Manifest Victory*, 42.

sense except actually belonging to that group. At one point in his fifties, Ed fell in love with a young woman and married, producing a large number of children. At the time Moseley related his memories of this man in the late 1930s, Hampton's widow was ninety-two years of age and the only living adult from Rufus's childhood days. Another rare soul was John Park, who had for many years been a schoolteacher. Rufus seemed to have two memories about him: that he had a horse and buggy that anyone could use at any time, and that sometime in his fifties had gotten a diagnosis of consumption or tuberculosis, and was told that he had not long to live. Rufus remembered that Park wore the saddest countenance he had ever seen, like a man on the way to his own funeral. Park went to another doctor in nearby Mount Airy, North Carolina, and was there told that if he abstained from bad habits and engaged in healthy eating, he could expect to live for a long time to come, which he did.[16] With family, friends, and the idyllic Blue Ridge Mountains as his backdrop and preparation, Rufus Moseley was about to enter a new world he could not at first anticipate.

At age sixteen, Moseley was reluctantly offered a position as teacher at the Gum Orchard school further up in the Blue Ridge Mountains. I use the word "reluctantly" because he was very small of physical stature. Some of his students were nearly twice his size. Sickly from early in his life, some on the school board making the hiring decision were dubious of his ability to handle the position. He was hired, in part, because at least one of the men on the board was a close friend of Rufus's father, James, and had served with him in the Civil War. If he could last the summer term, it was decided, he could also teach the winter term. Aware of their apprehension—it was voiced in his presence—Moseley met with some of the student classroom leaders and asked for their help in making the term a success. This honesty disarmed his would-be persecutors, who apparently planned on giving him the business, and he gained their promise to keep things in line. Going back to the lessons learned from his father, utter sincerity and willingness to face problems head-on served him well, and he taught additional school terms as a result. The next phase of his life, however, was to be an intellectual revolution for him, for he had decided to attend college.[17]

Paying for a college education for even one of their children was not something the Moseley family could afford. When it came time for Rufus to go away to university, the financial means were simply not there. Moseley had saved some money from his teaching and borrowed more from friends to help in this, but it still was not enough. His parents believed enough

16. Moseley, *Manifest Victory*, 43–44.
17. Moseley, *Manifest Victory*, 43–44.

in Rufus that they were willing to sell their creek field property, land that Moseley later indicated was the most valuable the family possessed. He could not in right conscience allow for this, and instead the family came to an agreement on how to facilitate his college education. His older brother Charles had attended a business college in Bowling Green, Kentucky before he entered medical school. Some of his costs had been handled as a result of academic scholarships. It was therefore mutually decided among the Moseley parents and children that the first one to go to college, Charles, would help to pay the tuition of the next to go, in this case, Rufus. He, in turn, would see to the support his younger brother Millard when it came time for him to go to school, and likewise Millard would pay for the youngest boy, (James) Winfield. The last of the family to attend college was Maude Moseley, the baby of the family, whose college costs Winfield presumably covered.[18]

At some point before he returned to business school, Charles informed Rufus that there were scholarships available at Peabody College (now part of Vanderbilt University) in Nashville, Tennessee. Although initially turned down for such financial aid because of the poor quality of his penmanship, Rufus did receive help during his second year with the support of several professors and even the college president.[19] But before leaving for Nashville, Moseley met with his parents and had a most poignant discussion about his future. His father, a relatively uneducated man, told his son, "Rufus, I know nothing about the world you are to be in. I have no advice to give. I trust you." It was one of the most important things ever spoken to him and he remembered it to the end of his days.[20] Rufus did not disappoint. He was to soon distinguish himself as a bright and perceptive student, and was encouraged to look into graduate school with an eye toward a life in academia.

COLLEGE AND GRADUATE SCHOOL

As stated earlier, Rufus Moseley entered college with the intention of becoming a lawyer as a springboard into public service. From his earliest years, he had been told of and himself witnessed the importance of serving others. It seems that, like modern-day college freshman, Moseley was not entirely sure about his major toward that end, but found himself drawn to history, political science, and philosophy. In particular, the ancient Greek philosopher Plato held him spellbound. He believed, as did many in the

---

18. Conversations with Diana Moseley Vinson, October 2015.
19. Moseley, *Manifest Victory*, 47.
20. Moseley, *Manifest Victory*, 47.

early church, that God had blessed the world with preincarnate wisdom that foreshadowed the coming of Christ. In that sense, like Anselm and Thomas Aquinas, Moseley was something of a scholastic. He was to say of both Plato and Socrates:

> Socrates was happy facing Eternity after the most enlightened city of the ancient world [Athens] condemned him to death because they could not stand the questions he put to them. His noble and sincere life was a rebuke to those about him. There was a pureness about him that convicted his enemies, and rather than repent and become enlightened themselves, they sought to get rid of the light that made them feel so dirty and look so black. Plato, seeing this attitude of men set in their ways, observed that when the perfectly just man comes they will take him to the Cross. And they did.[21]

Rufus described being absolutely lost in intellectual delight as he studied ancient history and philosophy, finding happiness in the sheer joy of learning. When he was likewise introduced to the Transcendental and Victorian poets and writers, this joy of learning was kicked into overdrive. Ruskin, Arnold, Thoreau, Hawthorne, Holmes, Tennyson, and Emerson were his favorites, especially the latter two. Moseley described this period of time as one of being introduced to the "question mark" as he engaged in freewheeling and widespread contemplation of the great writers. The poets and playwrights, especially Alfred Lord Tennyson and Henrik Ibsen, were a source of great inspiration to him, and prompted him to say that they had a greater understanding of the spiritual realm than many theologians. In the midst of his learning, however, the young man from Elkin, North Carolina was to have a most definite encounter with Christ.[22]

In 1889, when he was a sophomore at Peabody College in Nashville, Tennessee, Rufus attended a revival service at the nearby Central Baptist Church. An evangelist named Penn preached the salvation message, using the story of Naaman the Leper as his text (2 Kings 5). As Rufus later shared, the message came home to him so powerfully that he felt as if it were being preached to Moseley the Leper. Each reservation Naaman had given for not dipping in the Jordan River as commanded were Rufus's own against following Christ. Although initially reluctant to do so in the presence of his peers and professors, he arose from his place on the pew and went forward when the preacher made the public invitation. Rufus could not foresee it at the

---

21. Moseley, "Our Divine Appointment."

22. Moseley, *Manifest Victory*, 49–56; See also Brooks, *Flowering of New England*, for an overview of Transcendentalism.

time, but it was the beginning of a great spiritual and intellectual walk for him that would lead him down many paths. Thereafter he proved to be possessed of as great a hunger for spiritual things as he had for his studies. His newfound faith would carry him forward to his time as graduate student, young scholar, and professor.[23]

A couple of nights after he gave his life to Christ, Rufus attended a dedication service for those who had come forward. Moseley shared the following about this event:

> Monday night was rainy and only a few people were present in the lamp-lit barn of a church at the service to witness my open dedication. Going to the altar was far easier this time . . . the evangelist, as he stood near and over me, remarked that his small congregation with only one at the altar might seem like a minor consequence, but that he had the witness, which he felt was from God, that the young man at the altar would mean far more in the Kingdom than he himself had yet meant.[24]

Moseley also found that this second step toward a life with God was far easier than the first, as were all steps thereafter toward God. A few days later, he was water baptized. Rufus expressed disappointment that he did not, upon coming up out of the water, experience the falling of the Holy Ghost upon him, as had Christ after John the Baptist had baptized him in the Jordan River. He had not yet heard of the doctrine concerning the baptism of the Holy Spirit, but wanted to follow Jesus' example and experience it as he came up out of the water. Undaunted, he found his new birth pushing him to an ever greater level of intellectual learning.

On the following Tuesday, while reading the Gospel of John, Rufus shared that he had the witness and experience of the presence of God to such a decree that it would confirm in his mind his sense of calling:

> More than ever before, I felt sure of being at that moment in the joy, peace, and fearless love of the Kingdom of Heaven. But I did not treasure it enough to keep it as a conscious perpetual possession, for years I would go out and return, not always understanding why. There was much that I thought I wanted that experience had to teach me I did not want, before I was ready for the secrets of the Kingdom. More and more, being in conscious identification and union with Jesus, being in the Kingdom of Heaven, became so precious (and everything outside so

---

23. Moseley, *Manifest Victory*, 51–52.
24. McLain, *Resurrection Encounter*, 42.

unsatisfactory) that I was made ready to let go the things that led me out and kept me out.²⁵

It is not as if he came to this revelation all at once either. As he was to state time and again, it was over the course of many years, and many spiritual lessons in the wilderness, where he was taught to treasure this conscious, moment-by-moment Presence above all else. What is apparent, however, is that as he did dedicate himself to the highest, his intimate sense of God grew to amazing proportions.

Having successfully earned his bachelor's and master's degrees from Peabody, the administration and faculty, notably President W. H. Payne and professors Sam Jones, A. P. Bourland, and Wycliffe Rose, encouraged Moseley to attend the newly opened University of Chicago for further graduate study. These professors and others were so impressed with Rufus that they went to lengths to aid in his further education in any way they could, including sending him money to carry him through a tough financial spot shortly after arriving. At Chicago, he sat under some of intellectual giants of the nation and era such as Henry Pratt Judson, John Dewey, George Burnham Foster, James H. Tufts, George Herbert Mead, James Breasted, and Henry von Horst.²⁶ Rufus also so impressed his Chicago professors that they sought to create a position for him there after he finished his studies, and a paid fellowship for the duration of his time there was given.

It was also while in Chicago that he met Henry Drummond, the great Scottish scientist and Christian writer. He made a lasting impression on the young Moseley, and his book, *The Greatest Thing in the World*, with its clarion call to the Love Life in Christ, remained one of his favorites. At the time of Drummond's visit to Chicago, the spectacular World's Fair was underway, and he invited Moseley to attend. Years later, Moseley said that nothing in the vast exhibit fascinated him more than simply watching Drummond take it all in. It seemed every detail was of the most profound interest to the scientist. Decades later, as one reads Rufus's words, one can also hear the echoes of Drummond's love message.²⁷

While in Chicago, Rufus Moseley also met and was influenced by a preacher named David Swing. Swing had been the target of conservative members of his denomination, the Presbyterians, who sought to have his pastorate at the Westminster Presbyterian Church taken from him. Though he was acquitted of heresy charges, Swing resigned his position and created the Central Church, and took a large portion of the Westminster

25. Moseley, *Manifest Victory*, 37; McLain, *Resurrection Encounter*, 42.
26. McLain, *Resurrection Encounter*, 44.
27. McLain, *Resurrection Encounter*, 55–56.

congregation with him. Moseley came into contact with him some years after his run-ins with the orthodox, and was impressed with his honesty and some of his liberal positions. Transcendentalism, a movement begun in New England and lead by such luminaries as Ralph Waldo Emerson and Henry David Thoreau, was a driving force in Swing's life, and which at the time was also of great interest to Moseley. Swing, like Moseley, found in liberal thought much liberating spiritual truth. Rufus was to later say that he became a liberal in order to treasure conservative thought. Each by themselves, he realized early on, were at best shadows of real Truth. By not shutting himself off to all thought outside of his comfort zone, Moseley (like Swing) found value in all Christian traditions. Swing's words and life inspired the young Moseley, and as he was to say, "caused my feet to hit the sidewalk in a new way, providing me with a sense of hope and a zest for the future."[28]

In time, Rufus coined the word "Totalist"[29] to define his religious and ideological positions, a belief system in which both sides are united, learn and gain from the other, and fall into each others' arms, informed by the Love of Christ, the Great Reconciler.[30] Hitching one's star to either religious or political conservatism or liberalism at the expense of the other was a tragic mistake, and something that Moseley would warn against over the years. In the 1920s, he witnessed a harsh division firsthand between liberal and conservative religious mindsets—the "modernists" and "fundamentalists," as they became known. This rift was seen nowhere more explicitly than in the area of evolution, and in the public spectacle that became the 1925 Scopes Monkey Trial in Dayton, Tennessee. Moseley had friends in both camps, and himself held views that were from both sides, but throughout, he managed to speak of it only when in and through love. While he was never afraid to state his views, he was cautious to ensure that whatever he said for or against a particular position was done in love.

At the University of Chicago, Moseley threw himself into his doctoral studies, carried (he contended) with this new life in Christ. Proving to be an intellectual of the first order, he quickly came to the attention of his professors, who recognized in this young man a remarkable ability to summarize in a sentence or two some profound truth, be it with regard to his studies in history, political science, and philosophy, or in his spiritual life. In one instance, he said something so profound to John Dewey that he asked Moseley to expound upon it. Rufus, who disliked elaboration if he felt the point had

---

28. Moseley, *Manifest Victory*, 55.
29. Moseley, "J.R. Moseley Writes Card."
30. Moseley, *Manifest Victory*, 55.

been made, simply replied that he had already said it.[31] Indeed, this is one of the keys to understanding Rufus's writing: there are great nuggets of spiritual truth peppered throughout his work which will, if the reader is wise, keep him or her looking for them. He so impressed his Chicago mentors that it was arranged for him to spend time at Harvard University. As at the University of Chicago, Moseley began to shine under the brilliant professors in Cambridge, Massachusetts.

At Harvard University, Rufus Moseley met and was befriended by a truly stellar academic lineup. He learned from and rubbed shoulders with men such as Josiah Royce, then called the dean of American philosophers; George Santayana; and William James, of *The Variety of Religious Experience* fame. Apparently working as something of an aide to James for a time, Rufus was among the first to read his early lectures and articles that became the immensely influential book on religion mentioned earlier. James was also to introduce him to Christian Science and New Thought, two modes of thought that were important to Moseley in his early spiritual quest. It was also with the backing of his mentors that he taught a class at Harvard, though what it was is not known.

With the support of these intellectual giants, along with those in Chicago, Moseley was recommended for and accepted a part-time position as a professor of history and political science at Mercer University, at the time a conservative Baptist school in Macon, Georgia. He accepted this opportunity with zeal, especially since Mercer allowed him to return to Chicago and Cambridge to continue his graduate studies during the spring and summer terms. He also took in a semester at Heidelberg University in Germany during this time.[32] It was during these heady days of education that Rufus Moseley came to realize something that was to be a hallmark of his ministry.

The discovery he described came to him sometime in 1892, when he began to see the possibilities of a life in the Holy Spirit he had never seen before. He came to believe that it was not, in fact, widely known. He was to state it as having

> the intimations of the possibility of a wholly different principle of living than is generally known or lived. This principle was associated for me with Jesus as I had read of Him in the gospels. The possibilities so stirred my imagination that I began yielding to its urge . . . those seasons of actually being in the Kingdom of Heaven spoiled me for everything outside of this realm.[33]

---

31. McLain, *Resurrection Encounter*, 64.
32. Moseley, *Manifest Victory*, 49.
33. Moseley, *Manifest Victory*, 49.

Though he did not know it at the time, he would come to describe this way of living as "Life as Love," or living in a place where one gives out God's perfect love and only that love all the time. In so doing, believers never leave the conscious, moment-by-moment life in heaven while still on earth. He did not come to that place immediately, but over the course of learning—he did not say "over time"—for it is in yielding and surrender, not necessarily a process of time, that one enters and abides. Moseley once said we needn't take ages to become overcomers, but that we can have it as quickly as we are willing to surrender completely and without reservation. Thus equipped and part of his fellowships at Chicago and Harvard, he left for Mercer University. He brought with him his liberal views, coupled with an intense desire to live out the life in the Spirit he came to believe was available, even if he did not as yet know how to fully enter into it.

MERCER UNIVERSITY PROFESSOR

So it was that beginning in 1894, at age twenty-four, Moseley moved to the site of his new employment in the central Georgia city of Macon. Mercer was still a very small school at the time, and Rufus lived in the same building where his office and classrooms were located. University catalogs from this period show that he taught general history, history of modern Europe and the United States, comparative politics, American political and constitutional history, comparative economics, psychology, ethics, and a short-lived class called "Lectures on Pedagogy."[34] Despite his youth, faculty and students alike looked upon Rufus as a brilliant scholar and teacher. Moseley protégé Wayne McLain shared a story about a late 1940s retreat in Greensboro, North Carolina that Rufus attended. Also participating was a Baptist minister who some fifty years earlier had Rufus as a professor. Not initially recognizing Moseley, the minister exclaimed upon the discovery, "Why, I know that man! I attended Mercer University. He was known as the most brilliant man on campus!"[35]

Sometime in the late 1890s, a Mercer colleague named B. D. Ragsdale, professor of Bible and self-appointed guardian of the school's orthodoxy, confronted Rufus over his perceived lack of Christian conservatism, and told him it was a problem. Moseley asked if there was something he had said or done to incur his wrathful accusation. Ragsdale responded by saying that the fruit in Rufus's life was good, but that he did not speak the language of orthodoxy. Both observations were quite true, and Moseley admitted as

---

34. "J. Rufus Moseley.".
35. McLain, *Resurrection Encounter*, 47.

much to his friend. Rufus asked his accuser to pray about it and seek God's opinion on the matter. A couple of days later, when he was leaving campus to post a letter, he ran into a changed Ragsdale. "I have heard from God," he said, "and you will never find me saying or speaking anything against you again!" Both men hugged each other and professed their love for one another; a potentially divisive situation was thus averted, and a lifelong friendship cemented.[36] This confrontation between a liberal and conservative, with utter sincerity and Holy Spirit guidance, was to result in a unification of the two political and spiritual viewpoints. The experience was to be repeated throughout Moseley's life and ministry.

Moseley gained a reputation among undergraduates and faculty alike for his involvement with students. This involved his participation in campus activities meant to encourage a combination of intellectual endeavor and spiritual pursuits among the student body. Many of these were particularly noted for their profundity. As seen in the Ragsdale example, he was always seeking ways to bring people together, and he included students in this effort as well. There was a regular informal student meal-time gathering in which he participated that became known as the "Transcendental Club" for the depth of the discussions and the topics covered. Another such student group was dedicated to the sharpening of critical thinking, critical writing, and debating skills.[37]

He also engaged his students in proper eating habits and frugal living techniques. Moseley and his students even came up with a system whereby they could live on as little as twenty cents a day, or just under six dollars today. Even at this stage, proper eating had become increasingly important to him, though nowhere near the centrality it would hold in his later life. As he was to say throughout his life, it is amazing how truly little a human being needs to meet his or her daily needs. In his later years, he would encourage other believers in this matter, and himself practiced a lifestyle of self-sacrifice and frugality. This was not done in a dogmatic fashion, but rather as a proper witness to the world of the good stewardship shown in "the least of things," money, and to not be wasteful, extravagant, or self-absorbed. It is when needs are replaced by wants that all manner of difficulties arise.

A second incident at Mercer concerning orthodoxy arose in 1900, when Moseley announced to the president and board that he had decided to investigate the claims of two new movements of the times, New Thought and especially Christian Science. He had been introduced to the teachings of these two groups during his time at Harvard. Professor William James had

---

36. Moseley, *Manifest Victory*, 59.
37. McLain, *Resurrection Encounter*, 51.

told Moseley that the Mind Science movement, especially New Thought, was perhaps the most compelling new spiritual trend since the Reformation. With such an endorsement from one of his mentors, and along with his own quest for physical health, Rufus believed he must see for himself if the movements' claims had any merit. Having been ill with a variety of ailments for most of his young life, notably those dealing with the digestive tract, any promising health claim would attract his attention. His own family doubted that he would have a long life.

Having read some of Christian Science founder Mary Baker Eddy and New Thought Phineas Quimby's works, the promises seemed attractive enough, but what of actual practice? Moseley did not come to his decision overnight, and given the nature of his character, it is likely that he studied, prayed, and asked opinions about the Mind Sciences. While at Harvard, he attended services at a Christian Science church in Boston, and it was there that he met Judge Hanna, the first reader in that congregation. He reported taking part in a communion service there when he witnessed a gentle glow on and above the table containing the bread and wine. He described himself as being "lost in an ocean of love." It was one of those early experiences he was to have where the Holy Spirit's presence and calling reached out to him in spite of being at a Christian Science function. He was quite aware that there were increasing concerns among orthodox Christians about the nature of the new movements, and as one can imagine, most of the opinions of these two new groups were not generally positive. Rufus was to later realize there were some public misconceptions, but also real reasons for concern.[38]

Cognizant of what Mercer's reaction was likely to be, Moseley thought the most honest thing would be to voluntarily resign to protect the university from any controversy or embarrassment his involvement in Christian Science might bring. Because he was greatly loved by both faculty and students, the board sought a number of ways to retain the young scholar, even offering to keep his professor's chair open until he could conclude his investigation. One of the things suggested to him was that as he involved himself in study of Christian Science, he stay away from Christian Scientists. Downtown Macon had an active Christian Science reading room, and Mercer administration and faculty were concerned about one of their own being seen attending meetings there. Of course, this was an untenable solution, for it was tantamount to studying biology and chemistry without time in a lab.

By the spring of 1900, after only six very successful years at Mercer, Moseley's interest in Christian Science became so great that he considered

---

38. McLain, *Resurrection Encounter*, 53.

and voiced his intention of tendering his resignation to the conservative Baptist school. Mercer President Daniel Pollock was especially fond of Rufus, and despite the resignation continued to seek out ways that might allow him to explore Christian Science and at the same time stay at Mercer. Moseley's best friend at the college, William Heard Kilpatrick, who was to go on to international fame as a Columbia University professor, took Moseley aside and asked him to consider staying an additional ten years. So great was Moseley's influence, Kilpatrick and Pollock believed, that he would transform the school and the state of Georgia by staying. Rufus smiled at the compliment and replied, "If I were to seek to save my position, even to have a good influence, I would lose the very thing that made me vital and worthwhile." Kilpatrick agreed, saying "You are right."[39] It is interesting to note that a few years later Kilpatrick himself would leave as a result of his liberal religious positions. He and Rufus remained the closest of friends to the end of their lives, and often shared stories with laughter.

After a lengthy university board meeting in the spring of 1900 in Griffin, Georgia, made up primarily of Baptist preachers from around the state, many suggestions and demands were made to resolve this impasse. Some cajoled, but all agreed that Rufus Moseley's leaving was done out of honest intentions. Rufus said of the parting that whenever he gave himself over to follow truth when it disagreed with the conservative nature of Mercer, he found periods of great joy. Even though it preceded his entry into a questionable group such as Christian Science, honesty and staying true to the path he was on held precedence. It would be those same qualities of character that later helped him to leave that organization. The Mercer board and administration therefore decided to accept Moseley's resignation with regrets. He departed two months later, at the end of the spring term. They parted, as Moseley was fond of saying, "in a love feast and in each other's arms."[40] Still, Rufus was not without other offers; his reputation as a fine professor and scholar was such that Walter B. Hill, chancellor of the University of Georgia at Athens, wrote Moseley and offered him a position where he would be free to teach anything he wished. If a chair did not exist, Hill was intent on creating one for him. Moseley refused this as well, feeling that while it would allow greater freedom than Mercer was able to give, it still held potential for limiting his free spiritual investigation and exploration.[41]

---

39. Moseley, *Manifest Victory*, 60.
40. Moseley, *Manifest Victory*, 60–62.
41. Moseley, *Manifest Victory*, 215.

EXPLORING CHRISTIAN SCIENCE

One of the great truisms of Rufus's life was that he was a spiritual seeker. While he held to basic Christian beliefs concerning salvation, the bible, and the cardinal doctrines, he had found from the time of his youth that in orthodoxy there was often harshness. Truths may well be spoken from the conservative end of the faith, but it was sometimes done with a distinct lack of love and thereby repellent to him and any other genuine seeker. It is here, as Wayne McLain stated in his Moseley biography—and I quite agree—there exists one of the greatest weaknesses in today's charismatic world: they may well have truth, but there is a widespread failure to go on to walking the Life as Love, lessening the impact the movement could otherwise have. This shortcoming is not, of course, limited to "spirit-filled" believers, but is a malaise within the Body of Christ that instead of attracting the lost and the seeking soul, repels them with the addition of many superfluous things ranging from politics to spiritual stances that are not, in the greater scheme of things, imperative.[42]

When Rufus Moseley left Mercer University to follow Christian Science, he did so with mixed excitement and trepidation. The movement, after all, was relatively new, and despite some outside evaluations of it from Professor William James, and his own study of it, Rufus was weighing its claims and studying its teachings. He was to later say of his association with Christian Science that it was not the organization, books, or visible church and leadership that attracted him—their shortcomings were readily apparent. It was the spirit behind the letter, the reality behind the visible that attracted him. [43] He firmly believed that all real divine healing is the action of the Divine Spirit, and claims that Christian Science, whether Mrs. Eddy believed it or not, was from that source. He was to say, "It was only in this sense that I could think of being a Christian Scientist, for I was keenly aware of much that did not appeal to me in the first efforts of Mrs. Eddy . . . I was never meant to be a disciple of a disciple; I can only be a disciple first hand of the Teacher of Teachers."[44] Nonetheless, Rufus genuinely hoped that Christian Science had a key to unlock new resources from the unseen spiritual realm: Here one can see his love of Plato shine through. He also knew of and was attracted by its claims for physical healing through the use of "treatments," wherein a person embraces their true identity as Christian

---

42. McLain, *Resurrection Encounter*, 73.
43. McLain, *Resurrection Encounter*, 55.
44. Moseley, *Manifest Victory*, 65–66.

Science taught it, through personal "positive affirmations," or by another on someone else's behalf.

Moseley found himself quickly greeted and warmly welcomed into the local Christian Science center in Macon. Rufus's great reputation as a first-rate mind was well known to the other practitioners, and it must have been seen as something of a coup to have him join their group. When he left Mercer, where he was also living on campus, he took up residence in a local Macon landmark on the corner of Georgia Avenue and Orange Street as a boarder. In the 1900 city directory he lists himself, in bold letters, as "*Christian Scientist.*"[45] One gets the feeling that if he could have included an exclamation mark, he would have. Ever the spiritual seeker, Rufus meant to explore the possibilities of the movement to its fullest extent.

Although he never gave up his orthodox Christian beliefs—indeed, they would in time prompt him to leave Christian Science—he did see possibilities he had never seen before, however incomplete. For instance, he came to understand that the Mind Sciences taught that the love and wisdom of Jesus were like unto laws that were workable truths, and anyone who exercised them in honesty could see results, however limited. It is, in part, for that reason that Christian Science's claim to some sort of "scientific" truth initially attracted Rufus. He also early on had come to realize that within Christian Science there were two distinct camps: On one hand, there was a minority, like himself, who held to orthodox Christian beliefs about the death and resurrection of Christ and his place as the deliverer of the human race, and others who took a path away from that position into distinctly non-Christian dogma closer to Gnosticism. Christian Science's founder, Mary Baker Eddy, took the latter route. He found many Christian Scientists honest, loving, and caring people, while others repelled him. With Moseley's efforts to try to bring Christian Science and the Bible together to form some sort of tenable, orthodox belief system, it became one of the increasing divisions between himself and Eddy, and would be instrumental in his eventually walking away from the movement.[46]

Within a year of entering Christian Science, Moseley began to hold prayer for others seeking healing through the movement's prescribed methodology. In 1901, for instance, he prayed for a child with serious eczema problems. The mother of the child, pregnant at the time with another, was also dealing with her husband's terminal case of tuberculosis. In the midst of this tragedy, Rufus was summoned to pray for the whole family, including the unborn child. As he did so, the woman claimed that the child in her

---

45. *Polk County Directory*, 1900.
46. McLain, *Resurrection Encounter*, 53–54.

womb, which had been essentially lifeless, again came to life. The child was later born, but due to other complications passed away shortly thereafter. This was to have an impact on Moseley in the sense of wondering why the child did not live if, as he had come to believe and Christian Science taught, the healing methodology was "scientific."[47]

Decades later, Rufus made mention of the shortcomings of the Christian Science and other New Thought beliefs when he stated, "The weakness of the new movements that take Jesus only as a way-shower and teacher and seek to overcome apart from vital identification and union with him, is that at best they are only doing partially when the Holy Spirit has already done fully and perfectly."[48] In any event, he was finding Christian Science prayer and methodology to be tough sledding when compared to the leadings of the Holy Spirit. Numerous times after 1910, Moseley stated that there were some general similarities between Pentecostalism and Christian Science's approach to healing, but only general ones. To see Jesus simply as an example and perfection with which to identify is not enough. In fact, it places one only at the beginning of the search for truth.[49] "Whoever receives Jesus as God with us, and God in full triumph, receives power to become like Him. This lifts us quickly into realms that effort and [Christian Science] treatments simply in terms of the divine idea might be arriving at, if ever arrived at."[50]

Rufus nonetheless participated in healing prayers and efforts for any number of people, such as a Geneva, Georgia man. It was here that he witnessed what was perhaps his first divine healing. The man for whom he prayed had an abscess on the brain that was revealed during an X-ray. Admitting his fear that there was nothing he could do, at least not with the Christian Science "treatment" of affirmation, he instead found himself praying along the lines of orthodox Christianity for the man's healing: in other words, not seeking positive affirmations, nor denying the reality of the illness, but rather seeking the Holy Spirit to perform the miracle. When a subsequent X-ray found that the abscess had disappeared, he began to realize the serious, stultifying limitations of the Christian Science approach, as well as the genuine power of the Holy Spirit through Christ. He was to later admit that he knew of no one in Christian Science who had sufficiently

---

47. Moseley, *Manifest Victory*, 70.
48. Moseley, "Ministry of the Spirit."
49. Moseley, *Manifest Victory*, 312.
50. Moseley, *Manifest Victory*, 312.

yielded to the Holy Spirit to have Jesus revealed to them as he was to the early church.[51]

A few years later, he was called to a local Macon hospital to pray for a railroad worker who had been badly scalded in a work-related accident. When he arrived and looked at the injured man, he had to look away due to the severe pain registered on the face of the victim. Rufus then turned his eyes heavenward in prayer. When he again looked at the man, he found to his surprise that the railroad worker was smiling. It convinced Moseley that if we look to Christ as our all in all, despite our personal shortcomings and misunderstandings about healing, he was generous and willing to help, even in our blindness. Some have mistaken God's generosity and love in healing for an active "science" which may be tapped. As Moseley found out, this quite misses the point. [52]

In the summer of 1901, Rufus Moseley—who from youth was constantly afflicted with digestive problems—began to experience serious pain in his abdomen. As stated earlier, his own family doubted he would have a long life due to poor health.[53] While he prayed for healing, and had others stand in on his behalf, the pain became so acute that he sought the advice of a physician. The doctor warned him of an impending appendix failure, and told Rufus that surgery was necessary. Refusing all medication for pain, Moseley went home and drew himself a hot bath as he continued to pray. When he slipped into the water, he noticed the pain beginning to fade, and the water in the tub turning green from the infection leaving through his pores. When he got out of the water and dressed, the pain was gone. Fifty years later, he shared the story of this healing before an audience in Denver, Colorado, and proudly indicated that he still had his appendix.[54]

For her part, founder Mary Baker Eddy had stated that Christian Science was a divine revelation given specifically to her, and her textbook of the teachings were God's statement to the world. She was of the firm opinion that she was specifically chosen to present it to humanity at large. With such high opinions and egos, Rufus Moseley had increased difficulty. Christian Science leadership specifically asked him if he would leave all to follow Christian Science without reservation. He replied that he would follow it to the point when the Holy Spirit would say otherwise. This wasn't quite the answer Christian Science leaders wanted to hear, but they did not press the issue when Moseley added that, if he knew anything of Mrs. Eddy's mind,

---

51. Moseley, *Manifest Victory*, 67–68.
52. Moseley, *Manifest Victory*, 70–71.
53. McLain, *Resurrection Encounter*, 54.
54. McLain, *Resurrection Encounter*, 88.

she would hold to the same opinion. She did not, and as the first decade of the twentieth century came to a close, his staying in the movement became increasingly difficult.

Around this same time, thought to be 1906, Moseley was called for an interview with Christian Science leader Archibald McClellan of Boston, and was told that Mrs. Eddy had the impression that Rufus was writing what he saw as true and helpful, but without any special interest in correlating it with Christian Science teachings. Moseley wholeheartedly agreed with that assessment. He had reached the point where he realized that if he could not be utterly sincere in his writings for the movement, his time with the organization was nearing its close. Christian Science, and Mary Baker Eddy in particular, were demanding he acquiesce to their teachings, something he increasingly could not do in right conscience. Earlier in the decade, he had changed some things in his writing about which they objected, but he believed that to do so any longer would be dishonest.[55] What he changed at their behest, or they later changed in his writings without asking, is not told. In some of their publications, such as *Christian Science Journal*, he attempted to bring Christian Science beliefs within a more biblical framework, but found that it was something leadership increasingly frowned upon. But as the first decade of the twentieth century was drawing to a close, Moseley understood that as a Christian it was difficult to justify staying in Christian Science.

As his years in Christian Science passed, the question for Moseley became whether he should learn healing or a walk after God from a flawed human being and movement, or as what he later would call as a "first-hander," or learning directly from the Holy Spirit. In the beginning, he thought he was doing just that, but it had become apparent that Mrs. Eddy and the majority of Christian Scientists saw faith quite differently than Moseley and orthodox Christianity. Although there was an attraction for him, he came to see that it was false and its claims at best superficial. Years later, wanting to make sure others understood that he in no way endorsed Christian Science or New Thought, Rufus commented, "I have had what seems to be a warning in the Spirit that the various assertions of New Thought and kindred efforts, with religious names or without them, should never be used as substitutes for the perfect healing salvation and redemption that are in Jesus Christ, nor for Jesus Himself.[56] One could, for instance, study how Pharaoh's priests were able to duplicate some of God's miracles wrought through Moses and Aaron, or seek the God who overcame Pharaoh. Approach was one thing to

---

55. Moseley, *Manifest Victory*, 88.
56. Moseley, "Religious Quest."

Moseley, reality quite another. But before he reached that place, there was a request for his services in the academic world: His old alma mater, Peabody, in Nashville, Tennessee, was in danger of closing.

PEABODY COLLEGE CALLS FOR HELP

In 1901, Peabody College was faced with the very real possibility of having its doors closed and its funding from public and private sources shared elsewhere. Vanderbilt University was on the rise, and some sought to incorporate nearby Peabody into its fold. While that would happen in time, it was something Peabody administrators and many graduates sought to avoid. Rufus Moseley was chosen as one of the leaders of a committee to find a way to keep the college open and at the same time not interfere with Vanderbilt or any other southern school's mission. For a period of some five months, Moseley traveled to and from Nashville and to other points meeting with influential and powerful donors. One of these was President Theodore Roosevelt, a Peabody board member, who, though initially in favor of closing Peabody, came to the view that Moseley's proposal was sound, and backed it. Roosevelt met with Moseley to discuss his support, as well as to inform him, as a Macon resident, that Harry Stillwell Edwards (also from Macon and a Moseley friend) would be seconding his nomination for the presidency at the 1904 Republican convention.[57]

Of all Roosevelt's comments, Rufus most remembered the President intimating that he had contempt for a man who, because he won a reputation in one field, presumed to pass upon matters in other fields until he took time to inform himself as well. To whom he was directing this comment is unknown, but Rufus thought enough of it to include it in his autobiography. In any event, Roosevelt told Moseley that he would not be attending the board meeting in Nashville, what with the Panama Canal and other pressing issues demanding his time. He did, however, hope to attend a later meeting, and told Moseley so. Roosevelt did indeed attend a later meeting on his way back to Washington, D.C. from a Mississippi bear hunt. When he arrived, he immediately gave support to the program Moseley had suggested, and his presence helped to prompt the gathering to support it instead of sending it on to yet another committee for discussion. The school thus saved, a grateful Peabody sought to bring Rufus back, if only to live on campus. Wycliffe Rose, one of Moseley's professors at Peabody, had made the invitation with

---

57. Moseley, *Manifest Victory*, 72–77.

the backing of the administration. But as he had at Mercer, he declined the generous offer in favor of his spiritual quest.[58]

EARLY LESSONS IN UTTER SINCERITY

Rooted in his upbringing and spiritual beliefs was what Rufus liked to call "utter sincerity." He spread this same notion among his Christian Science friends and became recognized among them as a true peacemaker. Moseley asked all to consider that if as believers we are willing to be dishonest with others on however small a scale, in all probability we would also be dishonest with ourselves and with God. Even at this early juncture, Rufus understood that God wanted us to speak to him as a friend as well as a Father, and wants us to come boldly and speak our mind, state our concerns and fears, and bring to him all that we know (and perhaps don't know) keeps us from a deeper walk.

Rufus was fond of saying, "I have found the Lord everywhere I have looked for him, and especially in sick rooms, in prisons, in death cells, and in every meeting of evil with good."[59] His youthful lessons with sincerity and honest were magnified over the course of time and with the clarification of the Holy Spirit. He would later write in great detail about a state of being wherein the believer is totally honest in all his dealings. This was also to mean that no thought, word, or deed was to be identified with what was self-aggrandizing or harmful to others. In all things and at all times, a person is to be walking in the Life as Love, faith that works by love, to the point where any dishonesty is so distasteful so as to repel the believer.

Rufus genuinely believed that such an approach was liberating beyond words, freeing us from all sham and pretense. It is the highest reality and the out-working of that reality, setting us free from any and all bondages. As he said in his autobiography, "The Spirit of utter sincerity and truthfulness working by love opens our understanding and makes us good soil for the planting of the Heavenly seed and for bringing forth the Heavenly harvest."[60] Rufus liked to quote poet and playwright Maurice Maeterlinck on this topic: "In owning our faults we disown them, and in confessing our sins they cease to be ours."

Rufus once said words to the effect that the devil will go with us almost everywhere, except to full confession. While Satan can easily couch himself in creeds, churches, and good works, he will not go to full confession of our

---

58. Moseley, *Manifest Victory*, 75; McLain, *Resurrection Encounter*, 264.
59. McLain, *Resurrection Encounter*, 264.
60. McLain, *Resurrection Encounter*, 251.

faults. Being exposed is one of the devil's greatest fears, and when we learn to freely tell our faults to others in a spirit of love and helpfulness, any bondage we may have had loses its power. Always be willing to tell others of our own faults, but not to divulge other's shortcomings. Moseley found over the course of his life that if people are willing to make confession of wrongdoing, they will have found release. He saw this as not just a spiritual principle applied to Christians, but to the entirety of the human race. Whether it was confession of things like theft or unforgiveness all the way up to murder, the person telling the whole truth of the matter was freed. Moseley found this to be true as a child and young adult, both before and especially after he was baptized in the Holy Spirit, and during his time with Christian Science, he continued to practice the absolute need for honesty and forthrightness.

As an example of this, in the spring of 1905 a Montgomery, Alabama businessman who headed one of the largest firms in that city contacted Rufus in an effort to rectify a situation with a co-owner that had become untenable. It is believed that the contact came as a result of Moseley's Christian Science involvement. The business had become threatened when the co-owner threatened to throw the business into receivership over a disagreement. Frantic to avoid this, the primary owner sought to buy his partner out, but without success; exactly what it was that caused this unfortunate situation is unclear, but the two, once friends, had become embroiled in a contest that threatened the well-being of both. Moseley traveled to Montgomery where he met with the man and family of the one who had contacted him. His immediate advice was for all of them to pray for the well-being of their adversary, asking God to bless him. The wife objected to this as an unreasonable request, but gave in and joined in the prayer. After a couple days' stay in Montgomery, Rufus returned to Macon, but apparently thought a followup trip might be necessary.[61]

Shortly thereafter, Moseley received word that a crisis point had been reached and was asked to again return to Montgomery. When he stepped off the train, the man and wife who had originally contacted him were all smiles. The crisis of which they had spoken had been averted. Unexpectedly, their partner came to them and said words to the effect of "If you want me out of your business, I will get out in a proper fashion." The two made up, with the offended party then telling his former adversary that if he was going to approach things in this spirit, he did not want him to leave. Surprised at this generosity, the partner agreed to stay. Decades later, the company was still in operation, the two families reconciled, and a potential negative

---

61. Moseley, *Manifest Victory*, 271–72.

situation avoided.⁶² As Moseley shared, "Any prayer that does not seek the best not just for ourselves but all others, and is not conducted in utter sincerity and good will, tends to limit the response. When we unselfishly ask for God's best for all, we get His best as do all concerned. It is a kingdom principle that will not and cannot fail. After all, 'Love Never Fails.'"⁶³

On several occasions, Moseley had dealings with people who engaged in dishonesty of various kinds, sometimes outright theft. One such incident pertained to a young man who had a seemingly constant desire to steal, even from those who had befriended him. Sometime in 1905 or 1906, this young person approached Moseley about his wrongdoing and asked his opinion as to how to come clean. Apparently when he was a student at a college, the school president had taken an interest in the young man. During his time as a student he had stolen from nearly all who had befriended him, including the university president. He left before his crimes were found out and came to Macon. He met and befriended the pastor of the First Presbyterian Church in that city, and asked if he could borrow money from him. Instead of loaning him the money, the pastor invited him to live in his home with his family. While there, he had stolen jewelry from his most recent benefactor. "What would you do?" he asked Moseley.

The highest thing he could do, Moseley told the young man, was to write to all of the parties that he could not see personally, and make full confession. In addition, he was encouraged to ask for the opportunity to make restitution as soon as he found employment. Although a difficult task, the thief agreed to do so and began writing letters to the victims of his crimes. Fourteen letters were posted. To the young man's surprise, each person he contacted forgave him and even forgave the debt and wished him all the best. Years later, he told Rufus that going to full confession and offering to make restitution destroyed the desire to steal for good.⁶⁴ With confession, to God and to each other, freedom comes in abundance and liberates the soul burdened with sin and bondages.

Around that same time, 1905 or 1906, another young man approached Rufus with a contrite attitude and confessed to him a long and deep-rooted practice of dishonesty. Stealing had become second nature to him, often resulting in the stealing of money or anything of value without a second thought. It had gotten to the point where he even stole from his employer, a man who had gone out of his way to help the young man. His conscience finally got the better of him, and he went to Moseley for advice on how to

---

62. Moseley, *Manifest Victory*, 271–72.

63. Moseley, *Manifest Victory*, 271–72.

64. Moseley, *Manifest Victory*, 271–72.

proceed. Before he could give his advice, the young man told Moseley he was resolved to go to his employer and come clean, letting the chips fall where they may. Rufus agreed that this was the best plan and prayed on behalf of the thief. A couple of days later, he returned beaming with joy. His employer forgave him, had no intention of bringing the law into the matter, and worked out a plan to repay the amount stolen. He even gave the young man a raise to facilitate the repayment and reward his honesty. When the employer was asked how he could show such mercy, he replied, "I had rather have a young man who has come clean as you have done, than to take chances with a new one." The thief, who had become physically ill from guilt, was immediately released of the malady and went on to do well.[65] Confession works not only against theft, but in much more personal situations as well.

Once a young woman and her husband came to Rufus with a problem that had to do with something another young man had said to her that was, as he put it, "just not the right thing." Feeling insulted and wanting settlement of the matter, she asked Moseley if there was something he could do. Rufus contacted the young man in question and asked if he, the young married couple, and himself could meet privately in such a way so as not to raise any suspicion that something was amiss. Responding to this request, the young man who had uttered the insult, as well as the husband and wife, came to the meeting. The woman repeated what had been said to her, and the accused again denied saying it. Rufus stopped the meeting at that point and asked that all four of them kneel in prayer about the matter. Before they even arose from their knees, the offending party admitted that he had, in fact, insulted the woman. By admitting to his lie, the offended party and her husband forgave the offense. The upshot of it all was that no one outside of the small group was ever aware that anything untoward had ever happened, and fellowship between all parties had been restored. Moseley stated that if necessary, he was prepared to bring the matter before the church for rectification. Happily, such a turn of events was not needed.[66]

But Rufus Moseley anticipated a delicate situation in his own life, his pending break from Christian Science. He knew that those same qualities of utter sincerity would be needed in that situation as much as any other. While seeking this road, he came into contact with a new spiritual movement that had made waves in Los Angeles, California and spread across the nation.

---

65. Moseley, *Manifest Victory*, 252–53; Moseley, "Wedding Garment."
66. Moseley, *Manifest Victory*, 253.

AZUSA STREET PENTECOSTALISM

By late 1906, Moseley had heard of the Azusa Street variety of Pentecostalism and began exploring its claims, a search that would last three years. By late 1909 and early 1910, he began an earnest quest for the experience called the baptism of the Holy Spirit. Word of the revivals in Wales and at Azusa Street in Los Angeles had spread far and wide, and there was considerable public interest in the phenomenon. One of his close friends had earlier received the baptism of the Holy Spirit and was to further increase his own desire for the experience. Exactly what this "baptism in the Holy Spirit" was at the time was subject to interpretation, as Moseley was to find out when he heard from both the new Pentecostals as well as the established Holiness groups. The Holiness movement, which was heavily influenced by John Wesley's teachings, sprang up during the Second Great Awakening in the United States, and by the 1850s was carried back to Great Britain. The new Pentecostals were advocating a different position than their Holiness counterparts, some stressing that speaking in tongues was evidence of the baptism. The older, more established Holiness groups, on the other hand, believed in a baptism via sanctification that may or may not result in speaking in tongues. It made for considerable confusion in those early days, and sides were increasingly chosen. Rufus was not immune to all of this, but as was his nature, he studied both sides before coming to a conclusion. Not all of his Holiness or Pentecostal friends would agree with him.[67]

At this point, Moseley simply wanted the experience as he perceived that his own Christian walk was lacking; he would sort out the theological fine hairs later. What is readily apparent is that his hungry, burning heart for God was pushing him forward yet again. As Moseley protégé Wayne McLain described Moseley's quest:

> He was not content—as multitudes apparently are—with a religion of ritual and mental assent to a creed or theological system, or even with a few experiences of the felt presence of the divine . . . His pilgrimage seems to have assumed that the divine presence should be man's portion all the time and should be experienced on ever deeper levels of thought and feeling." He would not be content with simply settling for conversion, followed by a life of waiting for the Second Coming, or death.[68]

---

67. For an excellent history on the dispute between the older Holiness Pentecostal movement and the new Azusa Street Pentecostals, see Synan, *Holiness-Pentecostal Tradition*.

68. McLain, *Resurrection Encounter*, 50–51.

Rufus was becoming increasingly aware that there was more, much more, to the Christian life, and he wanted to have an active role in it. The revelation he had as a student, that there was possible a way of life not commonly lived, was again calling to him. He ever had a seeker's heart, and would not let anything get in his way of finding Truth. There would be bumps on the road, personal losses, theological questions, and for a time rejection from the community around him, but it mattered not. If Christ was knowable in a deeper way as Rufus had come to believe he was, and if this meant the baptism of the Holy Spirit, he would earnestly seek for it despite the cost and his own misconceptions of it. This gentle pilgrim, seeker, intellectual, and mystic was about to enter a spiritual life he could not have imagined. His life would never be the same.[69]

---

69. McLain, *A Resurrection Encounter*, 50–51.

2

Locusts and Wild Honey
INTO THE WILDERNESS OF PREPARATION
1910–1921

The greatest glory in living lies not in never falling, but in rising every time we fall.

—RALPH WALDO EMERSON

The next phase of Rufus Moseley's life would provide him with a much greater understanding of the downtrodden in the United States and would become a key part of his ministry. Concern for the poor, a very basic part of Christianity which Jesus himself repeatedly emphasized, would become nothing less than a passion with Moseley, and in time was typified by his speaking out in power rarely seen or experienced at the time. He nonetheless understood that there was much work to be done in himself, far beyond what he could guess at the time, and that no one graduates from their time in the wilderness without dying to the pride of life and everything the binds and holds one down.

Moseley had gone from his salvation experience in 1889, to a nearly ten-year involvement with Christian Science beginning in 1900, to now actively seeking after what he had come to believe contained the very things he most sought. Although he (and others) would find an exact definition of the "baptism in the Holy Spirit" to at first elude capture, the great outpouring of the Holy Spirit in Wales and Azusa Street would provide the basis for seeking believers going forward. As mentioned earlier, Moseley himself heard differing opinions of the experience, and (like the Pentecostal movement in general) would seek to adopt a theological definition based on Scripture and experience. Rufus would be one of a multitude of people in those early days who wondered about what they were hearing, believed God was in it regardless of their uncertainty, and above all else wanted to experience all that God had for them.

EXPLORING PENTECOSTALISM'S CLAIMS

The American Pentecostal movement as it is known today was generally drawn from a series of events that took place beginning in 1906 at a place known as Azusa Street in Los Angeles, where speaking in tongues was the dominant feature, or at least the one that gained the most attention.[1] There were people at those meetings, such as William Seymour, who came to stress the idea that the initial evidence for the baptism was speaking in tongues. The issue of tongues was debated as to whether a person spoke in a known language that they had not learned, or whether it was a prayer language. A Southerner who at first resisted and then embraced the new Pentecostalism was Joseph Hillary King, a friend of Moseley and a man destined to have an impact on the movement. Like so many other early Pentecostals, he came from a Methodist and Holiness tradition, and like Rufus Moseley shortly thereafter, struggled with how to define the unmistakable move of God.

King was born in South Carolina to sharecroppers, and poverty early on necessitated that he work long, hard hours to help support the family. At age sixteen, King became a believer when a traveling Methodist preacher gave an altar call at revival gathering. A few months later, he had a spiritual visitation which he claimed sanctified him for ministry. Despite skepticism from his family, he began an honest and judicious quest to learn all he could. By age twenty-two, he was licensed with the Northern Methodist Church and began work as a circuit walker (as one author humorously pointed out, none of the churches he served could afford a horse[2]) for the denomination. By the late 1890s, his family having since moved to Georgia, he became increasingly dissatisfied with the Methodist church, feeling that a deeper move of the Spirit was not to be found in the churches with which he was familiar. In 1898, this dissatisfaction prompted him to join the Fire-Baptized

---

1. See Synan, *Century of the Holy Spirit*, for a fine overview of the events, personalities, and antecedents to the Azusa Street revival.
2. Jacobsen, *Reader in Pentecostal Theology*, 110.

Holiness Church, an organization he would come to lead just a few years later.[3] In little more than a decade, the Fire-Baptized group would unite with some Pentecostal Holiness groups and come to embrace the Azusa Street version of the Holy Spirit baptism. It was not without questions and reservations that this change was made, however.[4]

In modern times, "spirit-filled" Christians largely believe that the definition of "baptism of the Holy Spirit" has always been the same, when quite the opposite was the case. For instance, to Wesleyan-influenced groups, it referred to an experience after salvation where one was "sanctified," as a specific event itself, followed by the infilling and enabling of the Holy Spirit to live that life. It might involve speaking in tongues. King had heard of Azusa Street, of course, but like many of his day, was skeptical. A prodigious reader and researcher, he sought to understand the new phenomena as best he could. Another southern believer who had questions of his own, Gaston Cashwell, made the pilgrimage to Azusa Street to see for himself. He returned convinced, and thereafter preached the new Pentecostalism, and in the process gained the reputation as being an earnest proponent of it across the American South.

When members of King's Fire-Baptized Holiness Church returned with positive stories of Cashwell and his teaching, King knew he had to investigate for himself.[5] After carefully researching the topic and even publicly contradicting Cashwell, King came to the conclusion that Cashwell was right. In February 1907, the Holiness preacher and some of his aides asked for and received the baptism in the Holy Spirit in the "new" Pentecostal sense, and began speaking in tongues. Other members of his group did likewise, and it quickly spread through the Georgia Holiness community. It was into this mix of events that King and some of his associates periodically visited Macon, Georgia where they encountered Rufus Moseley. The fellowship between the two, based on mutual self-respect and honest seeking, was to prove a seminal event not only in the life of Moseley, but in the rise of Pentecostalism across Georgia and the South.

J. H. King was an influential person in the life of Rufus Moseley both before and after he (Rufus) received the baptism in the Holy Spirit in 1910. The two met in 1907 in Macon, Georgia, and talked at length about the experience King had recently embraced. An unnamed female associate of King's became very close to Rufus, and likewise encouraged and guided him

---

3. Jacobsen, *Reader in Pentecostal Theology*, 109–10; See also Moon, *From Ploy-boy to Pentecostal Bishop* for a study of Joseph King.

4. Jacobsen, *Reader in Pentecostal Theology*, 109–10.

5. Jacobsen, *Reader in Pentecostal Theology*, 109–10.

toward the baptism. In the following decades King and Moseley continued their friendship, but in those early days Rufus felt a special kinship. King, in turn, made a special visit to Macon in March 1910 and began what became known as the Moores Hall meetings, named for the building in which they were held.[6] It would not be the only such gathering in Macon concerning the new Pentecostal experience, as public interest began to swell.

BAPTISM IN THE HOLY SPIRIT

A week after the first Moores Hall gathering, and on the afternoon and evening of March 20, 1910, Moseley attended a series of meetings under the leadership of noted English revivalist and author Samuel Chadwick. The meeting was initially held at the downtown Macon Mulberry Street Methodist Church, but public interest was so great that the afternoon session had to be moved to the city auditorium. King was also in attendance. Through this and other meetings in the early spring of 1910, Moseley had become familiar with other middle Georgia Pentecostals of the time—to be sure, a small group—and spoke to them at length about the baptism of the Holy Spirit. Because Rufus was well-known in Macon, and his following of Christian Science was common knowledge, he was looked upon with considerable suspicion. One of those to whom he spoke who was aware of Rufus's interest in the Mind Sciences told him that he would have to become more orthodox, more conservative, before he could expect the baptism of the Holy Spirit. Moseley's response was that the promise was to those who ask, seek, and knock, not to the orthodox. Moseley related that, upon speaking those words, he was on the right path. He told of the spiritual and even physical working upon his body at the time in what he later came to understand as preparation for what was to come. Still, his non-standard answer did not garner him a great deal of positive reception from the others.[7] Moseley's intellectual brilliance, his academic credentials, and his lack of orthodoxy caused some to have doubts about him, both at the time and in the years that followed.

After the afternoon Chadwick meeting on March 20, 1910, Rufus attended the Macon Christian Science forum, where he announced to his friends his ongoing search for the baptism of the Holy Spirit. This was quite outside of the experience of his fellow Christian Scientists, but so great was their love for Moseley that they encouraged him in his quest. One of the

---

6. Synan, *Century of the Holy Spirit*, 1–6; Synan, *Holiness-Pentecostal Tradition*, 143–52; McLain, *Resurrection Encounter*, 70–72.

7. McLain, *Resurrection Encounter*, 70–71.

things that most bothered him was his sure knowledge that this new drawing of the Holy Spirit was about to take him away from these dear friends. After all, they had been an important part of his life since 1900; even his mother, Theresa, had followed him into the movement. How, he likely wondered, would it be perceived among his family and friends if he were to again leave one controversial group to join an even stranger, more intense one? It was a troubling time, and given that some of his new Pentecostal friends did not trust him anyway, this added to the burden he carried. In the eyes of the general public, regardless of religious persuasion, Pentecostals were not well-liked in those early days, and Rufus knew it.

At the close of Chadwick's afternoon gathering in the city auditorium that same day, an altar call was given for those interested in receiving the baptism in the Holy Spirit. Moseley was the only person in the large crowd to come forward. "I want God's best," he told Chadwick, "and if the baptism in the Holy Spirit is God's best, I want it." Because he had heard different accounts of just what the baptism in the Holy Spirit was, he was to say years later of that prayer, "I just put in an order for the whole thing, all that I knew about and all that I didn't know about."[8]

Of course, Moseley had also privately prayed for this experience, and had made a specific request of Jesus that if it were possible, he would like to have the baptism without tongues; but if not possible, he would take the baptism with tongues. Like many people of the time, reports of wild behavior associated with this particular gift and Pentecostals in general had given him pause. That evening, at yet another Moore's Hall gathering, prayers were made and Rufus continued to ask. As the building emptied, Moseley remained at the altar hoping and praying for the baptism then and there. By ten p.m., nothing had happened until he heard an inner voice tell him to "stop seeking and practice in love." Not entirely sure what that meant at the time, he arose and walked home. Unknown to anyone else, he was in the midst of the eighth day of a fast, and was "tarrying," and in prayer for the baptism. All the while, he was not entirely sure how to define what it was he sought. He simply knew that he wanted God's best and asked for it. When his prayer was answered, it was beyond anything he could have anticipated.[9]

Rufus lived close to downtown Macon on Georgia Avenue. As he walked home that night, he pondered the day's proceedings and message, and continued to pray as he made his way past Coleman Hill Park. At one

---

8. McLain, *Resurrection Encounter*, 69.

9. Moseley, *Manifest Victory*, 88–91; Moseley, Untitled speech in Washington, D.C., September, 1947.

point, he again felt his shoulders and back given physical realignment as he walked. This had begun a week earlier, but as he walked home that night, the sense of physical manipulation on his body intensified, giving him a burning sensation. He was later to say that he felt a physical upward pull that would, if he so chose, have carried him aloft. He also came to realize that the Holy Spirit is quite willing to intervene in the natural world at any time, and had much more control over the natural world than humans do over their own body. Christ seeks to make the body whole, something Moseley already believed, but he had not up to this time witnessed or experienced it for himself in this remarkable fashion. He believed it to be the final preparations for the answer to his prayer, a precursor to the Holy Spirit baptism he so intently sought. Upon arriving at the spacious antebellum mansion where he rented a room, he found he had the grand house to himself. The owner, Professor Edward Martin and family, had left for Atlanta that same day. Rufus later attributed this to the planning of the Holy Spirit, given what was about to transpire. He went upstairs to his room and again prayed for the baptism until around 11:00 PM, when he went to bed. Before falling asleep, Moseley prayed aloud, "Jesus, if it is possible, come and live within me and be in me the life and principle of your own good life that will let me go your way."[10]

Moseley also recalled the words of Christ that "If ye love Me, keep My commandments. And I will pray the Father, and He shall give you another Comforter, that he may abide with you forever; Even the Spirit of truth; whom the world cannot receive, because it seeth Him not, neither knoweth Him: but ye know Him; for He dwelleth with you, and shall be in you" (John 14:15–17, KJV). Stopping there, he rested in his request, believing that it would be answered. Though disappointed he had not received the baptism when he went forward at the city auditorium and at Moores Hall, he knew beyond words or thought that it was about to happen, and retired with a sense of expectancy and joy. He doubtless thought of many things before he slept, the paths that led up to this point in his life, a belief that God had something important for him to do, and he also harbored a great hope that someone with whom he had fallen in love would become his wife.

In the wee hours of that fateful morning, around 3:00 AM, Rufus awoke and took a seat at a table. With pencil and paper, he recorded some thoughts he believed would be of benefit to a female friend (I believe to be his love interest), an unnamed woman whom he refers to as simply the "Woman in the Wilderness." I also believe it to be the same woman associated with J. H.

---

10. Moseley, "Baptism of Fire"; Moseley, "Everything in Christ"; Moseley, *Manifest Victory*, 95–96.

King's ministry, someone who had likely known Moseley for a few years. She had earlier encouraged Rufus to attend Chadwick's meeting as well as King's Moore's Hall gathering, and attended both with him. Perhaps as early as 1906 or 1907, he had heard from her about the baptism of the Holy Spirit, and her avidity was such that he described her as positively "lit up." The thoughts came to him rapidly that morning, and he wrote as quickly as possible all that was being given. Rufus reported experiencing a growing joy as he wrote, again sensing that something more was about to happen. At the same time, he reported experiencing the limitless joy of Christ, where there was complete and total happiness, satisfaction, and delight. He found he had nothing but thanks to offer; nothing else seemed worthy of him but to fully give himself to the growing Presence in the room.[11]

Like a child at Christmas, Rufus related, he was in a place of glee and excitement as one thing after another unfolded before him. He had no thought of asking further, but like that child on Christmas morning, sat back and watched as one spiritual blessing and revelation after another was taken from the stocking, each one more delightful than the one before it. Rufus said of these few hours before Jesus manifested himself to him, besides his writing, he became aware of a holy possession that began at his head and descended to his lips and then to the rest of his body. To the end of his life, he found it impossible to adequately describe the event in terms of what he saw, heard, and felt, but was never more certain of anything for the rest of his days, and his life shown with the joy of it.[12]

As Moseley found himself by the moment entering a more heightened sense of spiritual awareness, a place some philosophers called "cosmic consciousness," he was cognizant that his encounter was radically more lofty than this. As he continued to submit himself to the Holy Spirit, and with volition not entirely his own, he arose from the chair until he stood upright. "Teach me about your blood!" he called out at one point, and as if in answer he raised his arms outward, taking the shape of a cross and began singing under the influence of the Holy Spirit: "Jesus, Jesus, how I love You, interposed His precious blood." As he sang, Moseley was shown what he later called the "reverse side of the cross," where all of the suffering Jesus had endured on behalf of the human race was so the exact opposite would be available to his yielded children. Rufus would later humorously say that the Holy Spirit took over his vocal cords and sang, as he was incapable of singing a single note.[13]

11. Moseley, *Manifest Victory*, 95–96.
12. Moseley, *Manifest Victory*, 95–96.
13. Moseley, *Manifest Victory*, 103–7.

As soon as his singing began, he became aware of a physical Being standing immediately in front of him, possessing immense sanctity and power. When in later years he was asked if he was relating a vision, he emphatically stated that the person of Christ in actual objective physical form stood before him. He told that he could have counted the paces between the two of them, or touched the outlines of his form. Overcome, Rufus fell at the feet of this Visitor, he said, "like one dead, yet never more alive in my life." At that point he was "infused" with the Holy Spirit. He continued singing praises and broke forth into prophesying (in English), something that continued until sunrise. To the theological chagrin of some of his Pentecostal friends, he did not speak in tongues. Indeed, it was not until the following November that he uttered anything in a special prayer language, but he did from time to time speak as given utterance in known languages that he had not learned, as well as encounter powerful dreams and visions. At some point before sunrise, someone rang the doorbell. Rufus initially felt a lessening of the Spirit's control on him as he considered whether or not to answer the door. He decided that he had an appointment with heaven that was more important than whoever the early morning visitor might have been. He later said he was never so happy to have shut the outside world out as he was that day. Moseley further related that, while at the feet of Jesus, the testing began in earnest:

> In the light of the witness of the Spirit and subsequent confirmations, the all-important tests were, by his enabling, met in his will. Those I did not answer aright held me in God's school in the wilderness until I gave the right answers.
>
> This question had first of all to be answered: "Is this manifestation and in-breathing of Jesus that had just been granted the coming of Jesus that the apostles looked forward to?" I answered "No, it is the preparation for His visible appearing and reigning upon earth." I also said I prefer for him to come in all, for me to be his servant and friend, and the servant and friend of all, to anything else. This saved me from the special temptation of our time, to set oneself up as another Messiah, or Christ, or as God. I was invited to ask what I would. I thank God I asked for the redemption and best possible for each and all on earth and everywhere.[14]

Moseley went on to say that before he left the room that morning, he had received the call to go to the people at the bottom of human despair—the down-and-outs—and share the good news that Jesus is alive, and he is

---

14. Moseley, *Manifest Victory*, 105–6.

longing to baptize with the Holy Spirit, to manifest himself to all and draw all into ineffable fruit-bearing union with him. Sometime thereafter (he didn't state exactly when), his call would include those on top of human privilege and would find him in the presence of presidents and governors, as well as religious and economic leaders. But first and foremost, and thereafter, he was to go among the poorest of the poor.[15]

> The light was clear. I must start at the bottom of human need, visiting the sick, the imprisoned, and the condemned. I was not only to go in love but without any responsibility for external results. The responsibility would be His, not mine. I was made keenly conscious that the highest judgment of values is not in terms of miracles or seen achievements, but in terms of love. I dedicated my life to moving among the needy, seeking to be loving and brotherly. I also agreed to begin telling people that I had only a few certainties, but the most precious, the certainties that Jesus lived and taught as the Good Spirit led Him and that the Spirit is also leading us.[16]

His ministry had now begun in earnest.

One cannot help but think of Francesco di Bernardone, Saint Francis of Assisi, when Moseley had his encounter with Christ. Francis, a reveler and party-giver par excellence, was one night in the midst of his merry-making when he was stopped in his tracks, "wounded by Love." His fellow party-goers were taken aback by his sudden change and still further outraged when this young man later became a mendicant follower of Christ. For Rufus, intellectual and spiritual seeker, he had wandered far and wide in his spiritual quest, and on this March night in 1910, he came face-to-face with the One who had all answers and who, as with Saint Francis, wounded him with love.

There is in Rufus Moseley's experience in those early morning hours something of profound significance to the history of Christianity. If he is to be taken seriously, as did those who knew him best, it is a repeat of the resurrection encounter the first disciples had the evening of the first Easter Sunday. While Rufus eventually shared this encounter in the succeeding decades, it never got widespread reporting among the religious world, in part because it would not have been widely believed, and also because his ministry was to the down-and-out. Rufus Moseley's encounter with the Living Jesus was a profound experience that gives testimony to Christ's ability

---

15. Moseley, *Manifest Victory*, 106.
16. Moseley, *Manifest Victory*, 106.

and willingness to appear to those whom he will, and reinforce the words and experience of the first disciples. As Wayne McLain reported,

> Such a report should have electrified the thought world of our century, for it assumes that Jesus is objectively alive in his body today just as he was in the days immediately following his resurrection and can appear to believers today in exactly the same way he did to his friends in the first century. If his report is true, it means that we had in Rufus Moseley in our time, a witness to, and an apostle of, the resurrection in exactly the same sense as were James, Peter, John, and Paul: . . . further, it gives rise to the daring expectation that Jesus can manifest himself in all his glorified objectivity to us today just as he did believers in the first century.[17]

Although he was to share this encounter from time to time over the years, it garnered little attention and gained even less traction. Especially in the early years, it is quite likely that it was written off as the delusions of a religious eccentric. One Macon clergyman to whom Rufus shared this story told him that while he believed him, he would likely be thought insane if he shared it widely. Another bluntly told him, "These things you have been telling me are of God and are true, but many people will think you crazy.[18] Simply put, his humility and personality were, like the apostle Paul, to limit its telling and to mute its credibility. It nonetheless does not limit the spiritual implications of such an encounter, and the fruit of this remarkable life gives greater credence to the possibility that Jesus Christ, in his resurrected body, visited a humble seeker in a rented room in 1910.[19]

Of course, Rufus also told his Pentecostal friends of his remarkable experience. They rejoiced with him, but almost immediately he was asked to define which side of the particular Pentecostal fence he was on. After hearing Moseley share his experience, one of the Holiness pastors asked Rufus if what he described was his "second blessing" subsequent to conversion, a term meant to describe the Holy Spirit baptism. Moseley responded by saying, "I don't think I have counted exactly, but it may have been about the seventeenth!"[20] It was but one of many examples of how Moseley defied definition himself, and was throughout his life something of a mystery to Pentecostals and Christians of all stripes. An exceptionally honest seeker, he did not really care how others defined him so long as he walked according

---

17. McLain, *Resurrection Encounter*, 86.
18. McLain, *Resurrection Encounter*, 84; 106.
19. McLain, *Resurrection Encounter*, 79–80.
20. McLain, *Resurrection Encounter*, 50.

to the light shown to him. He had gone down many different paths, found them all lacking, and now found that baptism in a firsthand relationship with Christ gave him what he sought.

Rufus never saw the baptism in the Holy Spirit, or salvation for that matter, as one-time events alone. He saw both as ongoing realities that would inform and direct the life of the believer to ineffable union: the true purpose of both experiences. Both salvation and baptism in the Holy Spirit were seen as having happened on specific days, but he held that they were intended to lead one to union, and to be daily experiences. He already had witnessed that some considered the baptism to be an end in itself, and with it the beginnings of sectarianism based on that experience. This happy troubadour avoided that trap, though he was not always understood and sometimes criticized for his approach.

What was apparent to all at the time and in the years to come was the unmitigated joy that he seemed to perpetually exude. Moseley seemed to have understood from the earliest days of his post-Holy Spirit baptism that it was going to be an ongoing, never-ending journey to find the best God had to offer. Though he was spiritually content, he was never satisfied and was ever listening to his inner Voice directing him onward. From early on, Rufus avoided the temptation to replace intimate fellowship with Christ with meetings, leaders, spiritual gifts, spiritual experiences, or the latest revelation from afar, something seemingly common today. Rufus saw this in his own day as well. He was unwilling to go along with the crowd if he genuinely did not think something was of the Holy Spirit or if someone or something acted as an intermediary. As far as he was concerned, he just didn't have that kind of time to waste.[21]

A STILL-BORN ROMANCE

There was one thorn in this otherwise fragrant rose of an experience: his female friend, his "Woman in the Wilderness" for whom he had developed unrequited romantic feelings. Moseley later wrote that, after he had entered into the baptism of the Holy Spirit, he mistakenly assumed that his feelings for the young woman were likewise brought forward and glorified, and that marriage was to be the result. It wasn't, and he describes having to give up his desire to be with her:

> It cost me much—more than it is well to attempt to tell—to make me ready to accept happily His superlative; not only for

---

21. McLain, *Resurrection Encounter*, 50–51.

me, but also for the one I loved. I died hardly and ungraciously. But after the death, I found that I had lost nothing but what had caused the suffering and the death, and kept me out of paradise where all things on ever higher levels are mine and yours and everyone's. After all, it was perhaps in letting go that I prevented myself from the actual loss of her. I would have been a poor husband, and the loss of a marriage is little compared with the loss of such a friendship.[22]

He would refer to her as "The Woman in the Wilderness" to the end of his days, but never named his lost love. It was a loss he keenly felt, and in a way explains the intense loneliness in which he lived out his days. Painful as this was at the time, he had another issue with which to contend: leaving Christian Science on loving terms, as after having received the Holy Spirit baptism he knew it was something he must do.

LEAVING CHRISTIAN SCIENCE

Rufus stated that, a week prior to his baptism in the Holy Spirit experience, he felt moved that the time was now right to be free of Christian Science. "You are ready for your release from the Christian Science organization,"[23] were the words be believed to be the Holy Spirit leading him forward and out. The very next day after his empyrean experience, he went to his Christian Science friends to report it. Their reaction was rather muted, as they did not understand the nature of the Holy Spirit of whom Rufus now spoke. Rufus dearly loved these individuals and wanted to part with them in the most loving way possible. As with his leaving Mercer University to follow Christian Science ten years before, he knew his departure had to be done in love and for the best of all concerned. While he did not break off all friendships, he made it known that the spiritual path before him now led away from Christian Science and Mary Baker Eddy. Because they loved Rufus, they reluctantly agreed with his decision, but were quite guarded against the Pentecostal world he was to enter. Nonetheless, for a few months they continued to call upon Moseley to pray for the sick, and he did so according to the new Pentecostal light he was given.[24]

---

22. Moseley, *Manifest Victory*, 110–11. Moseley, Untitled Manuscript of a 1950 speech, in the J. Rufus Moseley Collection, folder 4, Middle Georgia Archives, Washington Memorial Library, Macon, Georgia.

23. Moseley, *Manifest Victory*, 90.

24. Moseley, *Manifest Victory*, 89–90.

In retrospect, Rufus said of his experience with Christian Science that he knew of no one in the movement who was open to the baptism of the Holy Spirit, nor was there much interest in saying or doing anything that would contradict Mrs. Eddy. Rufus also said that any efforts toward sincerity, healing, or peacemaking were not as a result of Christian Science's teaching and methodology, but as a result of the Holy Spirit acting upon him and drawing him forward.[25] But it was not as if his new Pentecostal friends were without controversy either: the issue of speaking in tongues, and then the Oneness or "Jesus Only" doctrine, quickly came to the fore and threatened to undermine the nascent Pentecostal movement.

GIFTS OF THE SPIRIT

As noted earlier, when Moseley was baptized in the Holy Spirit, he did not speak in tongues in the sense of it being a prayer language (glossolalia). He was initially unsure about the gift, and thought it the realm of the mentally unstable, a common public opinion about those practicing it. From that time forward, he did find himself speaking in languages he knew existed, but had never learned (xenolalia); but to some Pentecostals, this was not the "tongues" that was allegedly the evidence for the baptism. On a few occasions that Rufus shared, he apparently spoke several sentences in Cherokee and was told by a native speaker what he had said. On another occasion, a French diplomat, fluent in several languages, heard Rufus speak in a few languages that he (Moseley) did not know, but all of which had the same message.[26] It would not be until November 1910 that he would have the experience of what charismatics today would call "speaking in tongues." Moseley did not overemphasize nor idolize the gift, something he saw among some Pentecostals, and in any event did not consider it as "the" evidence of the baptism in the Holy Spirit. He would, from what I could find, rarely use this gift in public. He was to say of it:

> when I sought for the Holy Ghost baptism, I had a measure of the general popular prejudice against tongues, and told the Lord that if he could give me the baptism without the tongues I would prefer it, but if not to give me the baptism with the tongues. With the great visitation, control, and glory that came, the speaking and singing was in English. In this glory and control the Lord definitely came within. Later, when I prophesied something that was to come to pass, but did not at the time realize that it was

25. Moseley, *Manifest Victory*, 89–90.
26. Moseley, *Manifest Victory*, 128.

prophetic, the Holy Ghost took control of my lips and tongue and I began to speak, or the Spirit began to speak through me, foreign words and phrases. Since then, the speaking has been both in English and in tongues.[27]

Decades later, he stated that he knew of few things that the ordinary human mind objects to more than speaking under the control of the Holy Spirit in languages unknown to the speaker, but understood perfectly by the Spirit giving utterance. He was to say, "I find that I can leave all this entirely in the hands of the Holy Spirit. He never makes a mistake."[28] Rufus was known to have considered exaltation of the gifts of the Spirit at the expense of the "Life as Love" as producing poor or even nonexistent spiritual fruit. Chasing after gifts or spiritual experiences was eschewed for the Life as Love.

Over the course of the week following his receiving the baptism of the Holy Spirit, the day visions and dreams he experienced were so profound that it caused great concern among his family, prompting them to fear for his sanity. Moseley's mother, Theresa, was frightened about what Rufus's new experience might mean. She had, of course, heard of Pentecostalism, and her family shared the widespread negative perceptions of it as a movement among the uneducated and poor, or worse, the mentally unhinged. At her urging, doubtless backed by Rufus's siblings, including brother Millard and his wife, Effie, they suggested that he enter a Dr. Allen's private sanitarium in nearby Milledgeville, Georgia for a time of reflection and observation. This was not the state institution there, but a private facility of considerably more progressive practices than was common in mental health facilities of the time.[29]

Upon his arrival at the sanitarium, approximately a week after he received the Holy Spirit baptism, Moseley continued to experience day visions difficult to explain and even more difficult to understand. He described seeing facility farm animals walking about with a grace and beauty he had never before seen; even the trees and grass took on a heavenly glow of glorification. This special gift, of seeing and living in the glory of what Rufus called the fourth empire or heavenly realm, was one that was continually repeated throughout his life. One of his young protégés once reported that it was not unusual to be riding with Moseley across the countryside or shopping in a grocery store when he would suddenly erupt in exclamations of thanksgiving for the beauty of the surroundings or the bounty on the shelves.[30]

27. Moseley, "Perpetuating Pentecost"; Moseley, "Spiritual Gifts."
28. Moseley, "Holy Grail at Home."
29. Moseley, *Manifest Victory*, 111–12.
30. McLain, *Resurrection Encounter*, 106–7.

Thanksgiving and gratitude were two gifts that Mr. Moseley would exhibit throughout his life and were to make him far more open to the moves of the Holy Spirit than many of his peers. In any event, he simply saw the world differently than most believers. With this gratitude came other gifts that ranged from uncanny discernment of spirits, words of wisdom/knowledge, prophetic words, healings, and even more dramatic manifestations. But in those early days at the sanitarium, nurses found it extremely difficult to wake him due to the intensity of the dreams he was experiencing.[31]

Rufus reported seeing the face of Christ in the faces of his caretakers, and felt a tremendous love for them and, indeed, everything he encountered. Moseley was under a physician's care at the sanitarium for thirteen days until Dr. Allen decided his patient was not delusional, merely in the midst of an intense religious experience. Within a few days, Rufus was working on the grounds and tending to the pecan trees he found there. When he returned to Macon sometime in April, he believed that he had to live down the sanitarium experience. After all, he feared some would relegate his experience as the product of an unstable mind. To his delight, old friends came to him and invited him to publicly speak numerous times on a variety of historical and philosophic topics. Rufus never forgot this simple act of love and confidence on the part of prominent Macon residents.[32]

His growing personal desire for and walking in the reality of the baptism was to burn within him for the rest of his life, and its corresponding love ethic would come to define him thereafter.[33] Moseley briefly described the early revelation of Christ he had been given, though was to find it a near impossibility to adequately put into words:

> I was given the greatest clarification, understanding, happiness, and bliss and put in almost unbelievable light, revelation, and glory. So much was given that I did not think of asking for anything . . . I entered into a realm above all conflict, where everything was reconciled, fulfilled, harmonized in love. I was given to feel and to see something of the wonder of the realm Jesus entered after his incarnation, crucifixion, and resurrection, the realm that has been named in my understanding the "fourth empire" or human-divine.[34]

---

31. Moseley, *Manifest Victory*, 112–15.
32. Moseley, *Manifest Victory*, 102.
33. Moseley, *Manifest Victory*, 112–13.
34. Moseley, *Manifest Victory*, 71.

THE FOURTH EMPIRE OR THE HEAVENLY REALM

Rufus would talk about there being four empires of existence: the first being the natural, the second being that of the human race, the third being that of the Divine-Human (Jesus) when he was on earth, and the fourth being that mentioned earlier, of the Human-Divine—which is to say, the resurrected Christ on the throne next to God in complete victory, and from that place of victory drawing his children to live his life anew through each of them. He was to explain, "I saw that heaven longs greatly to come to earth . . . we say we want to go to heaven, but if we were to go there would find heaven anxious to come here."[35] In this fourth realm, Moseley believed man was "made a whole being, possessing the faith of childhood, the vitality of youth, the maturity of middle age, and the wisdom of age. Here there is neither ignorance nor decay."[36] This "fourth realm" was what Rufus would later come to describe as "Life as Love," a place where when we are seated at rest, we give out love and only love to each and all of creation. The baptism of the Holy Spirit, to Moseley, was the gateway through which the believer can enter and abide in this place. As he was to say:

> It institutes a ministry of those who have begun to inherit its tremendous possibilities and cannot rest until they have seen it realized in their whole life. In their inmost being, they are already in the fourth empire, and are thus ministering spirits and angels of mercy to all other empires. This ministry continues until all realms of life are redeemed, fulfilled and brought to completion.[37]

Failure to move on to what Moseley called "Ineffable Union" (he also used "Perfect Everything" and "Life as Love" in place of Ineffable Union) was a shortcoming borne out of ignorance of its availability. To Moseley, it meant a spiritual journey that leads to moment-by-moment conscious union with Christ. He never claimed that he "arrived" at this, but that the spiritual journey toward it results in increased awareness and possession of Christ's presence. All of our experiences are meant to bring us to this place of dwelling in the fourth empire, the superlative union of conscious moment-by-moment union with Christ, what many earlier mystics referred to as contemplation, or one unnamed mystic described as the "Cloud of Unknowing."[38] We are taught by experience the folly of giving out anything but Christ's love, as we

---

35. Moseley, *Manifest Victory*, 199.
36. Moseley, *Manifest Victory*, 49.
37. Moseley, *Manifest Victory*, 99.
38. See *Cloud of Unknowing*.

get back what we give out. This is heady spiritual stuff, and a spiritual walk Moseley himself had difficulty explaining. This did not prevent him from trying, as throughout his life he often described his experiences using the great Victorian poets, playwrights, and writers he so loved.

The Norwegian playwright Henrik Ibsen's *Emperor and the Galilean* was one of Rufus's favorites, and considered the dialogue in that play between the Roman Emperor Julian and his Christian servant, Maximus, to be very close to what he was being shown of the spirit world. The apostate Emperor Julian, who had persecuted Christians and sought to make the world "Galileanless," is taken in a dream to another world. The world upon which he found himself was older, vaster, possessed of a golden light with multiple moons orbiting its tremendous girth. He then witnessed a procession approaching him, led by soldiers and weeping women, followed by the Galilean carrying his cross, whose influence and name he had sought to eradicate from the earth. "Wither Away Galilean?" Julian called out to Jesus, who, though bloody and beaten, smiled and replied, "To the place of the Skull." Julian was then horrified when he realized that the Galilean, whom he sought to eradicate, lives and dies for all his creation, and that his work on earth was but one stop in a universal effort to redeem his creation wherever it might be. Rufus did not believe that Christ had to die again and again, that his one sacrifice was for all, but he did believe that Ibsen, and a good many other writers whom Christians generally do not read, had much to tell us. For a well-read intellectual like Rufus, combined with his inner drive for the Life as Love, there was much to be revealed in a variety of writings if we have the ears to hear and eyes to see.[39]

FAMILY TENSIONS

Rufus's spiritual experiences were quite beyond the ken of his family, and would be met with concern and, in time, outright opposition. After his two weeks at the sanitarium, Rufus was encouraged to move into the two-story home his brother Millard and his wife occupied in nearby Byron, some eighteen miles south of Macon. Because Rufus had relieved Millard of the responsibility of paying for their youngest brother's college education as per family agreement, thirteen acres of pecan orchard land outside of Byron was deeded to him. It was to provide him with an income for his modest needs; near the end of his life, he deeded the land back to Effie, Millard's wife, from whom the land had come. A fire destroyed their house in 1930, and a brick

---

39. Moseley, *Manifest Victory*, 31–37; See also Ibsen, *Emperor and the Galilean*, esp. 188–89.

home was built on the site that same year and was to be his and his brother's family home until Rufus's death in 1954.[40]

Almost immediately after moving in, Rufus found that his new faith did not go over well with his housemates. Rufus's family thought him at best eccentric and at worst a holy-roller, with all the derogatory images the term implied. Yet I have not found anywhere where Rufus spoke ill of his relatives, nor said anything about them that was not in the highest love ethic. Nonetheless, I do not doubt that life in that home was a real challenge for all concerned. Why he never chose to find a place of his own in the following years is, I regret to say, something of a mystery to me; at most, I could offer little more than speculation. But within the confines of Millard and Effie's house, Rufus's room was strictly off-limits to all, and apparently this was especially guarded. That was a minor thing, however, as there would be public events over the next two years that would prove especially trying to his brother and his wife, as Rufus's very public and highly vocal religious stances grew into public opprobrium, and a source of supreme embarrassment for family and friends alike.[41]

It was nearly twenty months between the time of Moseley's return from the sanitarium and his engagement in highly visible religious activities in and around Macon. Beyond periodic editorials to the *Macon Telegraph*, little is known of his activities between the spring of 1910 and the early winter of 1911. During the summer of 1910, it is known that he hired himself out as a cotton picker with local growers, as well as worked in the family pecan grove. He also engaged in evangelistic work among some of the black field workers and took in meetings outside of city limits. When he did emerge, he gained a reputation as being a quirky, religiously odd local figure. As he doubtless recalled later, just as Francis of Assisi had become the object of scorn and ridicule among his former friends and family, so this gentle southerner was to encounter opposition to his message, and most definitely the manner in which it was presented. One can imagine the general and familial reaction to seeing a brilliant young scholar go from one unusual religion such as Christian Science, to another in Pentecostalism. The period between 1910 to the end of World War I was Moseley's own time in the wilderness, and would see his reputation in tatters, his life that of a pariah. Rufus had, in the eyes of many, become a fanatic, and it would

---

40. Conversation with Diana Moseley Vinson, October 2015.

41. "Refused Admittance to Church"; see also Rufus's response a few days later, "J.R. Moseley Writes Card"; additional details supplied by Diana Moseley Vinson on October 2015.

take years before he and his message would be appreciated in Macon and beyond.[42]

THE DAVIS SISTERS AND STREET MINISTRY

While it was doubtless a time of adjustment for Rufus, it also was a time when his religious views began to come to the attention of the city of Macon. Later in 1910, he met and befriended two twin sisters from Macon, Suzie and Carro Davis, who had themselves experienced salvation and the Holy Spirit baptism that summer. These two sisters, from an aristocratic family who lived on a plantation outside of the city, had been raised by an aunt when both parents died. From the ages of five forward, "Aunt Minnie" would see to the girls' education and religious instruction. Their aunt came into contact with Pentecostalism around 1909–10, and excitedly told her nieces about it. They were not impressed until they made a trip to Chicago in the summer of 1910, and there heard Andrew Urshan and William Durham speak on the baptism of the Holy Spirit. Carro experienced the baptism immediately, while Suzie was to have the experience shortly after returning to Macon. These two schoolteachers resigned their positions and began preaching, like Rufus, to the down-and-outs and racial minorities in the area. It was inevitable that the three should meet, and for the next several years they were inseparable ministry partners.[43]

In December 1911, the three of them apparently thought it a good idea to attend services at Macon's First Presbyterian Church on Mulberry Street—a church Suzie and Carro attended as children—and there disrupt the service with boisterous worship, presumably involving tongues. Outraged at this exhibition, the pastor demanded that they leave. They took their worship to the street that day as well as other occasions, all of which garnered considerable public and newspaper attention. Carro Davis loudly sang hymns, her fine voice could be heard for blocks and only added to the public draw. African-Americans made up the majority of the public crowd, and there were reports of healings among them during these meetings. It was symbolic of Moseley's work among the poorest and neediest, and also helped fuel his already-strong belief that racial segregation was a great social evil.[44]

On Christmas Day, 1911, despite the fact that they had obtained permission from law enforcement to hold street meetings, their group

---

42. McLain, *Resurrection Encounter*, 109, 111.
43. Pickard, *Davis Sisters*, 13–21.
44. Moseley, *Manifest Victory*, 127–31; Camp, *Ineffable Union*, xxvii–xxviii.

apparently became unwieldy, some reports said over a thousand were in attendance, prompting the police to ask them to move. Gathering in front of the Knights of Pythias building in downtown Macon, Rufus reported years later that when asked to break up the meeting, he responded to the police officer that he was not in the business of stopping meetings, but of helping them along. This elicited laughter from the crowd and angered the officer who then took steps to arrest Moseley. Realizing that he had offended the officer, Rufus apologized and said, "If you love me half as much as I love you, we will get along just fine." The policeman smiled and Rufus was released before a trip to the local station was made.[45]

These were part and parcel of his early post-Holy-Spirit baptism days in which the local population and his family considered Rufus a true oddity, the cynosure of a strange street cult. An old friend of his, poet and scholar Professor George Herbert Clarke, even made it a point to visit Macon specifically to see Moseley. Clarke, perhaps at the behest of some of Rufus's Mercer University friends, sought to get Moseley to tone down his very verbal and erratic public religious demonstrations. Clarke failed, but did report to a third party about Moseley, "There is greatness there that you [meaning the friend to whom he was talking] and I can hardly begin to understand."[46] The amazingly redemptive thing about it all is that ten years later Rufus Moseley would become one of the city's best-known and beloved citizens, and was a frequent guest speaker at churches all over town, including the First Presbyterian Church. Those days were not in the least indicative of his anointing, but rather of his own early enthusiasm.

Just as he had come to know early Pentecostal leader Joseph King during the movement's formative period, so too would Moseley meet and butt heads with one of the era's most controversial Pentecostal figures, Andrew D. Urshan. Urshan was a Persian-born Christian who had attended the American Presbyterian Training College near his Iranian home in Urmiah. He served as a missionary among the Persian people until in 1902. Following a visit to Europe, he migrated to Chicago. Having a number of relatives in the city, he began attending services at Moody Church until he embraced the Pentecostal message, at which point he was shown the door. He went on to establish the Persian Pentecostal Mission in Chicago. Around 1914, he and others believed they had a new revelation about the nature of God

---

45. "Refused Admittance to Church"; see Appendix II at the end of Camp, *Ineffable Union* for full transcriptions of these newspaper articles; McLain, *Resurrection Encounter*, 107–10; see also Pickard, *Davis Sisters*, for a detailed account of these two remarkable Macon women and their participation with Rufus Moseley between 1910 and 1917.

46. Moseley, *Manifest Victory*, 130.

which departed from traditional Christian teaching on the Trinity. Instead, the new movement embraced what was to become known as "Oneness Pentecostalism" or "Jesus Only" teachings. It was a rejection of two millennia of doctrine and practice that held that God was manifest in three distinct personalities: Father, Son, and Holy Spirit, and replaced it with a belief that the totality of the nature of God was manifest in Christ alone. In observance of this, and perhaps its most recognized feature, water baptisms were conducted in Jesus' name only, leading to the name.[47]

As earlier noted, the two Davis sisters had met Andrew Urshan in Chicago, and would later embrace his Oneness message when he came out with it a few years later. Urshan apparently also had a romantic interest in Carro Davis, and for a time was a guest at their plantation home near the Lakeside district outside of Macon. While Carro respected Urshan, and embraced his Oneness message, she did not share his romantic feelings and told him so. It is interesting to note that Urshan thought Rufus Moseley a rival for the affections of Carro, something that, if true, Moseley never mentioned. The two would thereafter permanently disagree about the Oneness message, Rufus remaining a confirmed Trinitarian to the end of his days. When combined with his mistaken suspicions that Moseley was a rival in love as well, Urshan angrily broke off fellowship with him. They did patch things up, albeit a few years later, when Urshan asked Rufus's forgiveness for his attitude toward him. By then it became apparent that Moseley had remained celibate and Urshan himself married someone else. The renewed friendship was something for which both men were grateful. Whenever Rufus was in the Chicago or New York area, he made it a point to visit his friend.

WORLD WAR I AND LIFE AS A PARIAH

In the years following the street meetings and before the 1914 outbreak of World War I in Europe, Moseley's activities were much more low-key. Between 1911 and 1912, he met with nearly every pastor and spiritual leader in Macon to share his testimony. Many of them found his tale interesting, some even believing him, but for the most part his reputation as an eccentric Pentecostal had been written in stone. He expanded his circle of testimony-giving to include business leaders, hoping to provide them with the message that Jesus lives, and wants to baptize in the Holy Spirit and live again through all believers. This was not always understood by hearers, and many laughed at his perceived fall from a respected scholar to what many

---

47. Moseley, "Happy Days in the Kingdom"; Jacobsen, *Reader in Pentecostal Theology*, 151–52; See also Segraves, *Andrew Urshan*.

considered to be a religious nut. Nonetheless, during this period, his writings reflect a joy at being, an anticipation of becoming, and an excitement at what the Life in Christ was to mean. He was enough of an example to other believers that some sought him out for advice.

Prior to the outbreak of World War I, a young Macon, Georgia man known simply as Crockett contacted Moseley to seek his opinion about a business venture. The young man was a believer and owned some property that another was interested in renting. The problem for Crockett was that the man wanting to rent intended to turn it into a bar. He was of the opinion that nothing in his possession must be used for or profit taken from something that worked ill to others. When he came to Rufus and set forth his problem, Moseley told the young man that he already knew the answer, and in fact had stated it as well as anyone could. Crockett told the prospective renter he would not allow a saloon on his property, prompting him to look elsewhere. Almost immediately another man came to Crockett, seeking his property with the intention of setting up a small grocery store. He was to stay in that property for over twenty years.[48] Other incidents in Moseley's life during the second decade of the twentieth century were more unusual. One such example of the Holy Spirit leading him to unusual things and people had to do with someone Rufus came to call "Friend John."

"FRIEND JOHN"

In January 1914, Moseley heard an unusual report of a diminutive black man being held in a Valdosta, Georgia jail. This prisoner had refused to give his name and referred to himself as "God." A friend of Moseley's, a former student at Mercer named J. B. Copeland, lived in Valdosta and practiced law there. Rufus contacted his friend and asked him to represent the prisoner until he could arrive from Macon. When he reached the Valdosta jail cell and introductions were made, Moseley asked the unusual man if he was calling himself God so that his total identification was not in his physical being, but that he might make God his all-in-all. The man smiled and said, "You understand me better than anyone else."[49] Nonetheless refusing to call him "God," Moseley simply chose the name John and thereafter, in Quaker fashion as he did to all he met, called him "Friend John."[50]

After his release from jail, Friend John would occasionally send Rufus a card or letter, or would look him up if he was in town. During one such

48. Moseley, "Wholly the Lord's."
49. Moseley, *Manifest Victory*, 137.
50. Moseley, *Manifest Victory*, 138.

occurrence in the summer of 1914, he sent word to Moseley that he and his group of followers were out at a suburban recreation area near Macon, Georgia. When Rufus arrived and asked the followers the whereabouts of Friend John, he was told that "God" had gone for a walk. For a couple of years, Rufus did not hear from or about Friend John, until he received a message from one of Georgia's state mental institutions in Milledgeville, informing him that his name had been given by one of their new patients. Rufus told the officials what he knew of the man and he was, sometime thereafter, released. It would over twenty years before Moseley would hear of him again, and it proved quite an eye-opener.[51]

In the late 1930s, Rufus Moseley heard of a black spiritual leader in New York City who was to go on to nationwide fame under the name Father Divine. As he read details of his life in an article, it came to him that his Friend John and Father Divine might be one and the same person. During one of Moseley's speaking trips to New York City, he stopped by Father Divine's headquarters and asked to see him. The secretary informed Moseley that Father was not in, but that she would pass on his name and information, including some memories from 1914. He simply wanted to know if Father Divine remembered a Mr. Moseley from Macon.[52] Some months later, during another trip to New York City, he again stopped by Father Divine's headquarters, where he found the secretary very friendly. Yes, it seemed Father knew of a Mr. Moseley from Macon, but that it was not Mr. Moseley who befriended Father, but the other way around. Nonplussed, Rufus was shown into the office of Father Divine where he shook the hand of his friend. Father Divine, as leader of his cult, would not allow anyone to speak to his group. His willingness to let Moseley do so was remarkable, even though Divine and his followers did not agree with Rufus's message. A hallmark of Moseley's ministry was his willingness to share with any groups the truth of Christ. Divine told Rufus that the man he had known as "Friend John," at the time he knew him, had lived in the realm of Jesus. But now, Moseley was solemnly informed, he lived in the realm of the Father. When Rufus tried to correct Father Divine—apparently this was not often done—about Jesus being the only begotten embodiment of the Father on earth, Divine responded, "I am not on earth."[53]

---

51. Moseley, *Manifest Victory*, 138.
52. Moseley, *Manifest Victory*, 137–39.
53. Moseley, *Manifest Victory*, 138.

FIGHTING RACISM'S UGLY LEGACY

By the time of World War I, Rufus stepped up his ministry to minorities or any he perceived to be treated unfairly. This ranged from preaching to field workers during lunch hour to speaking at black churches in and around Macon. It sometimes mandated action to prevent the undercurrent of racism from becoming violent. On one occasion, Rufus stopped the lynching of a young black man who had been driving his white employer's truck, something about which one white resident and his myrmidons in Byron, Georgia took umbrage.[54] Moseley, all of five and a half feet tall and weighing perhaps one hundred and twenty-five pounds, fearlessly confronted the angry mob intent on murdering the black youth. Shaming them into releasing their intended victim, Rufus later commented that some in the crowd repented of their activity and attitudes, as evidenced through later behavior. It must be remembered that, from the time Reconstruction ended in 1877 to the year 1920, Georgia led the nation in lynching. On average, a black man was murdered every month, often with watching crowds and photographs taken of the grisly event and passed around like macabre trading cards. Over the next forty years, Moseley's activities in any number of minority churches across the United States gained him opposition from considerable numbers of whites, both Christian or otherwise.

PLATO DURHAM

It was also during the World War I era that Rufus Moseley was to meet and become close to another most remarkable man, Plato Durham. Dr. Durham was the dean of the Candler School of Religion at Emory University in Atlanta between 1914 and 1918; Rufus described him as an "idealist, mystic, and dreamer." Moseley, of course, was all of those things as well, and it seems Durham shared his reputation for being something of an eccentric. They immediately became friends. By the 1920s, when Rufus was working as a religion writer for the *Macon Telegraph*, he would periodically be invited to Emory University to speak to graduate students. Durham himself had been a Chautauqua speaker in Macon, likely where the two met. He also was known to preach extemporaneously at places like the steps of a courthouse. This gifted but quirky man was said to be a first-rate philosopher and Christian, but lacking in the skills necessary to run an academic department. Durham believed that there was something special about Moseley, and told him so. He encouraged Moseley not to be limited to the works of God in the

---

54. Manis, *Macon Black and White*, 127.

past, but to be ever open to what he might be doing now. During another one of their visits, Durham looked Rufus in the eyes and perceptively and prophetically said, "Something is coming, I am watching you; it may be through you."[55] Durham reminds one of Rufus himself, perhaps something of a look at Moseley had he remained in higher education.

OPPOSITION TO AMERICA'S ENTRY INTO WORLD WAR I

During the lead-up to World War I, Moseley began to write and speak about the horrors of war. He was a steadfast pacifist, not as a result of simply being against taking up arms against one's fellow man, but because of the kingdom way he was beginning to see. It was possible, he liked to say, to be too low-down to fight—that is to say, a coward—and such a position is just as much a moral failure. His opposition to the America's involvement in World War I had as much to do with wanting to keep the United States out of the madness as it did with the false premise upon which the war—any war—was based. His distinctly kingdom-of-God approach to war, even in these early years of his ministry, often flew in the face of conservative religious and political belief. Could a Christian take up arms? Yes, he believed one could be like the apostle Peter, who drew a weapon and used it in defense of Jesus in the garden of Gethsemane, but who later denied him. Or one could be like the apostle John, who took no weapon in defense of Christ, but stayed with him without denial in the hour of supreme shame and suffering.[56]

When evil is used to shut down evil, it never really addresses the underlying forces that created the conflict in the first place. He believed that the Love Way, which in his opinion had never really been tried (other than perhaps during the first century), held the answer. He understandably faced criticism for this position, some even questioning his patriotism for daring to suggest that there was a different means available. Of course, he was cognizant that a good portion of the world did not hold Christian values, but he believed that practicing foreign policy based on the Sermon on the Mount would nonetheless work. "Love never fails," he would say, even though it might appear to do so. In the 1940s, when India sought its independence from Great Britain and Gandhi implemented the Love Way, he rejoiced to see nonviolent resistance win the day. To Moseley, it was proof positive that using love as a weapon, not to overcome and subjugate one's enemies but to

---

55. Moseley, Manifest Victory, 135–36; Bowen, *The Candler School of Theology*, 31.
56. Moseley, *Manifest Victory*, 134.

win them as friends, was the way to go. As he explained in the days prior to America's involvement in World War I:

> the perfectly loving and altogether beneficent attitude of Jesus, which will not strive nor contend about human rights and possessions, which resists not evil for evil, which turns the other cheek, which will not go to law or war, nor go on any mission except one of love, and good will, is the attitude that is to win against all others, because it is the worthiest of all to win. All men and all things, as I said, will yield to this attitude and only this, in freedom and joy."[57]

In any event, the idea of a "just war," such as Saint Augustine proposed, was repugnant to Rufus, and a poor way to meet aggression. If violence must be used, Rufus favored the creation of an international body to act as a police force—in this case, Woodrow Wilson's League of Nations. In the post-war years when Wilson sought to establish his "Fourteen Points" and chief among them the creation of a League of Nations, Moseley was onboard with his support. He believed that there had to be some sort of agency that would see to the limiting of dictatorships and aggression in the international community. In later years, his support for this and the United Nations made many of his conservative brethren wonder about him. After all, in the post-World War II era, there was a tremendous interest in end-times prophetic belief, and many saw such an agency as little more than the basis of a one-world government. Even today, such a position would not be understood. Rufus was to say, "the children of light fight with the weapons of Heaven, the weapons of light and love,"[58] Ever quick to quote Ralph Waldo Emerson, Moseley's views on war and nonviolence were nicely summed up with the Sage of Concord's words:

> The cause of peace is not the cause of cowardice . . . If peace is to be maintained, it must be by brave men, who have come up to the same height as the hero, namely, the will to carry their life in their hand, and stake it at any instant for their principle, but who have gone one step beyond the hero, and will not seek another man's life; men who have, by their intellectual insight or else by their moral elevation, attained such a perception of their own intrinsic worth that they do not think property or their own body a sufficient good to be saved by such dereliction of principle as treating a man like a sheep.[59]

57. Moseley, *Manifest Victory*, 133; McLain, *Resurrection Encounter*, 147–48.
58. Moseley, *Manifest Victory*, 134.
59. See Emerson, *Complete Works*.

Voicing opinions like this had two basic reactions: First, it would cause conservatives to call into question his motives, and second, it made the *Macon Telegraph* ownership take notice. In an odd turn of events, the liberal newspaper, with many of its stands in favor of the same things as Moseley, saw in him an articulate spokesperson for a segment of their readership. It would result in the two entering into a working relationship that would last decades.

Moseley and the Davis sisters made time during the First World War to minister to the soldiers stationed at nearby Camp Wheeler. Again locating out of doors, this time on Camp Wheeler Road, soldiers who were soon to be transferred to France were given the opportunity to give their lives to Christ. Many of them understandably feared for their lives in the coming conflagration, but Moseley sought to assure them that if their life was hid with Christ in God, they were guaranteed safety so long as their work here was incomplete. He was to say on this,

> You are safe anywhere that those in authority over you may put you, as long as you are dedicated to do God's best and all that you are put here to do. This is just as true as its companion truth, that to put and keep first the Kingdom of God not only makes his highest of all sure for you, but also makes sure that all you need in the way of means to do God's will and work will be added.[60]

SOCIAL COMMENTATOR, ACTIVIST, AND CHRISTIAN REPORTER

Near the end of the First World War, Moseley became an increasingly active writer of editorials to the *Telegraph*, mostly dealing with the insanity of war, the needs of the poor and destitute at home and abroad, passionately speaking against the death penalty, visiting those on death row, the need to help the war-ravaged in Europe, and racial injustice. When World War I ended, Moseley redoubled his letters to the editor, imploring wealthy America to do everything in its power to feed and clothe those ravaged by war. "Shoot the hungry Germans with biscuits harder and faster than we have been shooting them with bullets,"[61] he wrote. Some of his letters were sent on to President Wilson and other political leaders, further enhancing his appeal as a soon-to-be newspaper columnist. His letters appeared in *Outlook* and

60. Moseley, *Manifest Victory*, 145.
61. Moseley, *Manifest Victory*, 140.

Saturday Evening Post as well, and were the first introduction of this gentle believer and scholar to a nationwide reading audience.[62] He also was active in raising money for any number of relief organizations, ranging from Chinese and Russian aid for the starving millions in those nations, to appealing for funds for the war-ravaged Jews and Arabs in Palestine. Unnamed Jewish organizations even publicly recognized his efforts. It would be the one among many such accolades he would receive in his lifetime.

The post-World War I days proved to ones of transition for Rufus. He began to travel more widely, monies often provided by the relief agencies for whom he wrote. When funds were not so provided, Moseley often found himself asked to act as an agent for local peach growers in Georgia.[63] As a result, he would visit New York; Washington, DC; and Philadelphia at the times when there were important religious meetings as well. He was able to do his work as a grower's agent during the day and then attend religious gatherings in the evening. He was often among Catholic, Jewish, Methodist, Nazarene, Baptist, and other denominational friends. He even met with Augusta Stetson, a controversial Christian Science leader who reportedly was at odds with Mary Baker Eddy, the group's founder.[64] It is likely that Rufus had first met her during his earlier involvement with Christian Science, about a decade earlier. What makes this particularly interesting is that these groups by and large held negative views of Pentecostalism, yet were very friendly with Moseley. Rufus was not shy about sharing his experiences, but such was his quality of his spiritual life that he drew others to himself. It was something that would only increase as the years passed.

Moseley's editorials gained him something of a reputation as a social commentator from a religious, even Pentecostal, point of view. He may well be the first Pentecostal whose views were perceived to be intellectually cogent and applicable to current events. Most of his Pentecostal peers suffered from the (perhaps unfair) reputation Rufus himself had just a few years earlier of being gauche, uneducated, and thoroughly out of touch with reality. Now, combining his spiritual experience with a first-rate intellect, Moseley began to present Christ to an audience who otherwise would not listen. His earlier excesses on the streets of Macon, and public perceptions that he was a "nobody," were finally fading for good.[65]

---

62. Moseley, *Manifest Victory*, 141.
63. Moseley, *Manifest Victory*, 143.
64. Moseley, *Manifest Victory*, 143–44.
65. Moseley, *Manifest Victory*, 140–41.

3

The Promised Land

Reporter, Activist, and Spiritual Leader

1922–1929

The Lord told me what he wanted:
He wanted me to be a new fool in the world.

—Francis of Assisi

In the previous chapter, I referred to the period between 1910 and 1921 as Rufus Moseley's wilderness experience. He had gone from a young and highly respected scholar and professor at Mercer University to one the public perceived unfavorably for his involvement in Christian Science and then Pentecostalism. His public demonstrations were widely noted in Macon, and the general opinion was that the once-promising historian and political scientist had, as a result of religious fanaticism, thrown it all away. But after what he called his "early enthusiasm" of those days, Moseley zeroed in on ministry to the poorest and most destitute in central Georgia. He increased his criticism of capital punishment, as well as ardently opposed America's entry into World War I. Rufus also stood in favor of desegregation and for the rights of women and the working class, and against the evils of accumulated wealth while others went without even life's basic needs.

These public stances increasingly gained him respect, and at the same time perpetuated the public perception of his being controversial, even quirky. These were courageous positions to take, given that the South was a bastion of conservative thought and even nationally one could get in trouble for publicly opposing the war once the United States became involved. In late 1919, the infamous Palmer Raids, named for the US Attorney General's persecution of those simply exercising their right of protest, had swung into action. It encouraged neighbor to spy on neighbor and report "suspicious" behavior, "unpatriotic" talk, or "questionable" reading habits. Nonetheless, Moseley and others across the nation defied such unconstitutional government overreach and made their voices and cause known.

SPIRITUAL REPORTER

The publisher of the *Macon Telegraph*, William Anderson, took notice of Moseley and also published his editorial letters in favor of the causes they both championed. Because the *Telegraph* itself was becoming increasingly liberal, Anderson saw in Rufus a kindred soul despite his public religious excesses a decade earlier. Realizing that the superbly educated Moseley had something to say, and the mind and vocabulary to do it, Anderson—also co-owner of the newspaper—asked Rufus to join the *Telegraph* staff in 1921. Moseley insisted that he receive no pay for his work as a semi-regular religion columnist, and was never listed as an employee despite eventually working there for thirty-three years. He believed that receiving money for what he termed "spiritual services" was repugnant.

Still, not paying Moseley was something that did not sit well with Anderson, and on a few occasions he secretly deposited funds into Rufus's bank account. On the same day that he became aware of the money in his account, by then some $2,700, equivalent to just under $39,000 in 2019 dollars, Moseley witnessed a woman being evicted from her home. Her furniture already out on the front lawn, Rufus rushed to the bank and withdrew all $2,700 and with it paid off the woman's mortgage, thereby saving her from destitution and homelessness. Moseley never shared this story, and it would not have become known if witnesses had not reported it after his death. He took seriously the scriptural command to do his good deeds privately. It was just the spiritual makeup that would make him such an asset to the newspaper.[1] Word that this Pentecostal/liberal/intellectual had joined the paper got around and endeared him to many readers who had, by the 1920s, become increasingly disillusioned with organized religion.

---

1. McLain, *Resurrection Encounter*, 112, 118, 128; Wayne McLain also published a collection of Rufus Moseley's newspaper columns entitled *A Heavenly View*; Moseley, *Manifest Victory*, 140–41.

Anderson's first assignment for Rufus was a request to provide a wide and far-ranging question-and-answer story to explain himself and his beliefs. The great freedom he afforded to Moseley was not restricted to him, but was typical for all *Telegraph* reporters during the "Anderson era." What made this particular assignment unusual was that Moseley was asked to provide the questions as well as the answers. Rufus related that he tried several times to do this, but each time believed it was not what he believed the Spirit would have him say. Finally, on an afternoon when he was working in the family pecan grove outside of Byron, it came to him, and he recorded his responses. A good example of this was in his opinion of the Protestant and Catholic churches in general:

> Protestantism has gone far afield in the substitution of a doctrine about the cross, and in the substitution of a theory of justification by faith for faith, the faith that works by love, as has Catholicism in substitution of ritualism for a new life in Christ . . . [I have] glimpsed or been permitted to see a larger, kinder, more universal sense of Christ that reconciles the essential truths of orthodoxy and liberalism, and will make it easier for Buddhists, Confucians, and representatives of all other religions to see the "universal Christ" emancipated from "imperfect interpretations."[2]

This was not to say that he held to a position that there were multiple paths to God, but that the One who came to save mankind, if properly viewed or understood, would be readily received by the world at large. Moseley often bemoaned the fact there was so much division in the Christian world, and that the divisions revealed hypocrisy, sham and pretense to the outside world. Mahatmas Gandhi, with whom Rufus periodically corresponded, famously said that he loved the Christian's Jesus, but could not abide Christians.

As his life and ministry went through these positive transitions, the revelation of a way of Christian living that he began to refer to as the "Life as Love" likewise began to take shape. As he further elaborated:

> Everyone must decrease that he may increase. This involves the daily dying that even the best of His disciples don't rejoice in . . . but my, how heaven opens when as we die to all that keeps him from living, growing triumphing in us! How blessed and glorious it will be when we can say it and mean it: "For me to live is Christ, and to die to self is gain," and that "it is no longer I but Christ who lives in me." For if we die, and as we die, we really

---

2. Moseley, "Viewpoints on His Religion."

live; and we do not live except as we die. We will find not only that Christ lives in us but that we also live in Him. "Thank God! Thank God!" We will never know our wonderful possibilities except as we find them in him. This is the heaven side of the life in union with Christ. The other side of the union is what crucifies self and prepares us for this freedom and glory in Christ.[3]

To Moseley, a vital part of this revelation was involvement in doing his best to alleviate suffering and injustice, to boldly speak against evils in the nation and world about him. This alone made him radically different from a sizable portion of the Pentecostal world that had come to reject any dealings with society whatsoever. At the time, Fundamentalism and Pentecostalism, with some exceptions, did little to publicly address social problems or offer any concrete solutions. Moseley's willingness to do so and to himself roll up his sleeves and help made him suspect in the eyes of many of his more conservative brethren.

UNFOLDING REVELATION

Sometime in 1923, Rufus Moseley was visiting some friends, a Mr. and Mrs. Ben Dryden, who lived in the Lakeside district outside of Macon, Georgia. At the time, their home was far enough removed from the city that it allowed for quiet out-of-doors enjoyment, especially walks meant for meditation and prayer. One of the evenings he spent there, Rufus went on his face in prayer and asked what he must do to be in God's conscious presence all the time. He tired, as does anyone who seeks after this goal, of going out and coming in, of not valuing the union with Christ enough to choose to stay there. Taking over his vocal cords, the Holy Spirit offered the words from Exodus, "My Presence shall go with thee and give thee rest. Go in love and I shall always be with thee."[4] Rufus rejoiced at this simple yet profound response. It was the secret, he said, the open secret of the kingdom, that if we give out love all the time, we can remain in that union all the time. Again, we live in what we give out. The "rest" was of particular importance too. As set forth in Hebrews 4, there is a rest for all believers to enter into: not just after we die, but in the here and now. It was the door that would allow him to experience ever-increasing joy regardless of where he found himself nor what he encountered. As these revelations increasingly became part of his life, Rufus Moseley had encounters in Macon and St. Louis, Missouri, that would solidify them.

3. Moseley, "Viewpoints on His Religion."
4. Moseley, *Manifest Victory*, 148.

ST. LOUIS MINISTRY

Sometime in early 1923 (the exact date is uncertain), a Oneness Pentecostal from St. Louis came to Macon to visit Moseley. How he came into contact with Rufus is unknown, as he did not travel widely at this time, and his newspaper columns were in their early years and not yet widely circulated. The St. Louis group sent this representative specifically to see Rufus, as they were of the opinion that he was to have a leadership role among them. Rufus agreed to travel to St. Louis to meet these new friends, but his having a leadership role was not something told to Rufus until the trip was underway. This unnamed individual, whom I believe Rufus left anonymous because of his inability to say much in agreement with him, even claimed regular angelic visitations. The St. Louis friend contended that these visits came at regular intervals, the first occurring when he was in the thirty-eighth day of a forty-two-day fast. The angel, it was claimed, was dressed in gray, and supposedly included verifications about things to come and of the need to stay "within the veil."[5]

The second part doubtless interested Moseley, as he was himself learning of what he called "ineffable union with Christ" or perpetually staying in a place of spiritual rest. Yet as Moseley heard it from the Holy Spirit, it was available to all; one gets the sense from Rufus's writing that his friend was telling him these things in a less than contrite manner. His friend then announced to Moseley that he had "heard it from the Lord" that he would not see physical death, that he would remain until the second coming in a glorified body. In fact, this particular belief about not tasting death had been making the rounds for a few years amongst some Oneness Pentecostal groups. By 1923, it was specifically addressed at a national Oneness conference in St. Louis, interestingly enough, and rejected as heresy.[6] What Rufus responded is not recorded, but the same day as this conversation was held, aboard a passenger train on their way to St. Louis, an unforeseen and tragic event unfolded that called into serious question his friend's spiritual claims.

On February 23, 1923, the "Dixie Flyer" passenger train Rufus and his friend were aboard jumped the tracks and crashed, killing and injuring many. A scene of terrible carnage, the nearby Calhoun, Georgia hospital was overwhelmed, and the injured were placed in any public facility that could be found to house them. Moseley escaped without injury.[7] Rufus reported that as he felt the train lifting, he closed his eyes and threw himself on the

---

5. Moseley, *Manifest Victory*, 146–47.
6. Tyson, The *Early Pentecostal Revival*, 243.
7. Moseley, *Manifest Victory*, 149.

bosom of Christ. An eyewitness shared that Moseley bounced like a ball as the train convulsed, finally landing between two shattered windows. His St. Louis friend, who had been forcefully arguing that he would not die physically, had been gruesomely decapitated. Rufus later saw his severed head on an undertaker's platter, reminding him of John the Baptist who, while announcing the kingdom, did not live long enough to see it.[8]

After the train wreck, Rufus returned to Macon, sending word to the St. Louis group of the death of one of their own. A few days later, Rufus accompanied the body back to St. Louis. The evening before his arrival, he felt impressed of the Holy Spirit to resist any efforts to designate him the new leader of the sect. Sure enough, some in that group apparently thought that it was God's will for Moseley to take over for the deceased leader. He firmly insisted that he was not interested in any leadership role and informed the group that they were not to be under his or anyone else's leadership. This was not received very well at first, and Moseley reported that he had to be firm in his conviction that he believed to be from the Holy Spirit. One of the St. Louis leaders, a remarkable woman named Mary Moise, went so far as to offer the deceased man's chair to Rufus, saying "We have been praying that you have a double portion of the Spirit," to which Moseley again reiterated, "I have heard from heaven about that. He is to have no successor. We are all to be taught of the Lord and led by His Spirit." Apparently they requested that he take over for over a year, and he repeatedly resisted their pleas and claims that he was to be a leader over them, or lead along with others.[9] Despite this, a strong bond between Rufus and the St. Louis group had formed, one that would last for many years to come and result in frequent trips, at least in the 1920s and 1930s, to St. Louis.

It is interesting that Moseley would make the trip knowing the mindset of the previous leader, and to know in advance what it was he would find when he went to Missouri. Nonetheless, he did have good things to say about some of those he met, and those for whom he could not give a good report he generally would leave unnamed or not mention them at all. One of these for whom he had great admiration was the afore-mentioned "Mother" Mary G. Moise. She was known throughout the St. Louis area and was hailed across the nation for her involvement in social work. She opened her doors to St. Louis' poorest of the poor, something that doubtless impressed Moseley, housing and feeding the female homeless, prostitutes, alcoholics, and those women the rest of society had tossed aside. Ministry centers such as the Door of Hope, Pentecostal Rescue Center, and the Dorothy Phillips

8. Moseley, *Manifest Victory*, 149.
9. Moseley, *Manifest Victory*, 152.

Mission, among others, were a few such outreaches. Mary Moise began her work under the Episcopal denomination, but when she embraced Pentecostalism around 1907, and later joined the Oneness faction thereof, her home also became the center for meetings, and even the raising up of ministers.[10] She also held views much like her deceased friend who died in the Georgia train-wreck, believing if a person had enough faith they would not taste physical death. In 1930, she passed away.[11]

In fact, it was during one of his visits to the Midwest that Moseley received one of his most profound yet simple revelations. He had been in active prayer as to how to proceed in any number of areas, including his new friends, and what and how divine guidance would look like. As he considered one option over another in this and other issues, the Holy Spirit gave him further clarification of things he had begun to see earlier: "Your only responsibility is the responsibility to remain in union with Me." This simple statement proved to be one of the most important revelations he was to receive: he was from that point forward freed from the incessant demands of time, people, and himself over what action should or shouldn't be taken in any given situation. He was to say:

> The Lord had been seeking to teach me this truth for a long time, but I had been too dull to see it. I would load myself with burdens that were too heavy for me to bear. Then I would turn to the Lord and he would deliver me from the burdens and make me glad and free. I would load myself again, and again He would deliver me . . . This continued until it became a reality to me that I had but one responsibility, to be in union with him all the time and that I was under one compulsion, to give his love alone, continuously, to all of life. If you are giving out God's love all the time, you will be in God all the time, for you will always be a part of what you are giving out.[12]

This would be what Moseley would come to call one of the "Keys of the Kingdom," profound in its simplicity, that by choosing to stay in conscious union with Christ, a moment-by-moment walk in this reality, we have fulfilled the one responsibility Christ has given us. The simplicity of it was to hold him in an elevated state of spiritual awareness, bliss, and joy for weeks on end; but it would still be a few years before he learned to value staying in that place of union above all else. While it helped him overcome the immediate pressure to assume a leadership position in any organization, it also

---

10. Warner, "Mother Mary Moise of St. Louis," 6–7.
11. Warner, "Mother Mary Moise of St. Louis," 13–14.
12. Moseley, *Manifest Victory*, 152–53.

laid the groundwork for his later ministry and gifting, one of which began to come to the fore when he was in Missouri.[13]

MINISTRY OF RECONCILIATION

Despite some of their Oneness and other unusual teachings, Rufus found himself caring deeply for this group, especially since they were committed to action on behalf of the poor. It is important to here reiterate a constant Rufus Moseley practice: Although he would disagree with people over articles of faith, he was loath to break fellowship with them if he detected sincerity and honest seeking. These St. Louis friends had also been influenced by Seeley D. Kinne, who had established apostolic outreaches in the city some years earlier. Moseley himself would come to know Kinne and later Ivan Spencer, both of whom would become important leaders at the Elim camps, and later the Bible Institute in western New York State. In time, both Spencer and Kinne would become stalwart adherents to the Latter Rain doctrines, some of which Moseley had difficulty accepting. Some have misinterpreted his willingness to maintain these friendships as proof of himself holding to similar teachings, which was simply not the case. His was a ministry of reconciliation. Although he did not himself belong to any church or denomination, he was ever seeking to bring people together, especially if hard feelings had been created as a result of animosities.

Rufus was fond of retelling a Civil War story about two of Confederate General Robert E. Lee's subordinate commanders, A. P. Hill and Stonewall Jackson. Both men had legendary egos and tempers to match. Once, when a disagreement between the two became so heated that it threatened any limited friendship they might have had, and certainly threatened their ability to work together, they decided to take the issue to Lee before it became irreconcilable. Both men had the highest regard for the commander of the army of Northern Virginia, and agreed to abide by his decision. The two met with Lee and each told their side of the story. When they had finished, Lee remained silent for a moment and then said, "Gentlemen, it has been my experience that the person least at fault is the one who first seeks reconciliation." Hill and Jackson were stunned, then looked at each other dumbfounded. At the same moment, they asked each other for forgiveness, thereby ending the feud.[14]

Rufus believed that all believers must be peacemakers, seeking to heal where wounds are deepest or even where they may seem superficial. Above

---

13. Moseley, *Manifest Victory*, 152.
14. Moseley, "Stop Strife and Strike."

all, we must seek forgiveness of those we may have offended, forgive those who have offended us, and seek as much as possible to make all people our friends. The things that divide, such as doctrines, politics, economics, and family disputes, can deeply wound and cause a breaking of fellowship. He witnessed all of these division-causing things across the span of his life, and it grieved him. Once, when he was before someone who in anger sought to out-argue him, Rufus reported that he found himself physically kneeling before the person. It so disarmed the disputatious person that he asked for Moseley's forgiveness. Rufus proved time after time that he was always ready to take the first step, show humility first, in the hopes of ending any divisive thoughts, words, or deeds.

DISCERNMENT OF SPIRITS

In the midst of his second stay in St. Louis in 1924, Moseley experienced the beginnings of one of the more unusual aspects of his ministry. While he had already begun to operate to a remarkable degree in the discernment of spirits, it was at the Moise home where I first found him describing the experience with what he termed the "discernment of animal spirits" in others. By this he meant that he would spiritually perceive and witness what "animal spirit" a person's character represented. For instance, it could be that Jesus' statement about Herod being a "fox" was an example of this. For Moseley, this was rarely meant in a negative way, given that each of the tribes of Israel were likewise symbolized by animals, and when he shared this with others, it was generally the cause of great encouragement and laughter. As he told those about him what he was seeing in the Spirit, others began to likewise exercise this gift.[15]

To his delight, Rufus found that when he returned home to Macon he was still operating in this unusual capacity. One of his friends in Macon, Mulberry Street Methodist Church pastor Walter Anthony, received the report in good spirits. Shortly thereafter, Anthony asked Rufus if he had ever noticed that a mutual friend of theirs, Methodist Bishop William Ainsworth, "was a bulldog." Moseley immediately laughed in recognition, and wondered how he had been so dull in the past so as not to see it. Later that night, at the Macon Cafeteria[16] on Cherry Street, Moseley saw Walter

---

15. Moseley, *Manifest Victory*, 167–69.

16. For those from Macon, Georgia or the immediate area, the old downtown Macon Cafeteria was bought out by S and S Cafeteria, which is still in operation, though no longer at the downtown site.

Anthony take the shape of a lion, and his uncle, Bascom Anthony, was also seen striding about as one.[17]

Moseley was to further comment on this discerning of animal spirits by saying that he found some people had the gift naturally, like something of an instinct. For himself, however, it only occurred when he was particularly "in the Spirit." Wayne McLain, commented on this:

> Rufus had this capacity to a rare degree. His discernment of spirits was not simply guessing what kind of spirit might be in someone he was seeking to help nor was it simply an idea given to his mind, but a manifest view of that spirit given to his eyes. It thus made his prayers for deliverance much more directly guided and effective.[18]

Moseley went on to comment that in his study he came to realize that George Fox, the founder of Quakerism, possessed it, as had apparently Jacob, Moses, and other Old Testament patriarchs. He rarely found these discernments to be negative, although he did note that George Fox had negative interpretations of those he perceived as having the "serpent spirit." Shortly after World War II, Wayne McLain again described the first time he encountered another of Rufus's gifts of discernment in operation:

> The first experience I had of his gift to see beyond the natural was at Duke University in 1945. A group of us had gone with Rufus to the Oak Room for dinner. While sitting watching him at the table I noticed an unusual movement of his eyes looking at me and giving me the sensation that he was looking through me or beyond me. Still I had no sense of fear or condemnation. I learned later that this capacity of Rufus was what St. Paul had termed the gift of discernment of spirits, the ability to see beyond the natural to the spirit or spirits dwelling in a person.[19]

Like all of his spiritual gifts, Moseley never made it an issue or bragged about it. He was content in that it was of service to other believers.[20] Still, to Moseley's mind, the closeknit nature of the discerning of animal spirits in people made him wonder about the natural ties between the animal and human kingdoms, and in the 1920s, this brought to mind the evolution controversy.

---

17. Moseley, *Manifest Victory*, 168–69.
18. McLain, *Resurrection Encounter*, 107.
19. McLain, *Resurrection Encounter*, 107.
20. Moseley, *Manifest Victory*, 166–69.

SCOPES MONKEY TRIAL

In July 1925, a most remarkable American courtroom battle took place that was to go down in the annals of legal and religious history. I refer, of course, to the Scopes Monkey Trial in Dayton, Tennessee, when schoolteacher John Scopes was tried for violating Tennessee's anti-evolution statutes, laws which made it illegal to teach anything other than the standard Genesis account of creation in public schools. Scopes, the schoolteacher charged with the infraction, had in fact volunteered to be a test case against the law. With the support of town officials, it was thought that a trial would bring in a great many visitors and help the community and region gain positive notice. It certainly did gain notice, but what resulted was nothing less than a carnival sideshow in which William Jennings Bryan, three-time presidential candidate, secretary of state under Woodrow Wilson, and fundamentalist believer, argued the prosecution's case; the newly formed American Civil Liberties Union (ACLU) and a handful of attorneys, led by Clarence Darrow, defended Scopes.

The eyes of the nation were on this trial, often producing scathing reviews of fundamentalist Christian beliefs. It was a trial of literalist Christian dogma against Darwinian interpretations of the origins of life, views which had become much more widely accepted. While Bryan and the prosecution won the trial, the effects on conservative, fundamentalist, and Pentecostal Christianity were profoundly negative. With ACLU lawyers Arthur Garfield Hays, Dudley F. Malone and Clarence Darrow's rapier wit, the literalist Biblical position was caricatured as ridiculous, and those holding to it likewise lacking in intellectual ability. Journalists by the score jumped in and mercilessly lampooned fundamentalism, but none more so than the *Baltimore Sun*'s H. L. Mencken. The public damage was complete, and the devastation lasting.[21]

While Rufus was a religion columnist for the *Macon Telegraph* during the trial, he writes virtually nothing about it beyond a casual mention here and there. This is odd given his otherwise thorough treatment of other topics of the day, including the difficulties that "modernism" and "fundamentalism" presented; but on Scopes, hardly a word. One can get a glimpse of perhaps one reason Moseley did not go into too much detail in what happened to one of his closest friends, Edwin M. Poteat. Poteat was a professor at Baptist Mercer University in Macon, and had run afoul of the administration's stand against evolution and was to eventually lead to his leaving the school. Poteat went on to champion opposition in North Carolina against

---

21. For a superb history of the Scopes Monkey Trial, I highly recommend Larson, *Summer for the Gods*.

Tennessee-style laws making teaching of evolution a crime. Rufus, having had his own problems with conservative religious and political opinions and leadership, sided with Poteat, but also asked the Holy Spirit about the truth of evolution. Given his own discernment of animal spirits, to him it seemed to suggest a greater tie between lower and upper life forms than fundamentalists were willing to see or admit. The response he received from the Holy Spirit was cryptic: "Evolution is not true, but seems to be true, and is truer than popular conceptions of it."[22]

How Rufus interpreted that answer is anyone's guess, but given that it was such a hot-button issue dividing believers, he kept his opinions about it largely to himself. Still, sometime later he related how he believed the Holy Spirit further elaborated upon the earlier word concerning evolution: "It does appear to the natural mind that the higher forms of life have come up out of the lower forms, but when My work is finished, it will be seen that all has come from Me."[23] He would often keep quiet about a number of issues, believing that the Love Mandate was such that it was part of his ministry to unite, rather than divide, over controversial things. As we will see later on, this held true concerning his views of the End-Times, something that garnered great interest in the 1930s with the rise of Hitler and Mussolini.

OTHER MIDWEST MINISTRY

Rufus continued his visits to St. Louis throughout the 1920s and came to consider the city something of a second or third home—he loved spending winters in Florida when he could—and that came to be a special place for him as well. He was in St. Louis long enough to introduce himself to some of the city's religious leaders, such as Archbishop John Glennon. He shared his testimony of receiving the baptism of the Holy Spirit, and Glennon graciously promised to pass on the report to the Pope. He told the Archbishop that if the Catholic Church would humble itself at the feet of Jesus and be used by him for immediate use, it would come forth in such a manner that would amaze even the most orthodox in that institution. Of course, he shared the same message with Protestant leaders as well. Most of them, while they respected and even loved Moseley, considered him something of an odd character and his message perhaps too good to be true or too fantastic to believe.[24]

---

22. Moseley, *Manifest Victory*, 169; Moseley, "Holy Kingdom."
23. Moseley, *Manifest Victory*, 170.
24. Moseley, *Manifest Victory*, 171–72.

Around the same time as his second trip to St. Louis, Moseley also came into contact with unnamed Pentecostal personages in Detroit, Michigan. Rufus mentions this group without identifying it in part due to his intention to show his love for them while at the same time distancing himself from some of their beliefs. As William Heard Kilpatrick, the great Columbia University professor, said of his friend Moseley, "Most admirable, perhaps, of all is Mr. Moseley's consummate ability to deal in a kindly fashion with any and all groups from whom he felt compelled to separate himself either as regards ties of defined organizations or as regards systems of thought."[25] The leader of the Detroit group had invited Rufus to attend some of their meetings in that city sometime in 1923 or 1924. In 1925, he took them up on their offer and, according to his own account, received a fine and generous welcome. The leader of the Detroit group had an especially strong will, something Moseley repeatedly encountered in others throughout his life, and the two found themselves on opposing sides before too many days had lapsed. Moseley's Detroit friends had insisted that the kingdom of God had come to earth, in Detroit no less, and that others who wanted to be part of it had to come through their good graces. Rufus, of course, resisted this, and stated that while the kingdom could indeed be in Detroit, it could not be localized there, and certainly not monopolized from that venue.

Moseley's friend tended to emphasize the externals of the kingdom, apparently in terms of who was to control it, and Rufus would then contradict him by emphasizing the internals of the kingdom walk. Before the kingdom could come outwardly, it had to come inwardly and be manifested as perfect love, purity, and utter sincerity. As Moseley was fond of saying, "If we have the power of the Kingdom apart from its Spirit, we are at best hypocrites, at worst antichrists." This did not go over too well with his new friend, who chaffed when Rufus further told him that instead of seeking a flock or personal following, he should be doing his utmost to point his people towards an intimate relationship with Christ for themselves.[26] It is not known whether or not the two ever met again.

In the spring of 1926, Moseley made a third, prolonged visit to St. Louis. It was during this particular stay that he received an inspiration, like most such insights given to him, as grand as it was simple. While in prayer at the Mary Moise home, and after laying forth his own petitions, he asked the Lord if there was anything he would like to say to him. Immediately realizing the ridiculousness of the statement—akin, he said, to spending an hour with the President of the United States and dominating the conversation,

---

25. Kilpatrick, "Foreword," xi–xiii.
26. Moseley, *Manifest Victory*, 156–57.

only to arise and say on the way out, "Is there anything you would like to say?" Now having his attention, Rufus related how the Holy Spirit spoke into his spirit the words "I want you in me all the time, and I give you the keys." Moseley realized that he, indeed all believers, were being called into that place of union to never depart again. Being out of union does not mean a believer losing his/her salvation, but rather the availability of entering into such a union and staying that there was a real possibility and all believer's predestination. This meant that living in the heavenlies was not limited to positional salvation in Christ, but ongoing union that produces moment-by-moment conscious experience. As he was to say,

> I had realized, since Jesus manifested himself and came within me and I had come out of the marvelous enveloping glory, my great need was to take up my abode in Jesus and abide in him without ever going out any more, just as he had taken up his abode in me to abide forever. We need to be in him perpetually, as we need him to be in us everlastingly. It is in this "double union" of him in us and us in him, and the bearing the fruit of that union, that we become like him and joint heirs with him in the services and in the inheritance of time and eternity. His full revelation in us and in our full revelation in Him is our full salvation, redemption, and glorification.[27]

He went on to explain that the "keys" of which the Spirit spoke were not something over which he had control or domination of others. Rather, he was to freely share these truths with all, that in order to stay in union with Christ, we need only "keep on the outside whatever it is that keeps us on the outside." That master key, was, of course, love. Giving out divine love to all is what opens the kingdom ever wider to us. We also learn that the door or entry is at the feet of Jesus and is exactly the right size. It is at his feet, so we enter humbly; it is just the right size, so that nothing worthwhile is kept out, and nothing unworthy comes in. What Moseley was stating was something that was, perhaps still is, largely missed in Evangelical Christianity: the possibility (certainly the invitation) to live in unbroken union and bliss in Christ. Rufus did not suggest that he had "arrived," to borrow a word from Paul, and still needed to learn to value this union above all else. Moseley shared this widely, but he was not often understood by those to whom he spoke. What does seem to be a common reaction, however, was a genuine love many had for Rufus despite either their lack of understanding or

---

27. Moseley, *Manifest Victory*, 164.

outright disagreements with him.²⁸ There would be other examples drawn from his St. Louis contacts of genuine kingdom attitudes.

In 1927, after a visit to Philadelphia, Moseley made what I believe was his last St. Louis trip of the decade. During this stop, a tornado swept through town, causing all manner of property loss, death, and personal injury. Rufus reported that he and his friends were in a meeting on that given evening and that, while the cyclone came near to their place of fellowship, they were unaware of the danger. Either the glory of the Lord was so pronounced, as Moseley stated, or they were worshiping so loudly that no one heard the approach of the dangerous weather. A couple of months later, Moseley traveled with one of his St. Louis friends to a nearby city for a series of meetings. According to Rufus, there was apparently a great deal of excitement about the conference among the goers, in particular because of Rufus's traveling companion.

This Christian leader, like others Moseley seemed to frequently encounter, apparently had a rather strong will and the habit of overpowering others into submission. It was something that Moseley generally did not like to be around, and it could be the reason he does not name the individual. Shortly before the event was to start, Moseley went to pray in a nearby city park and asked for guidance. He already sensed that this particular group had great potential in gifts and ministry, but their being dominated quenched the Spirit. Before the meeting, Moseley approached the preacher and spoke of his concerns. To his delight, at the opening of the meeting, his friend announced to those in attendance that it was God's will that they not be under his or any other's domination. They were to seek the Holy Spirit and only the Holy Spirit. In a remarkable change of heart, this leader shared that it was of vital importance for all of them to seek God for themselves so that, in the event of one of them stumbling, the rest could raise him or her up without themselves falling.²⁹ While Rufus was beginning to minister more widely to any number of Christian groups, there was an issue very dear to his heart, and one that he held from very early on.

In the late 1920s, while still in Missouri, Rufus learned about a death row situation back in Georgia that was to forever change his life. As early as 1910 or 1911, sometime after he received the baptism of the Holy Spirit, Rufus Moseley sent an editorial letter to the *Macon Telegraph* stating his beliefs on a number of spiritual and social issues, one of which was his opposition to capital punishment. Already an outspoken critic of racial segregation, his opposition to capital punishment would be in part due to the racist manner

---

28. Moseley, *Manifest Victory*, 163–64.
29. Moseley, *Manifest Victory*, 175–76.

in which it was applied. Although there are many examples in his writings about this particular topic, there was one in particular that greatly moved him. It involved a twenty-one-year-old black man, Robert Jones, and the work of the Holy Spirit in him prior to his execution.

A LIGHT IN A DARK PLACE

Between October 1927 and late June 1928, a series of tragic events occurred in Macon that was to have the most profound impact on all involved. On October 7, 1927, a twenty-one-year-old black man named Robert Jones killed one Wesley Short, an elderly white clothes cleaner over a monetary dispute involving a suit of clothes. It had been well-known that Jones and Short had been in loud disagreement over the issue, and on the Saturday morning in question, it apparently became heated again. Entering Short's business, Jones demanded what was owed him. When Short made a sudden move toward a drawer, Jones thought he was going for a weapon. Robert quickly grabbed the nearest thing with which to defend himself. Using an iron bar, he struck the old man, killing him in the process. He was arrested just a few days later and, while in custody, admitted to the killing. Robert was tried just ten days after his arrest, and despite what was thought to be self-defense, was found guilty of capital murder after a mere five-minute jury deliberation. He was sentenced to die in the electric chair, originally scheduled for the following December.[30] It was later rescheduled for June 28, 1928. Jones was then placed in the Bibb County jail to await transfer to the State Farm in Milledgeville, where the sentence would be carried out. At some point during his time in the Bibb County jail—thought to be sometime in early November—Jones underwent a conversion to Christianity so dramatic that it influenced everyone who came into contact with him; he had also asked for and received the baptism of the Holy Spirit.[31]

Jailhouse conversions are hardly novel, but there was in this instance something that so moved fellow prisoners and officials alike that it garnered the attention of the local press. Barely able to read or write when he entered jail, Jones quickly and almost miraculously learned to read well, and within a few weeks was able to memorize and quote long portions of Scripture. He also began to preach to his fellow inmates, who often joined him in loud singing of hymns. The circumstances surrounding this remarkable change of heart reached the ears of *Macon Telegraph* reporter Malcom Johnson, doubtless through Rufus Moseley. Moseley, as a columnist with

---

30. Johnson, "Trial of Negro Starts Monday," October 25, 1927.
31. Johnson, "Admitted Slayer"; Moseley, *Manifest Victory*, 266.

the *Telegraph*, was a fixture at the Bibb County courthouse and jail, and when he heard about the conversion of this young man, he informed his colleague at the *Telegraph*. Indeed, for several months prior to the execution, Moseley was with Jones nearly every day. On December 7, 1927, Jones dictated a short letter, presumably to Moseley, stating his sorrow at what he had done:

> I write these lines in the Bibb County jail. God has forgiven me [of] my sins and I want the people to forgive me. I did not mean to kill that man and I am sorry that I did it. I will never be guilty of a case in court for anything [again]. So God be with us until we meet again. Robert Jones[32]

Months later, the Monday, May 7, 1928 edition of the *Telegraph* begins with an account of Jones's loudly singing in the jail cell, eyes gazing upward in apparent ecstasy. Reporter Johnson relates how Jones's conversion had "taken" and that all he could talk about was Jesus and the change he made in his life. Not expecting, asking, or receiving any sort of last-minute sentence commutation, the young man seemed content to tell his fellow prisoners that they, too, could be free despite being behind bars. According to accounts, Jones became increasingly eloquent in his exhortations and sermons.

On June 25, 1928, Robert Jones was transferred to the State Prison Farm, where his execution was to take place three days later. As he had done in the county jail, he continued to offer exhortations and prayers for his fellow prisoners. Prison Chaplain E. C. Atkins was astounded when he witnessed prisoners on death row give their lives to Christ as a result. In some instances, Robert didn't have to say much of anything to have prisoners, now brought to Robert's cell on the chaplain's orders, fall under conviction and give their lives to Christ. Atkins told of even the most hardened criminals being remarkably changed simply by being in Jones's presence. The chaplain remarked that he had never seen anything like it before, and that if this young man were allowed to live, he could change the entire prison and beyond.

Over the course of his tenure at the *Telegraph*, Moseley wrote impassioned polemics against the death penalty and was quick to point out that black males were many times more likely to be executed than their white counterparts convicted of similar crimes. For Moseley, however, Jones was different; he had become not just a brother in Christ, but a friend for whom he deeply cared. Moseley involved himself in multiple efforts to sway public opinion on behalf of his friend. Writing in his own column in favor of a

---

32. Moseley, *Manifest Victory*, 266; Jones's letter to the *Telegraph* editor, December 16, 1927.

sentence commutation to life, he also wrote letters to the editor pleading that Robert and others be spared, and set forth reasons for it. Moseley found himself appalled that there were some letters to the editor that took positive glee in the electrocution of the condemned, causing him to wonder about the general interior life of those of that opinion. "Some people can have part in an electrocution with the levity and loud laughter that bespeaks the empty mind and the callous heart,"[33] he said in embarrassment for those he described.

> One of the tragedies about capital punishment is that it hardens everyone who has any part in it or who even approves of it. It is not the evil we receive from others, if we take in the Good Spirit, but the evil we consent to and approve of and have part in any way that hardens and hurts us. When one reaches the place that he desires, wills, and seeks to work good and only good to all and to meet all evil with good, the Lord turns everything into a blessing to him.[34]

He likewise used his arguments against capital punishment in general, hoping to appeal to those with influence to do what they could. Rufus recognized that those with money, position, and power would not be faced with the sentences doled out to the poor and needy. Because they could not afford top-notch legal counsel, their chances were understandably muted. Worse, when the very court and prosecutor were sometimes the ones to choose defense counsel, it made for the high probability for a conviction.

Supporting Atkins's testimony to Rufus about Jones, *The Macon Telegraph* reported on June 28, the day of his execution, that Robert Jones was "unusually jubilant this afternoon (June 27) for a man who had only a few more hours on earth." *The Telegraph* further reported:

> Jones is the fortieth person to occupy the death cell at the state prison, according to prison officials, [and] has been the most unusual of all prisoners that have gone away before him. In the past it has been the custom to bring Christian workers to the cell to pray, and to preach to the condemned men, but this practice has been reversed with Jones and under an order from the prison chaplain, four of the most indifferent prisoners from the Negro department were brought each evening to hear a message of salvation from Jones.[35]

---

33. Moseley, "Best That Can Be."
34. Moseley, "Best That Can Be."
35. Johnson, "Robert Jones Awaits Death."

On the day of his execution, Rufus Moseley accompanied Jones to the death chamber. Besides the officials in charge of the grisly business, there were also relatives of Wesley Short in attendance. Robert asked forgiveness of the Short family for what he had done, and that although it was his former nature that had done the killing, he was alright with his body being punished for it. Moseley was much more animated. His voice trembling with emotion, he said that he could no more pull the death lever than he could drive the nails into the hands of Christ. "This boy, a child of God," Moseley said with raised voice, "has the advantage over all of you," meaning those about to execute him. By this time trembling with emotion, Moseley cried, "This is a crucifixion! I would go to the chair myself if I thought capital punishment would be ended!" Then pointing to the electric chair, he spat out in disgust, "this hellish thing!" So vociferous were Moseley's denunciations that he had to be stopped by prison officials. As a result of his protests, he would never again be allowed to accompany a prisoner into the death cell.

Robert Jones continued to worship as his face was covered and the electrodes attached to his head and leg. Immediately prior to his execution, Jones cried out in joy, "I'm in him and he's in Me!" His prayers and praises were cut short when the first jolt of electricity tore through his body. Examined by the State Farm doctor present, it was found that he was still alive, and a second burst was then administered, killing him. The execution was performed shortly after noon on June 28, 1928.[36]

The story of this young man's life and conversion has implications these many years later. Had he been white, he doubtless would have received a lighter punishment. For Rufus Moseley, the greatest tragedy wasn't just the death of his friend, but of the opportunity lost for Jones to have an influence for Christ in prison and beyond. Chaplain Atkins and some guards and other prisoners were also badly shaken. Robert Jones was someone Rufus never forgot, and he frequently recalled his friend in public talks across North America until his own death in 1954. The deaths of both Wesley Short and Robert Jones were deeply regrettable and tragic for all concerned, but Jones's salvation proved anything but "a hellish thing."[37] After the execution, Moseley had this to say:

> With all the time that I spent with him in jail, during the last hours in the death cell, and the minutes near the electric chair,

---

36. Letter from Georgia State Prison Farm to the Bibb county Clerk of Court, June 18, 1928; "The State vs. Robert Jones," Grand Jury indictment, October, 1927; "Slayer of Short is Electrocuted," June 28, 1928; Moseley, *Manifest Victory*, 266–68.

37. Johnson, "Slayer of Short is Electrocuted, June 28, 1928; Moseley, "Christ in the Death Cell," July 1, 1928.

there was no indication of the least fear. Instead, there was an out-flowing gratitude, radiance, kindness, and consideration for and in the interest of others that made him the most uniformly victorious in Christian faith, peace, joy, and love of anyone that I have ever known. Robert's last months, days, and minutes is a striking testimony of what Christ can do for anyone, no matter what he had done previously, and when one repents, surrenders, and makes an entire dedication to do his will.[38]

At the same time as Robert Jones's incarceration and execution, there were two other instances of men receiving the death sentence that deeply affected Rufus Moseley. One of these was the chief of police from Cleveland, Tennessee, with the unlikely name of Homer Simpson, who had participated in a bank robbery in which someone was killed. Although Simpson did not do the killing, he was given the death penalty, perhaps as a result of his having been a lawman involved in a serious crime. Another was Bascom Morrow, who received the death sentence for a similar crime. Moseley spent over a year with the two in his frequent visits to prisoners on death row. He was pleased to report that both of them, before they were executed, had received Christ and confessed freely to their crimes. He described them as having "reached unusual moral and spiritual elevation" before they died.[39] As impassioned as he was against capital punishment, Rufus was also to repeatedly speak with equal force against another tragedy: suicide.

Moseley's periodic writings on suicide, other than addressing the tragedy inflicted on the person involved and the family and loved ones left behind, also prove something of a mystery. Throughout the 1920s and into the 1930s, Rufus would compose articles on suicide that would appear in the *Telegraph*, and in at least one instance was prompted when a local Macon clergyman and Moseley friend took his own life. To all outward appearances, the man showed few signs of the inner turmoil afflicting him. Rufus wrote of it with great passion and sense of loss, not only for his friend, but for what this beloved person meant to the kingdom of God. Suicide was little understood in Rufus's day, and was often written off as the actions of the pathetic and weak. Moseley knew better. It later came to my attention that his youngest sister, Maude, a schoolteacher, had taken her own life in 1910 at the age of twenty-eight. The pain of her loss was something Moseley never wrote about directly, but his polemics against suicide ring with the sound of his personal loss and sorrow.[40]

38. Moseley, "Christ in the Death Cell."
39. Moseley, *Manifest Victory*, 176; Stewart, "Real Homer Simpson."
40. Moseley, "Antidote for Suicide"; Moseley, "Ye are Gods"; Moseley, "Wonders of

CHRISTIANITY, POLITICS, AND THE SEPARATION OF CHURCH AND STATE

Moseley began to take increased interest in politics at all levels as the 1920s wore on, through not often in support of one candidate or the other. In what was unusual for the time—and especially now—was when he would write about candidates he made it a point to tell what he saw as the positive attributes of all concerned. In the 1928 presidential campaign, which saw Herbert Hoover run against New Yorker Al Smith, he decried the note of religious bigotry that had been introduced into the discussion. Smith was Catholic, and to many southerners, his membership in that denomination was tantamount to treason and blasphemy against the "true" faith. Editorials, letters to the editor, and public discussions in Macon were nearly universal in their denunciation of Smith: Not so much because of his political positions, but because of his religion.

In a July 1928 article, Rufus shared his support for the separation of church and state and the danger of having any one sect hold sway in government. Though he liked to quote David Lloyd George, British Prime Minister during World War I—that if we do not implement the principles of Christianity in government, the world faced even darker days ahead—it needs to be emphasized that Moseley was not in favor of some kind of a quasi- or openly Christian theocracy—a Christian Taliban—to rule the United States or any other nation. Such a system would ultimately lead to dictatorship (as the Puritans in New England found out) and fanaticism. Instead he favored a system whereby the Sermon on the Mount would provide the framework for the governing of nations, and the law of love the means of its implementation.

Moseley's attitude about politics in general, as in all areas of life, was firmly based on the love ethic. Regardless of one's political affiliation, Rufus was of the opinion that unless one's views and interactions were generous and kind, loving and peaceful, more harm was done than any good one may think a particular political position holds. He stated it as follows:

> The test of every discussion and contact with people is "has it made me love them more, or less? If I love them less, I need to acknowledge it and ask the Lord's forgiveness and ask the forgiveness of anyone that I have failed to love at least as much as before" . . . It is a good thing to indulge in political activities if you can do it with the increase of your fellowship with the Lord

---

Love"; Moseley, "All Things Possible"; and Moseley, "Antidote for Suicide" for examples of his writings on the tragedy of suicide.

> and with an increased love and charity even for those you have to differ from in order to be true to God's will and public welfare as you see them ... After we think about it, we can't help but regret everything we have done that has had too much heat and too little sense and love in it, but we need never regret and need to repent of having been too loving and too charitable in dealing with one another. Since God loves his enemies and is always trying to save them, we are only happy in him as we love our enemies, even our worst political enemies.[41]

Rufus's warnings about combining religion with politics were clear, and his words bear considering for American Christians today, some of whom seem bent on establishing the very system Moseley and our Founding Fathers sought to avoid.

> As much as I like the Methodists and the Baptists and other Protestant groups, I would not care to live in a world dominated by any of them. As to the Roman Catholics and Greek Catholics, as much as I like these that I know personally, I would not want to live in a world where the leaders of either of these were free to carry out all of their teachings and convictions ... All human religious leadership I have ever known tends to produce the attitude of a closed mind and the static condition of life.[42]

Moseley became a fan of C. S. Lewis during the late 1940s, and I am sure that I would agree with the Cambridge professor's take on the dangers of religious moralizers in positions of power to force their views on society. From C. S. Lewis's *God in the Dock*:

> Of all tyrannies, a tyranny sincerely exercised for the good of its victims may be the most oppressive. It would be better to live under robber barons than under omnipotent moral busybodies. The robber baron's cruelty may sometimes sleep, his cupidity may at some point be satiated; but those who torment us for our own good will torment us without end for they do so with the approval of their own conscience. They may be more likely to go to heaven yet at the same time likelier to make a hell of earth.[43]

Blaise Pascal, the great seventeenth-century French mathematician, philosopher, and theologian of whom Moseley was likewise fond, said it even

---

41. Moseley, "Hide in Me."
42. Moseley, "Christianity and Politics."
43. See Lewis, *God in the Dock*, 292.

more succinctly in *Pensees*: "Men never do evil more completely and cheerfully than when they do it from religious conviction."[44]

Between 1890 and 1954, Rufus encountered religious/political pigeonholing, with believers in that era sometimes piously deciding which candidate or political party was "Christian" and which was not. As in every area of life, Rufus believed politics could be redeemed though love and understanding. He gained many of these ideas from his own study of Scripture, history, and political science, but also from a few friends and acquaintances who would have a profound impact on him in the 1920s.

OTHER INFLUENCES

Toward the end of the 1920s, Rufus Moseley referred to and quoted a few of the spiritual giants of the day: E. Stanley Jones (1884–1973), Sadhu Sundar Singh (1889–1929), and Toyokiko Kagawa (1888–1960). Jones first came to the attention of Moseley when his book *Christ of the Indian Road* was published. In this remarkable book, the background and work of the great Methodist missionary was told, as well as his efforts spreading the Christian message across the Indian subcontinent. A gentle Christian mystic himself, Jones was to find in Rufus a friend with many corresponding interests, both secular and spiritual. Rufus liked to share Jones's story of his struggles with nervous exhaustion.

Feeling that he had reached the end of his rope, Jones cried out to God for help in the massive work undertaken in India. Once, while in prayer and not giving particular thought to India, he believed the Holy Spirit said to him, "Are you ready for this work for which I have called you?" To which Jones relied in the negative, "No Lord, I am done for. I have reached the end." The Holy Spirit then plainly said, "If you will turn it over to me and not worry about it, I will take care of it." Jones, seeing his answer, quickly responded, "Lord, I close the bargain right here!" Jones then reported an immediate release and the descending of the Holy Spirit upon him with great peace that permeated his whole being. Abundant life had been given to him and the nervous exhaustion left him, never to return. He afterwards stated, "I felt possessed of life and peace and rest in Christ Himself."[45]

After Moseley positively reviewed *Christ of the Indian Road* in his *Telegraph* column, the two met and became fast friends.[46] So much so that throughout the 1930s and 1940s, they would attend and speak at the same

---

44. See Pascal, *Pensees*, 894.
45. Moseley, "Christ of All Roads"; see also Jones, *Christ of the Indian Road*.
46. Moseley, "Christ of All Roads."

conferences and later serve on a yearly presidential advisory group. Another annual ritual for the two would be their meeting at the Mars Hill conference in western North Carolina. Many of Moseley's closest friends and associates would meet at this gathering and share their spiritual experiences. Jones's own Christian Ashram movement began around this time as well, and Moseley was occasionally an honored guest. In 1941 and 1949 respectively, Stanley Jones wrote the foreword and introduction for Moseley's two books, *Manifest Victory* and *Perfect Everything*. Jones would also share with Rufus the story of one of his friends from India, and he was to have a profound influence on Moseley as well.

Sadhu Sundar Singh was born in 1889 and raised a Sikh in the Punjab region of northern India. After the death of his mother in 1905, a young Sundar in desperation cried out to God, whomever he might be, to appear to him and heal his mental anguish. He gave himself a deadline, deciding that if God did not appear to him, he would end his life before morning on the railroad tracks near his home. Shortly before his self-imposed time limit, he witnessed a bright ball of light, in the middle of which stood Jesus. Sundar was shocked at this, as he had expected to see Krishna or some other avatar, not the hated Christ of the local missionaries. He converted that night at the age of sixteen, only to be met with a harsh family reaction that included disowning him and forced him out of the house; later, his father even sought to kill him by poison, nearly succeeding. Shortly thereafter he took up the saffron robe of the traveling sadhu, or holy man, and walked the length and width of northern India, and into Nepal, Tibet, and Kashmir spreading the Christian gospel.

Before the age of thirty he gained international fame as a Christian missionary, although Western denominations were not entirely welcoming. Sometimes called the "Apostle of the Bleeding Feet" because he wore no shoes and left bloody prints in the snow, Singh even traveled to Europe and the United States, though he was deeply offended at the worldliness of the Christians he found in the West. Moseley was deeply affected when he heard the stories and read the accounts of his life, often calling Singh perhaps the most Christ-like believer then alive. Rufus had hoped to meet Singh during his visit to the United States, and apparently made plans to do so. But if the two ever met, there is no record of it. A few years later, in 1929, Sundar Singh disappeared during one of his annual treks into Tibet and was not heard of again. Some claimed that he simply left to join his friend, the Maharishi of the Kailash in southwest Tibet, for a life of solitude and prayer, but the more likely result is that his already failing health and eyesight proved his undoing. His passing was mourned by millions around the world, Hindu, Moslem, and Christian alike.[47]

Another figure from Asia, Toyohiko Kagawa (1888–1960) also had a profound influence on Moseley as well, as he was involved in social concerns for the poor, women, and the threat of war. Kagawa was a Japanese Christian who led pacifist, labor, women's suffrage, and other reform movements during the rise of ultra-conservative Imperial Japan. He converted to Christianity as a youth after taking a Bible course. His conversion did not set well with his family, resulting in his being taken in by two American missionaries. He attended the Tokyo Presbyterian College, Kobe Theological Seminary, and studied theology and a number of other topics in the United States at Princeton University.

Kagawa believed that Japanese society could be formed around kingdom principles, as set forth in his book, *Brotherhood Economics*, without the use of force or coercion. He sought first to work among the poorest elements in Japanese society, and in 1916 published *Research in the Psychology of the Poor* which was based on these experiences. By the 1920s he began to run afoul of the increasingly militaristic Japanese government. After Japan had invaded Manchuria and then the rest of China, he publicly apologized to the Chinese people for his government's actions. This would land him in jail yet again.

Kagawa famously said words to the effect of "It seems that everyone is attacking me: the Soviet Communists, the anarchists, the capitalists, critics, newspapers, Buddhists who could not compete with Christ, and those many Christians who profess Christ but believe in a Christianity that is sterile." After World War II, Kagawa was made part of the post-war government. He was twice nominated for the Nobel Prize in Literature and twice more for the Nobel Peace Prize. He and Rufus met during one of his speaking tours of the United States, in this case in Atlanta. They spoke together about spiritual things, and Moseley found in Kagawa a true kindred spirit on a number of levels. Like Sundar Singh before him, Kagawa ran afoul of some American denominational leaders when he stated that love of wealth and possessions in the West seemed to be more important than caring for the poor and destitute. He even refused to stay in luxury hotel rooms provided for him, instead opting to stay in a humble inn located in the poorer part of any city where he spoke.[48] For one such as Rufus Moseley, who worked tirelessly among the poor, this must have resounded in his spirit.

---

47. See Thompson, *Sadhu Sundar Singh*; Singh, *At the Master's Feet*; and Parker, *Sadhu Sundar Singh*, for overviews of this remarkable man and his teachings.

48. Moseley, "New Testamentarian."

END OF THE ROARIN' TWENTIES

As has been demonstrated and will be further demonstrated in the next chapter, Rufus Moseley did indeed have political opinions, and he most certainly was not shy (though he was polite) in sharing them. His opposition to capital punishment, advocacy of economic justice, and strident outspokenness against Jim Crow and racial segregation are but a few already mentioned. But there were other important storm clouds on the horizon, winds of change that would alter America forever and bring with them the rising threat of revolution and war. There was, as the tawdry days of the 1920s drew to a close, a growing sense of despair that afflicts every culture that worships prosperity and pleasure. Young people became disenchanted, the elderly did not have an answer for them, and politicians and religious leaders seemed helpless to provide any solutions either. The rock-ribbed certainty fundamentalists and other conservative Christians had provided melted in embarrassment before the onslaught of modernism and skepticism. Their poor showing in Dayton, Tennessee only seemed to advance the notion that religious sentiments such as theirs were ill-prepared to deal with the questions of the time, or provide any sort of answer other than looking backwards. The savaging fundamentalists had taken at the hands of writers like Mencken, and the growing popularity of the intellectual approach of Bertrand Russell, seemed to leave the world in a place of questioning and in some cases, despair.

Nonetheless, there were some voices of hope at this time, such as Aimee Semple McPherson, who adapted the presentation of the gospel in a much more modern vein, and was light years ahead of many of her Pentecostal contemporaries. Utilizing radio and other modern means, she was able to project a nationwide message that became increasingly popular. Others, such as Rufus, possessed of a spiritual viewpoint as well as an understanding of history and economics, took an even more strident role in proclaiming the love of God, the union with Christ, as the answer. He did not dismiss secular criticisms of Christians for their sometimes backwards ways, yet continued to offer a different approach. But the miasma of doubt, the emptiness of wealth, and the rise of fascism and communism did not bode well for the future of the nation nor of Western liberal democracy. When the Great Depression finally swept aside much that had seemed permanent, it gave a sense of further hopelessness, this time with the added edge of unemployment, starvation, and war.

4

The Poor, the Downtrodden, and the Kingdom Response

1930–1935

What does love look like? It has the hands to help others. It has the feet to hasten to the poor and needy. It has eyes to see misery and want. It has the ears to hear the sighs and sorrows of men. That is what love looks like.

—Saint Augustine of Hippo

With the crash of the American stock market in October 1929, a time of prolonged social and economic woes enveloped the nation. For Rufus Moseley, it also saw a turning point in his writing and ministry; not in the sense that he changed his belief in the primacy of seeking after the kingdom of God, rather, became more convinced than ever that there was a need for the wealthy and government to work together to ease the pain the economic downturn had wrought. Moseley also increasingly addressed geopolitical realities, given the rise in tensions worldwide as a result of fascism in Italy, Nazism in Germany, and imperial control in Japan had unleashed on the world. The 1930s were also a time of remarkable spiritual change in Macon, and one in which Moseley took a very active part. Perhaps his most powerful writings in both secular and spiritual matters emerge during this decade. Over and above all of this was his increased insistence that the Love Way of Christ was the answer to all of it, that because love could not fail, it was the final and only workable answer.

As a historian and social commentator, he also felt it incumbent upon himself to talk about economics in the wake of the 1929 stock market collapse and the Great Depression that followed in its wake. From the late 1920s on, Moseley's newspaper columns take on an increasingly prescient quality. By the mid-1930s this is in full blossom and, leading up to the publication of *Manifest Victory* in 1941, act as a precursor for that seminal work. His freewheeling discussions of religion and philosophy in the 1920s is left in part for an intensive and focused presentation of what it means to live in the kingdom of God in the here and now.

GREAT DEPRESSION

In the early part of the 1930s, Rufus was understandably concerned about the effects of the Great Depression on those least able to bear its fallout. With unemployment well above twenty percent, and millions of families struggling to simply put food on the table, something drastic had to be done. At the end of the Hoover administration, Republicans had taken a "hands off" attitude toward the fiscal disaster, and believed that the markets would correct themselves. To commentators such as Moseley, this just wasn't enough, not with the immediate problems facing the common man. When banks likewise began to close, and those that stayed open experienced frantic customer efforts to withdraw their funds, it had all the makings for the kind of political challenges Europe was also experiencing. The threat of revolution was real, and Moseley pleaded with government and business leaders to take action on behalf of the poorest and most destitute to stave off such a possibility. There were already terribly destructive political ideologies at work in the world, and the Western democracies were increasingly under siege. Unless action were taken, it appeared that similar violence in the United States could occur.

When Franklin Roosevelt and the Democrats began instituting emergency efforts to deal with the multi-headed hydra of economic and natural disasters, Rufus was quickly on board. He wrote glowing accounts throughout the Depression of government relief efforts to help the poor: Works Progress Administration (WPA), Civilian Conservation Corps (CCC), Tennessee Valley Authority (TVA), National Recovery Act (NRA), and the other New Deal programs prevented difficulty from growing into despair and then revolution. Already possessed of the opinion that government should be in the business of helping the poor, Moseley believed that Roosevelt's quick action was just what was needed. He did, however, believe that industry should likewise be involved and hire back workers instead of taking profits from their absence. Some did just that, as shown below, and Rufus was quick to applaud any doing so.[1]

Rufus Moseley was not anti-capitalism; he was, however, of the opinion that Christian values should rule in the market place as surely as in the rest of life. He liked to share stories of businessmen and corporate leaders who had caught the proper spirit of giving, especially in the trying times of the Great Depression. Among these was one Patrick Henry Callahan, a Louisville industrialist who ran a varnish company in that city. Like every other business, his interests took a hit with the collapse of the stock market and ensuing economic downturn. Instead of laying off workers and cutting wages, Callahan took the initiative to first cut salaries at the top, then slightly reduce worker hours so there would be no layoffs. He also instituted a system of profit-sharing where employees shared in the prosperity of the company and the goods and services they produced.[2] Like one of his heroes, Tolstoy, Moseley would say that so long as he had more than others, it was his duty to share with those who had less, not take away the little they had. Rufus made several visits to Louisville where he was the guest of Mr. Callahan.

These two men—one Catholic, the other Pentecostal—understood each other remarkably well. With Moseley's full agreement, Callahan stated:

> There is no more justification for the continued existence of a business that cannot carry its normal working force in times of depression than for one which cannot pay a living wage. All ethical and religious standards worthy of the name must condemn the practice of dismissing workers in order to cut down cost and expenses, while dividends to stock holders and salaries to officers are undisturbed. Slavery will never quite be abolished until the faithful worker is given more share in the management of business, which in human principle is as much his as it is that of the man who puts money into it.[3]

To which Moseley added:

> The cutting should be from the top where the salaries are large and where accumulations are also large and never from the

---

1. Moseley, "More Divine Laughter."
2. Moseley, "All But Love Fails."
3. Moseley, "All Important Needs."

bottom where the wages are low and the workers too often accumulate debts rather than bank accounts. Every advance in industrialism makes the position of the worker at the bottom more precarious and slavish unless there goes along with this an ever increasing humaneness and the triumph of the Christian spirit and way of life.[4]

The seriousness of the money issue was something that did not just affect the individual, but as stated earlier, involved the spiritual health of the nation as well. When companies take huge profits and do not pass on wage increases, instead cutting the work force or eliminating benefits, it reveals an underlying condition of heart that sees the worker as merely cogs in the wheelhouse rather than human beings. Rufus believed that as long as those who possessed the capital and directed industry did not use their money, power, and influence to help those on the bottom, the threat of revolution was real, that in fact it was inevitable. And concerning the poor, Moseley contended that there is a great responsibility for those who have much in talent, resources, money, and industrial power for their right use for the benefit of all, not just the enrichment of a few. He further stated, "It should be impossible for one who takes the name of Christ not to give himself to the life of love and service for his fellow men. The day will come when unused wealth and wealth for selfish pleasures will be looked upon as representing one's unlikeness to Christ and resistance to His spirit and His way of life."[5]

Rufus Moseley and many other American and British Christian leaders of the early part of the twentieth century had markedly different views of economics than one finds among some present-day Evangelical Christians. It had little or nothing to do with the acquisition of wealth and possessions—such motivations were largely abhorred—and emphasized instead taking care of the weakest, poorest, and most destitute in one's own nation, and indeed, the world. G. A. Studdert Kennedy said words to the effect that economics and religion are not opposed to one another, but are two sides of the same coin, so to speak.[6] Rufus was of the firm conviction that great spiritual blessings would be bestowed those who use their economic might wisely and in love for the needy. Like the servant given ten talents, proper use of it is rewarded, while misuse is severely reprimanded. One of the greatest temptations in his day—and ours—is for the wealthy to behave as the servant with but one talent and not use it wisely for the

---

4. Moseley, "All Important Needs."
5. Moseley, "All Important Needs."
6. See Kennedy, *Wicket Gate*.

common good and the kingdom of God.[7] Such attitudes, whether taken by individuals, businesses, or governments, carries with it the seeds of their/its own destruction. On a macro scale, it is the stuff of which revolutions are made; on an individual scale, it is the very makeup of callous hearts and seared consciences. Both are an abomination. While his concern for the poor continued apace, Moseley again found himself in a most unusual situation, again involving a man scheduled for death in the electric chair. The outcome was a surprise and delight for all.

HONESTY, SINCERITY, AND A DEATH SENTENCE AVOIDED

A much more positive capital punishment case in which Rufus found himself embroiled involved a man known simply as Gay. In 1931, Gay had killed someone in a heated argument in rural central Georgia. He was tried and convicted of the crime, and sentenced to death in the electric chair at the State Prison Farm in Milledgeville, Georgia. When the time came to transfer the convicted murderer to his appointment with the executioner, the sheriff driving him there did something most unusual: he drove up to the gates of the State Farm and simply dropped Gay off, and then left. The convicted murderer stood outside the gate for a time, where he was observed, and eventually entered in the sight of the guards. When asked what they could do for him, Gay replied in a matter-of-fact fashion, "Well, I am here to be electrocuted."[8]

The guards looked at one another and laughed. But when Gay did not leave, they finally invited him to see the Prison Superintendant, Judge B. H. Dunaway. The authorities at the State Farm, of course, knew Gay was scheduled to be delivered for execution, but were dumbfounded when they realized he had been waiting outside, alone, as if standing in line at a movie theater. "Where is the sheriff?" Dunaway thundered. "Oh, he is gone," Gay replied, "He dropped me off and told me I would be shown where to go. I imagine you will want me in a death cell now." Stunned by Gay's honesty, his story was verified as to his identity and situation. A call for the sheriff who had delivered him was then made and asked to return and explain himself.[9] When the law-enforcement officer returned, he told prison officials that he knew Gay would not leave or try to otherwise escape. He had found the young man the very model of honesty and sincerity in the county jail where

7. See Kennedy, *Wicket Gate*, 1931.
8. Moseley, *Manifest Victory*, 256.
9. Moseley, *Manifest Victory*, 256.

he was being held, and had no concern that he would flee. Prison officials were doubtless angry with the sheriff, who then signed the paperwork finalizing the delivery of the prisoner.

The story was quickly published first by a local newspaper, then passed on to other newspapers in central Georgia. The Associate Press eventually heard of it, and likewise repeated this unusual tale; the *Macon Telegraph* made it a front-page story. Rufus Moseley heard about it from the State Farm prison chaplain, as well as reading it in a newspaper. He immediately made the trip from Macon to Milledgeville to meet this unusual man. Gay retold his story, authenticated by officials, and prompted Moseley to write to Governor Richard Russell in Atlanta. "Too much good here to execute!" he implored. Russell apparently thought so, too, and commuted Gay's sentence to life imprisonment. Moseley often visited his friend over the years, and happily reported that he had become a trustee and was of great service to his fellow inmates, as well as to the warden.[10] By being honest, Gay found forgiveness and his life was spared. As Rufus shared:

> In this ministry of enlightenment, it matters not what one has done nor what spirit one has been heretofore; everything is turned to good when there is receptivity and response to the Perfect One. The worse the spirit and the greater evil one has worked, the greater his destiny and services of helpfulness as he yields to the good spirit of the Lord.[11]

Rufus's views on capital punishment were in the minority, both among the general public and the Christian world with which he interacted. In our own time, it is not difficult to see that Moseley would be just as opposed to abortion. But Rufus would be equally against the cutting of state and federal funding that helped the woman who had the courage to keep her child. He understood that if Christianity stands for or against something, such as abortion or capital punishment, it needed to be backed up, both at the church and government levels.

There was another topic that was highly popular and hotly debated among American Christians in the 1930s, just as it is today. As such, one might expect that Rufus would write at length about this too, but as with the Scopes Monkey Trial, scarce notice was given to it other than passing mention. As times worsened in the 1930s, American believers became increasingly interested in prophetic end-times teachings. While Rufus looked forward to Christ's return, he was put off by the constant speculation, often fueled through wild conspiracy theories that blew across the land.

10. Moseley, "Christmas Every Day."
11. Moseley, *Manifest Victory*, 237.

RUFUS MOSELEY AND END-TIMES PROGNOSTICATION

Given the huge amount of interest in the end times, one may consider Rufus Moseley's relative lack of interest rather unusual. It wasn't that Rufus Moseley did not believe in a visible second coming of Christ—he most emphatically did—but he found the guesses and spiritual contortions many believers went through trying to pin down when it would occur, or who might be the antichrist, a hopeless and counterproductive exercise. As with his view that the veritable worship of the gifts of the Spirit or personal revelations over union with Christ was to be avoided, Moseley believed that end-times teaching was something that had to be put in its proper perspective. As such, he viewed many strident pronouncements about the Last Days to be detracting casuistry away from Christ's command to walk in Divine Love.[12]

Rufus barely broached the topic in the 1920s, but as the 1930s drew on and World War II neared, he did at least address the issue on a couple of occasions. In the decade of the Great Depression and Dust Bowl, many American believers were certain that horrible economic depression was proof-positive the end was near. Jeremiads were preached about the sun being blotted out, something a good portion of the population witnessed with Dust Bowl conditions, as well as warnings that a "mark of the beast" was at hand. Add to that the rise of extreme right- and left-wing dictatorships overseas, the isolationist policies at home, home-grown extremist groups threatening violence, and the rampant crime wave of that decade, and Americans in general thought something was seriously amiss and were heaven-gazing, looking for the end of the world.

When Franklin Roosevelt became president in 1933, far-right groups, some of them Christian, were convinced that his New Deal program was the beginning of America's slide into communism. One such critic was popular conservative Catholic priest Father Charles Coughlin. This Michigan-based priest operated a radio ministry that began in the 1920s, and initially dealt primarily with spiritual topics. By the mid-1930s, however, he became a virulent and venomous Roosevelt opponent and conspiracy theorist. In time, his weekly listening audience would number some thirty million Americans. Like some political and religious radio programs in our own time, Coughlin played on fears and uncertainties, which convinced millions of Americans that perhaps their government was descending into an end-times New World Order. Coughlin came to blame Jews, liberals, socialists, and others for the nation's ills, later engaging in claims that the Illuminati,

---

12. Moseley, "In Heaven on Earth."

Freemasons, and "International Bankers" (often a code word for "Jewish Bankers") were to blame. Unfortunately, as Coughlin's beliefs became more radical and incendiary, many American Catholic and Protestants came to believe his fantasies of hate and bigotry. By 1939, Coughlin's positive statements about Hitler and fascism finally caused his popularity to plummet. The Catholic Church itself stepped in and demanded that his radio program be shut down. Other radio stations had earlier acted on their own, removing him from the airwaves.

The 1930s in particular was a hotbed of extreme right-wing conspiracy theories and organized groups holding to such opinions. Groups like the Silver Shirts, the "Jawhawk Nazis" in conservative Kansas, the wild-eyed beliefs of Gerald Winrod, and other conservative preachers came to typify the venom many increasingly held against seemingly all institutions, especially government. Virtually all of them combined conservative Christian religious belief with conspiracy theory. Protestant preachers likewise attacked the liberal policies of Roosevelt as "creeping socialism" that would direct the United States into a Soviet-style government that would, like its Russian counterpart, lead to enforced atheism. Roosevelt's efforts to aid the destitute and his wife Eleanor's work on behalf of African Americans added fuel to the fire among conservatives that something satanic was afoot at the highest levels of government. The truth was that there was a concerted government effort in Washington to meet the threats of fascism and communism by providing aid to the poor and lower classes who had been hit hardest by the Great Depression. It was the beginning of a more socially conscious government, but it was not met with support from all quarters.

The combination of religion with politics was one reason why Rufus rarely involved himself in end-times discussions, in part because it drew all manner of wild interpretations and was often taught along partisan political lines in much the same way as it is today. When conservative believers of his time pointed to the National Recovery Act's emblem, allegedly having three sixes hidden in it (to create the Mark of the Beast, "666") as "proof" America had descended into the abyss of an antichrist system, he brushed such nonsense aside, knowing that such views generally did nothing more than create fear and hatred. One of the few times he wrote about the end times was in an article dated September 23, 1933, entitled "Mark of the Beast":

> All of us who refuse to do anything against anybody and through the spirit of Jesus and through Jesus himself seek, will, and work nothing but good to anyone, will escape all the bad things that are coming upon the earth and will find that everything is working together for our good. The warning in Revelation is perfectly

plain: all we have to do is to refuse to do any evil and to refuse to resort to any of the weapons of evil and also do all the good we can to everybody and be patient with everybody, and we will be perfectly safe and no mark of the beast will ever be put upon us because both the nature and methods of the beast have been escaped by us.[13]

Rufus added the following warning against believers engaging in fear-mongering, hatred, or other unchristian beliefs that conspiracy theorists propagated:

> Don't allow anyone to get you to agree to do any evil to anyone under the pretense that it is necessary in order that good may come out of it. Good only comes from good. You cannot do any evil without becoming a victim to the very evil you do. All who try to overcome evil with evil do not overcome the evil but are overcome by the very evil they tried to overcome . . . They who take the sword perish with the sword. Those who try to lead other people in captivity themselves become captives.[14]

Rufus was also to say, "There is no advantage in gazing up into the heavens [guessing when the second coming will occur], [but] there is great advantage in making yourself heavenly. Those who really look for Jesus in manifest victory desire to be manifest with Him are making themselves and everything else ready for this manifestation."[15]

There is some indication, both in print and spoken to trusted friends, that Moseley thought that, had the human race properly readied itself by yielding to the Holy Spirit, the second coming may well have taken place earlier. His view of manifest victory was that, if believers had followed up their conversion with baptism in the Holy Spirit and pursued the Life as Love in total abandonment to Jesus, it may have allowed for a much wider acceptance for and anticipation of his return. From a May 1929 article, Rufus states:

> With these early Christians, faith in Jesus Christ and the gift of the Holy Ghost turned the world upside down. From one hundred twenty, the number of disciples grew in one day, the day of Pentecost, to three thousand. But a short time later it swelled to five thousand, not long afterwards it was a multitude. Had the post-apostolic Christians continued in the simple faith of Jesus

---

13. Moseley, "Mark of the Beast."
14. Moseley, "Mark of the Beast"; see also Camp, *Selling Fear*.
15. Quote attributed to Moseley.

as the Christ as revealed by the Holy Ghost, and had they kept open to the guidance of the Spirit and lived in the Spirit and perfect love of Christ, the Kingdom of God might have long ago been victorious on this earth.[16]

The reasons for the falling away of church standards over the years are legion, but mostly involved a slow slipping into maintaining the old wine skins that suffocated spiritual freshness even as it excluded the very things that made the church so vital. Firsthand revelation gave way to institutional discussion of what those before them had believed and achieved, followed by the hair-splitting over doctrines which can, when it goes to seed, result in divisions, denominations, even inquisitions.[17]

These are things Moseley saw as a historian as well as a believer, yet his beliefs were informed by the need to stay in union with Christ above all else. He held out hope that he would see the second coming himself, but also wondered if believers as a whole were ready for it. After all, if the kingdom does not come to the church inwardly, it is not ready for its outward appearance. Moseley believed that one of the greatest deceptions the church can fall into is to seek the transformation of society by force, legislative or otherwise.[18] Instead, he foresaw the overcoming bride, prayed for its maturing, and understood that any victory was based in love and humility.

If this is understood correctly, Rufus Moseley believed that individual salvation followed with the baptism in the Holy Spirit were but early-stage preparations for the coming of Christ within each person, but also in the outer world. In short, being made in Christ's image inwardly is a precursor to full manifest victory of believers, and as such is an essential harbinger of the kingdom that is to come outwardly. He did not believe that believers could, of their own power, stave off or bring the Second Advent, but believers could, if in union with Christ, be vital participants in it. By failing to yield to Christ, as he often said, "Things on the outside will get worse and worse, while for those in union with Him it will get better and better." In this sense, the tribulation one hears about so often has as much to do with ongoing human rebellion and self-willed lives than anything else. The time of sorrows is self-inflicted.[19]

Moseley was also aware of the belief among many believers that with Great Britain's Balfour Declaration in 1917, which looked favorably upon the creation of a Jewish state in Palestine, a certain end-times marker had

---

16. Moseley, "Gospel Then and Now"; McLain, *Resurrection Encounter*, 196.
17. Moseley, "Secret of Jesus."
18. McLain, *Resurrection Encounter*, 198–99.
19. McLain, *Resurrection Encounter*, 202–3.

been reached. This view was strengthened when Israel was created in May of 1948. For many believers, then and now, more than any other recent world event, the creation of Israel seemed to signal the approach of the end times. Even before these two events, Rufus was highly active in campaigning for funds to help Jews in Europe and the Middle East. After Israel was created, he likewise asked his readers to give to charities to help both Arab and Jew in that part of the world. He did not state in so many words whether he deemed the creation of Israel as a fulfillment of prophecy and the "beginning of the end," but was most definitely concerned for the well-being of all peoples in that war-torn region.

There was another area among believers which was of interest both in Moseley's time as well as today, and on this he had most definite opinions.

MONEY AND FINANCES

Anyone who has given even a cursory look at portions of contemporary American Evangelical Christianity, at least among charismatics, will see that there has come to be an inordinate emphasis on money, ranging from topics such as tithing to expected returns on one's giving. Expecting returns was something that Moseley found offensive in his own time, when it wasn't widely taught; we see today that such teachings have become widespread. I do not think Moseley could have imagined it would grow to the lengths it has today. Rufus lived the simplest of lives, rarely had more than a few pennies in his pocket, his clothing was simple and often showed signs of wear, and his shoes were worn out. In some quarters of the American charismatic world today, he would be considered to be in a state of unbelief for it.

Rufus Moseley, besides embracing his own version of Francis of Assisi's "Lady Poverty," lived what Henri Nouwen later described as "voluntary downward mobility." In his *Spiritual Direction*, Nouwen writes that it is a voluntarily "going to the end of the line, staying behind the sets, choosing the last place."[20] It goes against the Love Mandate to get ahead or have advantage over others, even in ministry, and instead calls for the individual to be like Francis, like Jesus, and to choose the humble, the meek, the way of the poor and downtrodden. As Nouwen wisely pointed out, "We are called to follow Jesus on the downward path of ministry and to go to where God is leading, even if that place is somewhere we would rather not go."[21]

---

20. Nouwen, *Spiritual Direction*, 138; Walters, *Perfect Joy*, 56–57; Talbot, *Simplicity*, 109–14.

21. Nouwen, *Spiritual Direction*, 139.

The key to this life is that it is voluntary, a choosing of the humble and meek way that dismisses the incessant demands for money and position. For Rufus, it meant laying aside a career in higher education for doing the most menial of tasks for the poorest and most destitute. Like Francis of Assisi, he chose to identify with "the least of these," and in so doing identified with Christ himself. This is radical stuff, and a type of Christianity that is so rarely seen across the span of Church history; yet there it is, offering each and all of us the way to a greater life in Christ, a deeper walk with the Holy Spirit, and becoming wellsprings of hope and love to a nation and modern church that has largely sold itself to position, power, and wealth.

One of the things that caused some to wonder about Rufus Moseley, especially in his later years, was his physical appearance. While well-groomed, his clothing could be described as that of a tatterdemalion. He owned but one suit of clothing, usually the one he was wearing at any given time, and over the years it not only went out of style, but became ragged around the edges. During a 1940s visit to New York City where he was to meet with national religious leaders, some of his friends were appalled that he was going to see these prominent men in his tattered suit, and whisked him off to a haberdashery to purchase a new one. When it became apparent there wasn't enough time for fitting him with new apparel, they returned to his hotel room, made him take off his suit, and took it out for at least a quick cleaning. One can only imagine Rufus, sitting alone in the hotel room in his underwear, awaiting the return of his friends with his clothes.[22]

Stories like this were often repeated among those who dearly loved him, generally with copious laughter. Once, when visiting the Tommy Tyson family in North Carolina, Rufus answered the front door to find some boys seeking clothing drive donations. Having just had a suit purchased for him—presumably by Tommy—he nonetheless gave the gift to the boys at the door. Similar stories were told about his shoes, which apparently he wore until nearly falling apart. Tommy Tyson once purchased him a pair, apparently going with him to a store to ensure he actually made and kept the purchase. While at the shoe store, Rufus told a young Jewish clerk waiting on him that Jesus loved him mightily, and that he had told him to say so. "Well, I hope it is true," the young man replied. As they left the store, Moseley turned to Tyson and said, "You see, Tommy, even those who do not believe it hope it is true!"[23] Wayne McLain, a friend of Tommy Tyson, shared the following observation:

---

22. McLain, *Resurrection Encounter*, 124.
23. Tyson-Carter email communication with the author, June 2014.

Rufus seemed to live with very little anxiety about his appearance or his clothing. He once remarked that most of his clothes were given to him. Of course, his appearance at the time may have spurred such generosity. Though he lived in happy unconcern for clothing as a rule, I did hear him say that when he was to appear before the governor of the state to plead for the life of a prisoner on death row, he sought to wear good clothing and make a good appearance, for the sake of man he was trying to save.[24]

Rufus learned early on in his Christian walk of God's daily provision for him. As he was wont to do, he often withdrew a dollar or two from his bank account on Friday afternoons to cover his weekend expenses. Once, apparently having no money in the account, he asked the Holy Spirit to show him the truth and working out of trust for the least of things; that is to say, money. Seeing a person on the street in apparent need, Rufus felt led to give the single penny he had in his pocket. He found that on the following day he received a number of invitations to meals in private homes. It convinced him that if he would make available all he had without consideration for getting back, done in the spirit of love, God could be counted upon to see to his every need, regardless of how minor. By being willing to minister where led, to give when told to give, he never lacked for food or clothing. He stated that he never once asked for funds or otherwise had taken up a collection for himself. By going the Jesus way of even desiring to put first what should be first, by giving out love and only love, he was made far more secure in terms of ordinary needs than any other way of life.[25]

Moseley also went to considerable lengths to keep his own giving secret. At a Camps Farthest Out gathering sometime in the 1940s, a non-denominational organization Glenn Clark founded for spiritual seekers, he signed over a one hundred dollar check given to him by the CFO Secretary to a young man who was in need. As Rufus signed it and handed it to him, he added this admonition, "You take this and don't say anything about it to anybody!"[26] On another occasion in the 1930s, Moseley was given a bag containing seventy-five dollars for a speaking engagement, a sum of approximately $1,200 in 2019 dollars. He spotted a drifter in threadbare clothes on the street and handed him the bag, saying, "Brother, you look like you could use this more than me." Decades later, when his protégé Wayne McLain visited the *Macon Telegraph* offices, he asked employees if there were any

---

24. McLain, *Resurrection Encounter*, 124.
25. Moseley, *Manifest Victory*, 208–9.
26. McLain, *Resurrection Encounter*, 121.

who remembered Rufus Moseley and if so, what stood out in their mind. An elderly black gentleman said he remembered Rufus, and summed up his recollection of him as "If you had no coat, he would give you his."[27]

Stories about his generosity like these are many, but to Rufus, it was simply living in the kingdom of God, and certainly not something one would brag about. Moseley would never dream of himself sharing these stories, holding to the scriptural command to not let the right hand know what the left hand was doing in terms of giving. Indeed, the stories of his generosity I have shared would not be known if witnesses and/or the recipients had not shared them with others. There can be no doubt that Rufus had a giver's heart, often paying for a homeless person's meal while he went hungry himself. Rufus, like Francis of Assisi, held that to suffer and go without was a blissful honor if performed in the right spirit and motive.

Those ministries Rufus did give to he knew from firsthand experience to be honest and would use the money well. Conversely, ministries that used donations to build mansions and purchase expensive automobiles and clothing were practices he found repugnant. But asking money in and of itself was not wrong, as Rufus was to find out. On one occasion, shortly after his receiving the baptism of the Holy Spirit in 1910, he attended a meeting where he was asked to pass the plate for a collection. He responded, "I am sorry, but I am looking for a place to worship where money is not mentioned."[28] This caused great embarrassment to those who asked, as well as financial loss to the person for whom the offering would have been made; no collection was taken. Rufus underwent great travail over his action, and later met the person for whom the offering was intended and gave him well above what would have presumably been collected. Money, and its proper use, was important in ministry, and his self-inflicted pain in this particular instance was to change his heretofore opposition to others asking for money.

As far as a widely taught financial doctrine of today, tithing, Moseley rarely offered opinions about it. He was not in opposition to the practice, and recognized it could produce changed behavior. For instance, one person with whom Rufus was friendly told him that he overcame his personal greed when he committed to giving a tithe of his income.[29] For his part, Moseley thought it of the utmost importance that all believers recognize that everything they have is from God, and that the obedient believer may be called upon to give to whomever and wherever, and even all one pos-

---

27. Moseley, *Manifest Victory*, 208–9.

28. Moseley, *Manifest Victory*, 94.

29. Moseley, "Christ and Money"; I would also recommend Morris, *Blessed Life*, for a fine contemporary view of Christians, tithing, giving, and general finance issues.

sesses if so directed. Rufus believed that if the believer lived in that truth, the tithe was unnecessary, or the least one could do. While he did not oppose tithing, he was cautious of anyone who in their teaching insisted on paying the tithe, especially if they were the direct beneficiaries. He also pointed out that tithing in the Old Testament sense was not mentioned in its New Testament counterpart, other than Christ's pointing out to Pharisees that while they carefully tithe, they missed the bigger picture of love and compassion.

The reason for this, according to Rufus, was that first-century believers understood that the weightier matters before God were love, righteousness, and faith. And when God has given a particular person a task, Moseley understood that the means to perform the task would be there. Begging money for supplies was never the intended way, as the more we beg the more difficult it becomes for us, and we become a burden on others. Early believers were so possessed of this knowledge that they fulfilled the law and all requirements of God; in doing so, they were cheerful givers. Rufus was adamantly opposed to giving from obligation, or worse, because he/she was being leaned upon to do so. Still, Rufus would on rare occasion comment on the tithe:

> If you look to God for guidance about money matters and all the affairs of life and as your source of supply, putting him and His Kingdom of Love and righteousness first, it is the law of perfection that you will be led into the best services of love and that all you need for rendering those services and for living and for debt paying will be added . . . You cannot yield to the Good Spirit to do any deed of love or mercy, with the desire not to let one hand know what the other doeth, without God backing you.[30]

When he died, Moseley had very little other than his clothing, and the little he did have he gave away, including the family homestead land in western North Carolina.

Rufus Moseley was fond of quoting nineteenth-century Episcopal leader Phillip Brooks concerning money with words to the effect of "Show me the things a man spends his money for and the things he refuses for it and I'll tell you what kind of man he is." Rufus would further this sentiment by holding to the idea that when we look at our own use of money, we see how rich we are towards God and how much treasure we lay up in heaven, and how much treasure we lay up here below where it can be stolen, lost, or corroded. Christ himself said we cannot serve both God and mammon, for we will love one and hate the other. Moseley recognized that the misuse of money could be among the greatest obstacles to our entering in to

---

30. Moseley, "Christ and Money."

the kingdom of heaven. When Zaccheus, the redeemed tax collector from Jericho, had his life changed upon meeting Jesus, among the first things that changed was his attitude towards money. He promised to give half his riches to the poor and pay back at a rate of four to one all those whom he had cheated. His bondage, as real and formidable as any addiction, had been broken, and money no longer had hold of him. Of this, Moseley rightly said:

> It is easier to give up every other sin than it is the sin of covetousness. It is humbling to us to realize this, but it's so; and the reason that Christianity has made so comparatively slow progress is because so few have been converted economically. A minister of the Gospel or one who calls himself such, if he still loves money and still holds on to the advantages and the pride of life, may hinder the Kingdom more than he aids its coming. As Friend Walt Johnson so powerfully puts it, "The minister of Jesus must be glad to put himself on a level of the desperately needy that Christ would have to minister to." Until ministers and Christians generally are ready to make sacrifices for God and one another and for all men in the advance of men like Gandhi, how can they expect to draw men unto Christ, and into the Kingdom of God?[31]

The love ethic was the all-important guide in anything Moseley did concerning money or anything else. Giving out of a joyful and grateful heart was the first criteria to follow, with no expectation of getting something back. It was and is an issue of heart. I know that while he was generous with any money he had, he was also cautious about giving to people or organizations who utilized dubious tactics to solicit funds. He may well give all he had, as shared earlier, to a widow being evicted from her home, but was cautious about sending money to organizations who told the faithful to give to God and then provided their own mailing address.

WAR ATROCITIES AND SUFFERING IN THE FAR EAST

Moseley also wrote with some regularity in his columns about various natural and political tragedies that resulted in starvation and deprivation overseas. He wrote passionately about the famines in Russia and China during the 1920s and 1930s, as well as the great harm the Japanese invasion had visited on China. He was a champion for all displaced peoples, refugees, and

---

31. Moseley, "Bless and Help Everybody."

immigrants wherever they were, as well as Christian victims of persecution and martyrdom.

One story he liked to tell was of a Christian missionary in China who was captured by bandits, who then demanded recently collected funds for various ministry projects. When she refused, the bandits threatened to behead her. She began laughing at the idea, thoroughly confusing the thieves. When they asked her to explain herself, she stated that she had the thought of how glorious it would be to see her head roll down the hill as she ascended into heaven. Thinking the woman mad, the bandits left her without stealing the badly needed funds.[32]

On other occasions, Moseley shared the stories of ongoing Japanese war crimes against the Chinese people. When Japan invaded China (Manchuria) in the fall of 1931, the imperial government immediately set forth to brutally colonize the nation. Like any other minority, Christians felt the brunt of harsh treatment, often resulting in imprisonment or death. One such instance involved a young Chinese believer named Tsu Fok. Tsu had been an iron worker, but when the Japanese stopped him and saw his calloused hands, they assumed him to be a Chinese soldier out of uniform. He and the group of Christians with him were then arrested. Imprisoned and tortured, Tsu and the others prayed for deliverance. Tsu in particular drew the wrath of his Japanese captors, and for five straight days, for hours on end, he endured the most awful torture. At the end of the fifth day, Tsu again prayed for deliverance, and that night Jesus appeared to him in a dream and told him he would be delivered the next day.

The next morning, the Japanese commander called all of the prisoners out into the courtyard, demanding that the Christians stand off to one side. Fearing some new mistreatment, Tsu was stunned when the commander walked up to him and asked, "Who are you?" He responded by stating that he had had a dream just the night before, but did not give details. The commander replied, "I, too, had a dream last night. Tell me yours first!" Tsu then related the words of Christ to him about deliverance. The commander smiled broadly and said, "Your God appeared to me in a dream last night too and told me not to harm you further, but to deliver you." Tsu and the stunned group of Christians were thereupon given a pass and told to return home in safety. As they walked along, the Christians began singing hymns of praise and thanksgiving for the miracle.[33]

---

32. Moseley, "Christ Delivers."

33. Moseley, "Christ Delivers"; see also Moseley, "Glorify Jesus in Everything," for an example of his efforts to raise funds for those affected by war in Asia.

Presumably from his acquaintance Toyohiko Kagawa in Japan, Rufus heard of other accounts of the horrors being visited upon the Chinese people. Rufus felt urgency for the wealthy West to do everything they could to help the impoverished, the persecuted, and the imprisoned wherever they may be. So great and effective were his writings on behalf of suffering people that many charity groups thanked him and sought his help. His appeals on behalf of persecuted Jews in Germany and the Middle East were especially heartfelt. But as the mid-1930s approached, there was a local spiritual matter of importance on the immediate horizon, and acting as something of a harbinger was the visit of a nationally-known evangelist, for whom Moseley had the highest regard.

SISTER AIMEE

On February 22, 1934, Aimee Semple McPherson descended on Macon, Georgia for one of her "anti-evolution" debates with noted atheist Charles Lee Smith. As colorfully gentle as Aimee was, Smith was noted for his bombast. For instance, he was proud that he had been prosecuted for violating blasphemy laws ("A victimless crime," he quipped), and often publicly spoke of it. The two traveled together in public opposition, really more of a carnival than any semblance to a real debate. Despite sometimes heated comments during performances, they actually got along reasonably well. Rufus was asked to serve as a referee. Ever since the 1925 Scopes Monkey Trial in Dayton, Tennessee, when fundamentalism was dealt a crushing and humiliating blow at the hands of the American Civil Liberties Union (ACLU), there were efforts by a number of Christian leaders to try to salvage creationism from what they perceived to be the growing threat of "Darwinism," or evolution. The following was one such effort.

Sister Aimee and Charles Lee flew into Macon to considerable fanfare. The *Macon Telegraph and News* ran stories about the event leading up to, during, and after its completion. Semple McPherson, undoubtedly the best known Pentecostal and arguably the most famous private American citizen, was treated as royalty. Despite rumors and alleged scandals, Aimee remained a respected and much-loved leader. Oddly enough, perhaps her greatest opposition was not from atheists, secularists, or modernists, but within the Pentecostal movement itself. Some old-school Pentecostals did not like the idea of a woman preaching, and others did not like the theatrical gospel presentations she staged at her home church, Angelus Temple, in Los Angeles. Still others did not like the idea that Aimee wore makeup. As one critic of Fundamentalism and Pentecostalism, thought to be H. L. Mencken, once said of Aimee, "Sister Aimee did not, like many other Pentecostals, take a vow of unattractiveness."

The Macon "debate" was a disappointment to at least one *Telegraph* reporter, James Etheridge Jr. He was to say of it, "If the meeting was a religious service, it was innocuously irreverent; if entertainment, unspeakably dull; if joint lecture, hackneyed and threadbare. It was preaching to the choir."[34] For Moseley's part, he had the highest of praise for Sister Aimee, a woman he had years earlier admired for her working against the forces of social and religious bigotry, and on behalf of the poor. He spoke precious little about the "debate" itself, and as a religion columnist for the *Macon Telegraph and News*, stuck to the power of her spiritual testimony. Of Mr. Lee, he said far less, other than to indicate he did not think he won many converts in the Macon audience. Rufus Moseley's admiration of Aimee Semple McPherson was justifiable, not just for her Macon appearance, but indeed for the totality of her life and ministry. Moseley himself often encountered resistance from conservatives in a number of life's arenas, and found in Sister Aimee—and anyone else put upon by self-appointed "defenders of the faith" to fall in line—a kindred spirit.[35]

MACON PENTECOSTAL REVIVAL OF 1935

During the late winter and into the summer of 1935, a series of Pentecostal revivals broke out in Macon, Georgia that were as remarkable in their outcome as they were in terms of changed lives and reported miracles. Beginning in February of that year, the Blackburn Avenue Pentecostal Tabernacle and the Bellevue Church of God (Cleveland, TN) witnessed an outbreak of the Holy Spirit that quickly spread across the city and into the surrounding rural areas. Rufus Moseley, in his capacity as a religion columnist with the *Macon Telegraph and News*, reported on these revivals, often with the names and even addresses of those particularly impacted. In the midst of the Great Depression, which had hit Macon as hard as any community in the South, there were many missions (a good many of them Pentecostal) scattered about the downtown area, serving the poor and destitute, who had been made so by the economic collapse. Yet in the midst of this, as is often

---

34. Ethridge, "Aimee and Smith."

35. Aimee Semple McPherson is one of the the twentieth century's most charismatic individuals. Decades ahead of her time, this torchbearer opened the way for women in ministry like few others. Some books that will give the reader at least a sense of her life and ministry include McPherson, *This and That*; Sutton, *Sister Aimee*; and Blumhofer, *Aimee Semple McPherson*.

the case during hard times, there was a willingness and openness to spiritual things, and it spread like wildfire. Hazel Avenue, Spring Street, Walnut Avenue, and storefront ministries in East Macon saw sharp increases in attendance, as did many of the visiting tent revivalists who took up residence on the edge of town or in vacant city lots. Moseley himself had a dream of this some twenty-five years earlier in which he was given to understand that Macon and Atlanta would be pivotal in a coming revival. He said of his oneiric experience, "A rare friend, who received the baptism of the Holy Spirit twenty-five years ago [1910] and kept on yielding and praying and praising until taken up in the Spirit, saw Macon and Atlanta, along with the countries and isles of the sea all at the feet of Jesus."[36] He watched and waited for it from that time forward.

The Blackburn Avenue Pentecostal Tabernacle had been a staple of the Macon Pentecostal community for several years prior to the 1935 revival, and was one of the centers of this sudden spiritual outpouring. A high school now occupies the land where this church once stood, but in its day, this humble fellowship served as a focal point of spiritual renewal and interracial spiritual contact, a rarity in Jim-Crow-era Macon. According to reports, revivals borne of personal repentance quickly snowballed and spread, causing ever-increasing numbers to become convicted and fall under the power of the Holy Spirit.

The other center of the revival, perhaps its point of origin, was the Bellevue (then a Macon suburb) Church of God (Cleveland, TN), a place Rufus Moseley once described as a very dry church. In late February 1935, first one congregant, then another, came forward, confessed their respective shortcomings, and asked forgiveness of God as well as each other. Some of these were highly personal, making Moseley's inclusion of them in his newspaper accounts all the more noteworthy. Likewise, alcoholics in attendance found themselves freed from their vice, spiritual leaders found refreshment in the Holy Spirit, and there is even a remarkable report of a resurrection from the dead in which Moseley himself participated. Like most revivals, this one started out as a cloud the size of a man's hand (1 King 18:44), but when it broke forth, none who experienced it would forget it. Yet Moseley did not first hear of this revival in Bellevue, but rather at the Blackburn Avenue church. When he became aware of Bellevue's participation a few weeks later, it would be in a most remarkable manner.

In early March of 1935, in the course of writing his column, Rufus Moseley briefly spoke of incidents at the Blackburn Pentecostal Temple that were reported to him through attendees and the pastor, O. Kelly. Kelly, who

---

36. Moseley, "Joint Heirs with Christ."

had for years suffered from poor eyesight, suddenly found that he could see clearly without the need for corrective lenses. This happened to him after he had witnessed the healing of a boy with a broken kneecap in Dexter, Georgia in January of that year. When the boy, who previously could not straighten out his leg, was suddenly able to do so and even run, Kelly decided that he could likewise obtain healing for himself. He prayed for his healing to occur immediately, but it was not until early March that he suddenly realized that he no longer needed glasses.[37] He shared this with his congregation, who in turn were encouraged to seek God for their own needs, both physical and spiritual.

Other remarkable transformations of heart took place as well, one of which involved an unnamed pastor who held prejudices against those who claimed to have the Holy Spirit but did not speak in tongues as evidence. He prayed for the forgiveness of his hard-heartedness, and found, as he reported to Moseley, that the tongue controlled by the Spirit is of primary importance, and speaking in tongues secondary.[38] While Moseley himself spoke in tongues, he had long been of the opinion that the true evidence of the Holy Spirit was a life lived in divine love, and staying in that union. He rejoiced with his friend and added,

> The proof you have the Holy Spirit is that you are filled with the Spirit, are sealed with the Spirit, controlled by the Spirit, and in union with Jesus Christ, and are bearing the fruit of this union... [it] also means perfect release and freedom, and means the whole body, but especially the tongue, the body's rudder, shall be brought under the control and use of the Holy Spirit.[39]

It was in the midst of the growing Macon revival that something most remarkable happened, and Rufus had a front-row seat to it.

One of the things that came to my attention in the transcribing of Moseley's writings and speeches for my 2016 book, *Ineffable Union with Christ*, a collection of his newspaper columns, was that he was in the habit of never referring to himself when it came to his participation in answered prayer for others, healings, or even resurrections. In those early days of my research I rather wondered about this, given that the level of his spiritual walk was such that I was convinced such things accompanied his ministry. If so, why was there rarely any mention made of it? Yes, he would often report of such things, and if someone in a given meeting asked for and received some miracle or other, he was quick to mention the person in question.

37. Moseley, "Go the Second Mile."
38. Moseley, "Go the Second Mile."
39. Moseley, "Go the Second Mile."

The Poor, the Downtrodden, and the Kingdom Response

What I came to realize was that the overwhelming number of times when he was directly involved he would not mention it, instead opting to state something like "a brother in Christ prayed," and then tell of the miracle. I found concrete evidence of this in the spring of 2017, when I was contacted by a person whose grandmother had received a most remarkable heavenly visitation during the 1935 revival.

Suzie Kennedy Judd, along with her husband Matt, are ministers at the Good News Church in Augusta, Georgia. Finding me in a Google search in late 2017, Suzie contacted me to inquire as to whether or not I had ever read mention of her grandmother, Gladys (Perkins) Kennedy, in any of Rufus Moseley's writings. I performed a quick perusal of the period in question and found Gladys's name mentioned in an August 1939 Moseley article in which he briefly described the remarkable resurrection that happened to her. At first, that was the extent of what I could find, but Suzie was sure that her grandmother's supernatural encounter had occurred earlier, in 1935. The remarkable story had understandably become part of family history, though Gladys rarely spoke of it as the years passed. Although she firmly believed her grandmother's account, Suzie hoped for some kind of confirmation of the story. At the time, I had not yet finished transcribing Moseley's 1935 writings, so I did not know for certain until I again began that task in the late winter of 2017. It was then I found a most remarkable testimony that had to do with Gladys Perkins Kennedy, and as Suzie had insisted, the miracle was indeed in 1935 during the Pentecostal revival sweeping Macon.

Gladys was the wife of William Chester Kennedy, both of them members of the Bellevue Church of God (Cleveland, TN), a suburban congregation in the greater Macon area where the revival had first arisen. Moseley reported the initial outbreak at that church as follows:

> At the Church of God [organized] in Bellevue, where a young man received the Holy Spirit baptism, I am informed by the pastor that up to last Sunday night at least thirty-five people had been brought to repentance and to the Lord, and that as many as fifteen had received the supernatural gift and baptism of the Holy Spirit. As he puts it, "nobody planned the revival." It came by somebody yielding to the Lord. There is very little preaching in the revival. In fact, in some of the meetings, I am told, the Spirit seems to take such control that nobody can do anything except yield to the Spirit.[40]

The revival spread rapidly across Macon, Rufus describing it as

---

40. Moseley, "Union with Jesus."

the spirit of revival is working in many places. Not only at in Bellevue, but at the Pentecostal Tabernacle on Blackburn Avenue, and the Pentecostal Mission on Hazel Street, it has been impossible to carry out pre-arranged programs without quenching the Spirit. Of course, preaching is not entirely eliminated . . . but it makes uninspired preaching impossible.[41]

During this time of spiritual renewal at Bellevue, Gladys was taken increasingly ill with bouts of rheumatism, an agonizing condition no opiates could alleviate. According to Gladys, her pain was so profound that she prayed for either healing or death. Also suffering another unknown disease, her health quickly declined. She died on Good Friday, leaving a five-year-old son, Ralph, and husband Chester behind. Needless to say, the family and entire church had been praying for her recovery, but when she died they did not relinquish their prayers nor their belief in her return. Word was quickly sent to Rufus Moseley, a family friend, to come with all haste to their home and pray for her resurrection.[42]

Moseley was increasingly on the road during this time, frequently speaking at churches, conferences, or house meetings. He had just returned to Macon when his friends, in the depths of sorrow at the loss of the twenty-five-year-old wife and mother, found and implored him to come to her for prayer. By the time Rufus arrived, Gladys had been dead for perhaps twenty minutes. He instructed the family to wait outside the room where her body rested, and entered and sought the Holy Spirit about the matter. It is interesting to note that he often cleared a room when praying for others, especially if there was unbelief present among bystanders. I do not know if this was the case here, but he did ask everyone to leave him alone with Gladys.

Approximately twenty minutes later, he opened the door and asked Chester to come in. There was Gladys, sitting upright, "more of a presence than an ordinary person."[43] She was not able to immediately speak about her experience—that would come later—and she waved off questions put to her as she attempted to make the readjustment to terrestrial life. All were understandably overjoyed at this turn of events.[44] As Rufus prepared to go back to his home in nearby Byron, he stopped and prayed over Gladys's son, Ralph, something the boy remembered into his adult years as a spiritual turning point. Years later, Ralph was involved in the Full Gospel Businessmen's International group (FGBMI) in Augusta, Georgia, and was some-

41. Moseley, "Love Your Enemies, April 7, 1935.
42. Moseley, "Gloriously, Radiantly Happy," April 28, 1935.
43. Moseley, "Give Thanks for Everything," May 5, 1935.
44. Moseley, "Give Thanks for Everything," May 5, 1935.

The Poor, the Downtrodden, and the Kingdom Response 117

thing of a beacon for the regional charismatic renewal and teaching revival that later swept the area. He was also active in the Catholic Charismatic Movement, and hosted many charismatic leaders in his work. Adding to an already-impressive resume, he also aided in the establishment and growth of Oral Roberts University.

In a visit four days later, Moseley reported,

> Yesterday evening I went out to Bellevue again and called to see a friend who I described in an article as being to all appearances dead for about twenty minutes on Good Friday, and who had the experience of seeing the Lord, and her unfinished mansion, and being told by the Lord that her work on earth was not finished and to go back and finish it. She came back the most radiantly and gloriously happy person that I have seen in twenty-five years. She gives one the sense of the sanctity of the Lord beyond that of anyone that I have ever known.[45]

Word of Gladys's resurrection quickly spread among the Pentecostal community, especially at the Bellevue Church of God. Beginning in late April, Moseley included this remarkable event in his newspaper column for the next several weeks and offered additional details.[46] When Gladys finally did speak of the miracle, it was in front of the Bellevue Church of God, where she reported that she had "Crossed over Jordan . . . and went into the presence of Jesus . . . There is no pain, no sorrow; it is all bliss and ease!" Gladys joyfully reported. She had, Rufus stated in his newspaper account, but one desire: "Thy will be done in everything!"[47] This dear young woman, who had suffered a nervous condition throughout her life, found after this experience that her fear of death absolutely vanished. Suzie Kennedy Judd, her granddaughter, shared with the author that after Gladys's husband passed away years later, she handled it very well, knowing from firsthand experience where he was going and what awaited him. Gladys also expressed the desire late in life that, if she fell ill, no efforts to resuscitate her be made. Given what she saw, experienced, and tasted of the other side, can anyone blame her?

What makes the resurrection story so precious to me is that Gladys's granddaughter contacted me about this and it proved to be a blessing to both of us: First, it provided proof of her grandmother's story, and for me the proof I needed to confirm my own suspicion about Moseley that he

---

45. Moseley, "Give Thanks for Everything."

46. Email and Facebook messenger accounts of Suzie Kennedy Judd to the author, March 2018.

47. Moseley, "Gloriously, Radiantly Happy."

rarely reported his own involvement in any miraculous event. Once I saw this, it opened up the many times he reported in this fashion, showing the degree of the Holy Spirit's humble working in his life and ministry. Four years later, Rufus recalled his own involvement by saying that Gladys "had a friend who had love and faith enough to keep on praying until she returned to her body."[48]

Gladys Perkins Kennedy was proof positive to those around her of the healing and resurrecting power of Christ. There were many other reports of miraculous events during this Macon revival in 1935, too many to list here. But in the life of this one woman, it became the most superlative, sacred things to ever happen to her. As the years passed, she would share it only rarely because of the holy nature of the event, the things she encountered, and the Person she met. Often Gladys would tearfully tell a few family members, such as her granddaughter, and she left the unmistakable impression that she did indeed have a heavenly encounter.

On the heels of this remarkable event and still amidst the revival, there was the arrival of a sometimes-churlish evangelist whose words as often produced division and strife as they did the salvation message. Mordecai Ham had come to Macon.

MORDECAI HAM

The twentieth century was filled with notable Evangelical preachers, but few had the reputation quite like that of Mordecai Fowler Ham. A firebrand preacher with a no-holds-barred style, he angered as many as he may have led to Christ. Born in 1877 near Scottsville, Kentucky, he was named for his grandfather, one of several generations of Baptist preachers. He believed he was called to preach at an early age, and was ordained to that end at a Baptist church in Bowling Green, Kentucky. An independent evangelist, his pronounced support for temperance and Prohibition were to gain him particular fame. He was also a pioneering religious radio broadcaster. Unfortunately, at some point he picked up harsh views of all things Catholic and Jewish. His calumniations were nothing short of towering. He considered Jews to be "Christ killers" and beyond redemption, and he held Catholics only a rung or two above Jews in his spiritual hierarchy of the damned.[49]

Specifically, Ham would hold forth absurd conspiratorial and anti-Semitic canards such as there being a worldwide cabal of Jewish bankers who

---

48. Moseley, "Jesus Way."

49. See Balmer, *Encyclopedia of Evangelism*; and Graves, "Mordecai Ham: Outspoken Evangelist" for examples of his extreme views.

also controlled the governments of the world. They were, Ham contended, seeking to create a New World Order that would usher in the antichrist. He also held that Catholics were likewise part of this conspiracy, that the papacy was in fact working hand-in-glove with Jews, and that blacks were being used to destroy white, Protestant America. Ham had gone so far as to accuse the Jewish head of Sears and Roebuck, Julius Rosenwald, of operating prostitution rings. So many were his false statements that critics eventually created a "Book of Ham" and sought to catalogue as many of his ill-founded statements as could be gathered. He is also known to have taught a doctrine called British-Israelism, or Anglo-Israelism, which held that the white races of northern and western Europe were in fact the true Chosen Race of God. It is a sad footnote that these views are currently held by a number of white supremacist groups in the United States, and even among some believers.

Ham was no stranger to injecting his extremism into political issues and races of the day either. When the 1928 election pitted Republican Herbert Hoover against Democrat and Catholic Al Smith, Ham railed that a vote for the Catholic candidate might well land the person casting such a ballot in hell. His was an occasionally caustic Christianity which, while it appealed to some quarters, today rightly sounds vitriolic, cruel, and bigoted. He never swayed from his views, however, and would voice his opposition to all he deemed enemies of Christ. In 1933, he biliously proclaimed a worldwide conspiracy against Christianity in which some members of the United States government and religious leaders were participating. Along with Father Coughlin in Michigan, also a spinner of conspiracy theories, Ham would repeatedly make his unfounded accusations and breed the worst sort of social attitudes.

Ham's main sphere of influence was the American South, where his fundamentalist views on salvation and diatribes against Jews and Catholics found a more sympathetic audience. He fared better among rural and uneducated listeners, while his crusades in cities of any size were generally met with resistance from a number of offended groups. When he came to Macon, Georgia in May 1935, it was to considerable fanfare. As noted earlier, the city was already in the midst of considerable Pentecostal revival. Ham was not himself a Pentecostal, and did not hold very complimentary views of it, though his presence was not thought to be a threat to the meetings then in full swing. There were, however, stated concerns among the Jewish and Catholic communities about what sort of message he might bring.

As a religion writer for the *Telegraph*, Moseley was understandably interested in hearing Ham. First speaking at an unnamed church on Vineville Avenue in Macon, Ham later held outdoor meetings in the city's Coleman Hill Park overlooking the downtown area. It didn't take Ham long to begin his attacks on Catholics and Jews, and being friends with many of them, Moseley was asked to meet with Ham in an effort to have him tone down his vitriolic attacks. Rabbi Isaac Marcusson of Beth Israel synagogue, a close Moseley friend, specifically came to Rufus and asked for his help. Marcusson and other Macon Jews had already spoken out against Ham's bigotry, but to no avail.

Rufus first mentions Ham's visit to Macon in a March 24, 1935 article. With tongue in cheek, he exclaimed, "A lively time ahead for Macon!" He knew Ham to be a superb public speaker, but was also aware of the bigoted nature of some of his views, which soiled an otherwise good testimony. He was to say of the soon-to-arrive Ham, "He seems to have the boldness of the prophets in considerable measure, and let us pray that as he moves in his boldness that he will also have in good measure, the tenderness and compassion, the holy love of Jesus, who is perfectly loving as well as perfectly bold. It is easier to be bold than it is to be loving."[50] On March 31, shortly before the controversial evangelist's arrival in Macon, Moseley spoke of Ham as essentially being a three-part being when it came to his message. When he presented Christ in love, he did well; when he spoke of his unoffensive opinions, he was interesting; when he devolved into bigotry and hate, he was someone who falls short of what God intended for any preacher. Rufus had heard him speak many times in the past, and came to his conclusions about him several years before. As one who had dedicated his life and ministry to the Love way of Life, he could not abide the bile that Ham would sometimes spew.[51] Given the horror stories coming out of Germany at this time, it is understandable how anyone with a shred of decency would not hold to anti-Semitism.

> Since Jews are the victims of so much persecution (not by real Christians, for real Christians would never persecute anyone, but by nominal "unchristian Christians" as well as unbelievers), a real Christian should be especially on guard and in protest against everything that stirs up prejudice and hatred and that provokes persecution against them as well as against all other minority groups.[52]

If anyone should speak to or offer criticism of Jews, Moseley contended, it should be members of their own group, or perhaps converts of that group

---

50. Moseley, "Holy Love."
51. Moseley, "Union with Jesus."
52. Moseley, "Be Entirely Loving."

The Poor, the Downtrodden, and the Kingdom Response 121

to Christianity. Even then, it must be done in the love motive and ethic of the Holy Spirit. Anything less was simply hateful and unproductive noise.[53]

During the first week of April, the traveling evangelist had begun his Macon meetings to overflow audiences. When Ham visited any city, he rarely would have a time limit as to when he would move on. In Texas, for example, there were reports of meetings lasting many weeks. In Macon, with the resistance from Jewish and Catholic quarters, he may have decided to stay longer. As it was, some four weeks of meetings passed. In between gatherings, Ham would often visit bars or other areas of less than Christian practices and openly challenge people in such places. His supercilious approach with any who disagreed with him gained him understandable opposition.

Elsewhere, Moseley stated that true believers could only have the most profound respect and admiration for Jews. After all, without the Jewish people, there would be no Christianity, and even irrespective of that, they are (as is true of any minority) to be celebrated for their contributions and treated with love. Understanding that his printed words were not enough, even though Ham read them, he sought to privately meet with the evangelist and discuss the growing angst in Macon over his harsh statements. Ham was convinced that his enemies were God's enemies and would not budge on the issue. On at least one occasion, Moseley was successful in having a face-to-face meeting with the evangelist at the end of an evening service.

He greeted Rufus and listened to his words telling of how good he (Ham) was when he spoke the salvation message, yet how profoundly offensive he was when he yielded to the other spirit. Moseley was ignored. Rufus sought a follow-up meeting at the hotel or perhaps a restaurant, but was rebuffed. Rufus nonetheless continued to seek out the evangelist, and in his newspaper column, he offered his prayers and reiterated his hope that the bigotry would be put aside.[54] The greater problem, of course, was that while bigotry was never appropriate, in the darkening days of the 1930s, when ancient anti-Semitic sentiments were being codified into law in Germany, it foretold of nightmares to come, though few in the United States could have guessed the levels to which it would descend. But even in this, Rufus Moseley was to find a constant in his spiritual life, and it was joy unfettered and unfeigned.

---

53. Moseley, "Be Entirely Loving."
54. Moseley, "Gloriously, Radiantly Happy."

c. 1895, when he was a professor at Mercer University.

c. 1941, when he was a columnist for the *Macon Telegraph and News*.

5

Approach of War
1936–1940

Abundance isn't about having as much as you want—
abundance is about having as much of God as you want.

—Ann Voskamp

The second half of the 1930s was a time when Rufus Moseley saw a maturing of the Life as Love in his own life, as well as in ministry to others. Though apparent by the late 1920s, his writings become much more involved and lengthy, and dealt somewhat less with politics than spiritual matters. It was also a period when friends and colleagues began to encourage him to write his life story, to set forth the nature of what he called *The Quest* up to that time. From this would come his autobiography, *Manifest Victory*. Above all else it was simply one man's testimony, a report Rufus set forth for others. Moseley continued to meet with people one-on-one, at house church meetings, and in prisons and hospitals much the same as he had prior to this time. It was also a time of important meetings with personalities who would later have great influence on what would later become known as the Charismatic Movement. But as always, first and foremost, was Rufus's clarion call to all believers to seek for themselves ineffable union with Christ, to pursue the perfection or maturity only Christ could provide, and to live in simplicity, honesty, and utter sincerity. As such, it is important that we take a look at some of Rufus's teachings and practices in those areas.

JOY'S RESTFUL DOMINANCE

Joy is perhaps one of the believer's most under-appreciated and experienced fruit of the Spirit, yet it is among the most vital. Rufus Moseley was one who perpetually encouraged all who would listen to walk in this place, given that it is our spiritual heritage and right to do so. Without joy, life—even Christian life—becomes dull and insipid. Worse, it can even cause the believer to sink into depression and wonder about the veracity of salvation. "Joy, bliss, and glory are the blessedness of being in union with Jesus, living with Him in the Spirit and the in-flow and out-flow of His love," is how Moseley put it.[1]

Christ was so insistent on our living in his joy that he gave it to his first disciples even as he was about to go to the cross. During those last hours, Jesus told his friends that it was imperative that they have the same close union with him and each other as he had with the Father. "These things have I spoken unto you, that My joy may remain in you, and that your joy may be full" (John 15:11, KJV). All believers look back to the first-century church and wonder at the power, glory, and joy readily apparent and how they "turned the world upside down," as was said of them in a Greek community. They understood that it was in union with Christ; that place where they entered it at the feet of Jesus, became as a little child, and then manifested it in a life of unfettered joy. Joy is not something you whip up in yourself, it is a gift of God to be received and lived. As Rufus once said, "Joy is not excitement or mere emotion; to be joyful is to be calmly happy."[2] Even better, if submitted to, joy cannot be interrupted when we are in union with Christ. Despite outward difficulties, challenges, and persecution, the early believers were able to rejoice.

With regard to this blessed union and fruit, Moseley stated that it is better to be in union with Jesus today than it was yesterday. And tomorrow will be better still, again, provided we keep an eye on our only responsibility: that of staying in union with Christ. We all are enriched by the experiences and joy of the new believer, just as the new believer is enriched by the experiences and joy of those more mature in the faith. In this fashion, the last shall be first and the first last: because we are of one Body in Christ, we all benefit from the experiences of each other. Rufus once said, "I realize that by His grace and by my late coming I have a quality of joy and bliss that far better friends of Jesus who came earlier did not have. Everyone entering in these late hours of God's great harvest day receives something new which

---

1. Moseley, *Manifest Victory*, 259.
2. Moseley, *Manifest Victory*, 259.

he contributes to all the rest." In this perfect way of Jesus, Moseley stated, "the last and the least become the first and the greatest in contribution to all the rest."³

Moreover, Jesus gives the way of joy—of joyous living, seeing and reacting to the point that we become lights ourselves and our lives become themselves prayers and service to others. It is intercession on a different level, not simply in prayer for others, but in ourselves being that prayer and answer. It is a highly attractive gift that most everything around us will respond to, even the harshest of enemies. It may not come about immediately, but because love cannot fail, the joy way, that of being in union, will win out. The only thing that can stop us in living this Christian life on this level is ourselves and our negative reaction to the things around us.

Moseley, as a student of ancient history and philosophy, liked to quote Plato's words, attributed to his teacher, Socrates. He found such wisdom in it, as did many of the early Church Fathers, that he considered them Christians born out of due season. Socrates was grateful for the life he had, even grateful for his querulous, petulant wife, Xantippe. Socrates was of the opinion that complaining about anything was counterproductive. This iconoclast was such an irritant to the leaders of the day that they finally resolved to silence him on the charge of "corrupting the youth" of Athens. When he meekly accepted the sentence, his students asked if it was acceptable for them to commit suicide to join him. He sternly told them no, that the body was on loan to every human, and no one had the right to misuse borrowed property.⁴ Yet in the midst of even a death sentence and the carrying out of the same, Socrates did not complain.

A much later writer, Ralph Waldo Emerson, Moseley described as "a rare union of the wise humanist and of the Christian spirit, [who] delights us and causes our minds to be perpetually smiling, often laughing, at the way he saw and interacted towards the whole drama of life."⁵ Christians must likewise be willing and able to see that all things work together for our good, and when bolstered with joy can greet anything in the proper spirit. "On the way to perfect everything which is our high call and predestination, we may have the joyous assurance that everything is working together for our good and that even when we fail to choose his best there is always provided the necessary whale to preserve us from drowning until we repent,

---

3. Moseley, *Manifest Victory*, 260.

4. Moseley, *Manifest Victory*, 260; Moseley, "All Taught of the Lord."

5. Moseley, *Manifest Victory*, 260–61; Moseley was an Emerson scholar, and along with the other Transcendental writers, found wisdom and beauty in their writings. He may not always agree with their conclusions, but he loved their willingness to see the best in all things.

rededicate ourselves, and call on our God. Then we are spewed out on dry ground and given the new chance," Moseley joyously proclaimed.[6]

Those who live in this place of ineffable union are so filled with the joy of the Lord that they could rejoice at seeing their money taken, their property seized, and even their lives snuffed out. You could do the very worst that man and the devil could think of, and still they could rejoice at the honor of being called to suffer for God's sake and give out his love even as they were being persecuted. Even if one is called upon to leave his or her body behind as a martyr, the great joy of returning for it and seeing it glorified is itself a reason to be thankful. When Stephen, the first martyr, was about to be killed, Scripture tells us that his face shone like that of an angel, so great was his joy and love for his Master.[7]

In this place of faith that works by love, of joyful obedience regardless of the cost, we must be able to rejoice in a spirit of victory even as we face seeming defeat. If we cannot do that, we are not in a place where we are able to live in the heavenly places while still here on earth. To be sure, it is a process, a pruning and tending to us that God is always performing, but this is the end result. A contemporary preacher in Rufus's time, Campbell Morgan, in his sermon "Our God is a Consuming Fire," said in effect that the same fire that is bliss and heaven for the saint might be hellfire to the unpurified, until purified.[8] "If this is so," Moseley added, "and I at least believe it is, our being in union with Christ can at once be attractive to the unbeliever as well as repellent. We are not responsible for their reaction, but only our own staying in union."[9]

HOLY FIRE

Moseley, then, was of the opinion that there was an eternal, holy flame and was constantly at work. A literary example of this can be found in Christopher Marlow's *Dr. Faustus* (1588) to show how Satan, while appearing to be out of hell, was in fact in it at all times, and by extension, so too can humans.

> Faust: Where are you damned?
>
> Mephistopheles: In Hell.

---

6. Moseley, *Manifest Victory*, 261.

7. Moseley, "Reverse Side of the Cross," 235–52; for a much older view of this, see á Kempis, *Imitation of Christ*, 55–56; See also Julian of Norwich, *Revelations of Divine Love*.

8. Moseley, *Manifest Victory*, 263.

9. Moseley, *Manifest Victory*, 259–60.

> Faust: How comes it then that thou art out of hell?
>
> Mephistopheles: Why, this is hell, nor am I out of it. Thinkest thou that I, who saw the Face of God and tasted the eternal joys of Heaven, am not tormented with ten thousand hells in being deprived of everlasting bliss?[10]

Moseley believed that there was a consuming fire in each and all, in believer and unbeliever: what is the fire of purification to the children of God is to those outside of him torment.[11] As Moseley pondered this, he observed:

> But whatever may be the last word about hell, even now Christ is ready to come within, fill us, and cover us with His everlasting, purifying burning, that at least starts in great earnest the full redemption of our whole being, mind and body as well as spirit and soul. Since today we can have both the beginning of redemption and the assurance of full redemption, why go any further towards woe and death?[12]

Christ can be lived everywhere and yet missed anywhere. The rub comes in our identification. Rufus found Christ powerfully present in death cells and chambers at prisons, with those dying of painful diseases, and among those suffering racial, religious, and ethnic discrimination. Our task is to be able to see Christ in everything around us and react with the love and joy he provides. As Moseley came to realize, we do not learn this overnight, but it is something he will bring us to if we but listen, yield, and abide in him.[13] But for one's joy to be truly full, one must learn gratitude.

THE PRIMACY OF GRATITUDE AND THANKSGIVING

In 2017, a dear friend told me of a most remarkable book, already several years old, on thanksgiving and gratitude. It is a contemporary work that in my opinion comes closest to Rufus Moseley's teachings on gratitude of any I have yet seen. Once I had the book in my possession, I found that I could not put it down, even though such a work necessitates careful reading and prayerful meditation. Written by Ann Voskamp, this remarkable book is entitled *One Thousand Gifts*. It is a meek and gentle call for believers to

---

10. Marlowe, "Tragical History of Dr. Faustus," 14.
11. Moseley, "Heavenly Hellfire."
12. Moseley, "Heavenly Hellfire."
13. Moseley, *Manifest Victory*, 264.

practice "eucharisteo," or gratitude, in all things, and to see the hand of God in the seeming most minor of life's details.[14] Through her own experiences, some of them quite tragic, Voskamp shows how she learned this simple yet profound truth of showing gratitude for all that comes one's way. It is a book extolling humility, of littleness, and for us to go lower in order to go up in the kingdom of God. This book captures what the saints of old understood: live in expectancy, not expectation, that gratitude precedes multiplication, that by serving the neediest around us we are in fact serving he who gave all for us.

Moseley likewise taught that there is no room for complaining in the kingdom of heaven at hand or to come. "We are not at the place of clear seeing until our whole attitude is one of gratitude, thanksgiving, and a longing for His will to be done about everything."[15] In these few words, one finds a summarization of the life and practice of J. Rufus Moseley. In that place of union with Christ, our lives become perpetual outflows of thanksgiving and praise regardless of what comes our way, and with the full knowledge that whatever we encounter has been allowed to show us the proper way to react to all things at all times. Because perfect love is the perfect fulfillment of all wisdom, it likewise results in free-flowing gratitude and thanksgiving. It works no ill to anybody, and it also works all possible good to everyone and never ceases to do so. It is therefore the fulfillment of the law and of everything. Jesus, being perfect love, wisdom, and power (and, frankly, perfect everything), is the inspiration and the fulfillment of perfect love.[16] The only reaction on our part that is worthy is one of thanksgiving in all things. One who does not live in a state of thanksgiving misses the core of Life as Love.

When we come into the place of living in that place of gratitude, we enter into the heavenly places where God multiplies back to us thirty, sixty, or a hundredfold what we give out to others. While today some Christians claim this in financial terms, God is more interested in expanding in us the life of Christ that gives without thought of return. Moseley spoke of this often, and caused him to reach the point where he prayed to be able to happily give up anything and everything that was not his best for him. Rufus had early on come to realize that material possessions meant nothing if it was not within the will of God and born of a spirit of gratitude, humility, and love. God may or may not call us to different work than we are currently performing, but what is of the utmost importance is that each believer be

---

14. See Voskamp, *One Thousand Gifts* for a truly remarkable treatment of this subject.

15. Moseley, "Victory Right Now!"

16. Moseley, "Best That Can Be."

thankful for where they are, what they have, and are open to him to make the greatest use of each of us. Moseley once said, "If Heaven is to come in the whole of life, it is a part of our education to find it in the humblest tasks and in the whole of life."[17]

Rufus believed that with a failure to live in gratitude, instead giving in to complaining, we become negative vortexes, drawing in the very evil we would seek to avoid. But the Christian who meets all with a thankful and grateful heart reveals that power of joy within them, and is a testament to the union Christ came to give to each believer. All of the negatives of life must be met in this spirit for there to be true manifest victory for us; failure to do so, or to do so in half-measures, results in a sullied life and limited joy. Conversely, when we give out the love, joy, peace, mercy, and meekness of Christ, it returns to us multiplied many times over. Of this attitude of gratitude, even when faced with opposition or difficulties, Rufus said,

> When those who have suffered most enter in they find that their sufferings have been light and for a moment as it were, and have worked all the greater glory. To those who enter in there are no regrets about anything that it costs to enter. It is all "thanks for everything!" All has worked together for good, or rather he has worked everything together for good. So every memory calls for thanksgiving.[18]

In another Voskamp book, *The Way of Brokenness*, she offers additional piercing spiritual insight when she speaks of the giving that gratitude generates:

> You miss him when you question who's needy enough to give to, who warrants the risk. He comes as the homeless guy, the refugee, the child drinking filthy water—and you get to decide. Are you going to fill your life with more stuff, more safety, or more God? What the world says is weak and small may be where Christ is offering himself to you most of all—and why do we want to be big people when God shows up as the little people nobody's got time for? You miss Jesus when you aren't looking for his two disguises: the smallest and the servant.[19]

In that place of inner union with Christ, we are blessed with a spirit of gratitude that opens so much to us. As she aptly points out, without gratitude,

---

17. Moseley, "Kingdom at Hand."

18. Moseley, "Walk in Love, Victory, and Glory."

19. Voskamp, *Way of Brokenness*, 211; see also Lawrence, *Practice of the Presence of God*, esp. 33–34 for a classic deep yet simple glimpse of this truth presented through a sixteenth-century Christian mystic.

there is no multiplication. As she further states in her latest (as of this writing) book, *The Way of Abundance*, "Die to pride, die to self, die to agendas, die to comfort, die to ease—and your life explodes with abundant life. Unexpectedly, the secret to abundance is not about self—but about *dying to self*."[20]

So it is with each of us—we must die to self and die to all that keeps us on the outside of that vital union with Christ. "Keep on the outside of the Kingdom that which keeps us on the outside of it," Moseley liked to say. In that place where the love of God is shed abroad in our hearts, and we give it out to each and all, we experience peace and gratitude for doing so. For of a truth, all of the fruits of the Spirit—such as peace—are not a thing or a place, but a Person.

MERCY AND LOVING JUDGMENT

The way of mercy, loving judgment, and truth, in the fashion that Jesus used and uses it, is the highest reality (as Moseley stated) and was also the highest form of consciousness. Born out of living in union with Christ, that blessed place where one receives and gives out his love, also has with it a divine sense of joy, bliss, and glory. It was and is the answer to any and all bondages, provides the deliverance we need at any point in our walk, and results in complete dependence upon Christ and Christ alone. This is a revolutionary walk in Christ, one that is often lost in the telling, misunderstood, and must of necessity be guarded as that pearl of great price. To Rufus, life in Christ is utter simplicity. It is not free of challenges or temptations—indeed, it can be formed and strengthened by suffering—but if lived in the union of Life as Love, it can and does result in celebration at the thought that we can suffer for his name.

One morning, Rufus Moseley awoke to hear the following words spoken into his spirit:

> He does not turn the light on to hurt, but to help. Happily for us we are going to be enabled to see every fault, error, and imperfection of thought, of word, and of act until these imperfections give place to his perfection. It would be tragic for anyone to miss the judgment of enlightenment, to miss seeing everything that it to be repented of and forsaken, and to miss seeing everything that is to be attained to, perfect union with Jesus and his perfect everything.[21]

---

20. Voskamp, *Way of Abundance*, 12.
21. Moseley, *Manifest Victory*, 233; Moseley, "Judgment of Enlightenment."

In seeing this great truth, Moseley found that he could increasingly react to all criticism with a "thank you" and a smile, and allow harsh and cutting words to be taken in the spirit of love. He seems to have found in this simple truth a great liberating view of interaction with others. It also caused him to increasingly take care as to what he said to others, even to the tone of voice in which it was delivered. What Rufus called the "judgment of love and mercy" was the means by which the Holy Spirit takes all of our failures and mistakes, our sins and self-righteousness, and subjects them and all of our thoughts, words, and deeds to the revealing light of divine enlightenment. It is in that place where we see things, ourselves, and others as they are. When we become aware of our own shortcomings, we will tend to be much less judgmental of others.

As a personal example of this, I once witnessed an incident wherein a middle-aged Christian woman was berating a young man, a new believer, for smoking cigarettes. He looked down at the sidewalk and diffidently replied, "Yes ma'am, I do have difficulty with this. I suppose it is like others who have difficulty with, say, self-righteousness." I do not know if the young man intended it to come out like that, but his words hit their target. The woman, realizing she was being self-righteous, spun around and walked away. If the woman had ears to hear, she hopefully came to the realization that the young man she sought to harshly correct put a spiritual mirror to her own face. I was somewhat relieved the young man had not quoted "Let he who is without sin cast the first stone," out of concern the woman would have stooped and gathered rocks.

Unlike the woman in my example above, God does not condemn us into shame. If we have sin in our lives—inward or outward—he is only interested in our repenting and coming to him for guidance, and is only dedicated to staying in union. He seeks to bring us to sincerity with ourselves, with God, and with others. This is admittedly not an easy path, for Christians, like anyone else, often seek to put the best foot forward, to make ourselves appear better than we are. As A. W. Tozer once put it, "I am sure that most people live in the secret fear that some day they will be careless and by chance an enemy or friend will be allowed to peep into their poor empty souls."[22] God's intent is to heal, to make whole, and to bring us into ever deeper union with himself. Insincerity, or a willingness to judge others, will halt our upward march into the heavenly places as surely as any terrestrial roadblock. He seeks to melt us, to mold us, to free us that we may in turn be used to free others of the stumbling blocks they may have in their lives. Only the ones who have themselves been in a spot where they

---

22. Tozer, *Pursuit of God*, 104.

were insensitive or unloving can minister to those in a similar place. What he frees us from, he then makes us ministers to the freeing of others from similar bondages.

Rufus had a friend, a poet and writer he chose to leave unnamed, whom he discussed in *Manifest Victory*. Subject to extreme periods of depression, his friend was put into a sanitarium. When Rufus visited him, his friend declared in despair, "Moseley, I am lost!" Apparently believing himself beyond redemption, he began to spill out his many shortcomings, sins, habits, and so on. Rufus told him that because he was confessing in such a forthright manner, he was nearer to salvation than anyone Moseley could think of. "Moseley, is it possible?" he implored. He led his friend in a prayer and wrote down several things for the man to reflect upon when the periods of darkness returned. Rufus was pleased to find on his next visit that his friend was transformed, freed from his fears and self-recrimination, as well as from the dark cloud of depression. He was released shortly thereafter and was able to resume his writing.[23]

Rufus often asked what better thing is there than to make an enemy into a friend; to bring restoration and be a bringer of peace where there are hard feelings over something in one's life? It is one of the reasons, I believe, that Christ instructed those who are at the altar to go to those against whom they have an issue (or vice versa) and ask forgiveness. Hardness of heart and attitudes among believers can be especially vicious, for like the priest and the Levite passing on the other side of the road from the injured traveler, some may deem themselves too good to stop and help. There were few things Christ attacked with more force than religious and spiritual arrogance and self-righteousness.

It is terrible to be persecuted, but it is even worse to be one of the persecutors! Those who do so, either for religious or secular reasons, need to come to a place of realization of the hellish nature of their behavior and repent. When this happens, it is a double blessing; one has only to look to the life of Saul of Tarsus and the man he became to see this. So it is that those who have the most to be forgiven themselves are those who love most deeply. The ones who have been the persecutor, either secular or religious, are among the brightest lights when they drop their hellish behavior. Loving judgment as God himself practices takes the worst of us and makes us into the best witnesses of his love. When we live in this reality, we can look at the worst of people we see around us and recognize that we were perhaps even worse. In taking our manmade hells and transforming them into heavenly testimonies of victory and love, it shows others still trapped that there is

---

23. Moseley, *Manifest Victory*, 240–41.

not only hope, but help. With compassion, we can reach out to them from a place of understanding and freedom and offer them the same liberation we have ourselves experienced. If we are truly children of the King, we must, like him, become the servant and friend of all.

Rufus Moseley often wrote of the importance of living a life or mercy towards others and ourselves. Some friends of his in Philadelphia came to a sudden understanding of this sometime in late 1939, and as a result began a ministry of service to others in a number of areas. "Victory Right Now!" was their cry, and when Moseley encountered them, he was amazed at the level of understanding and experience they had in this area. One of his close friends in Philadelphia, Frank Buglo, was among the most active in making himself available to service wherever Christ led. At a time when Moseley, who did not drive, was in need of transportation, Buglo took it upon himself to drive Rufus wherever he needed to go. Once, when Rufus mentioned his intention of going to Florida to minister, Buglo drove from Philadelphia to Macon and offered to take him there.[24] Moseley admitted that he had his own ideas of how to get about, but came to believe that "when we do not get from God what we think is best for us, and in the same way we expect it to come, it is always because he has something better for us and a far better way of bringing it to us."[25]

This way of loving judgment could sometimes transpire in actual courtrooms. Rufus was something of a fixture at the Bibb County Courthouse in Macon as he visited prisoners and sat in on court cases. He was on a first-name basis with the judges and city and country attorneys, as well as many defense attorneys. Some of these officers of the court had been students of his at Mercer University years before. Rufus would sometimes be asked to come forward to help adjudicate a case with the judge. One such occasion was between a local Pentecostal church being sued for excessive noise during the worship services. Some of the neighbors did not appreciate the racket, nor for that matter did some of the nearby businesses. The judge was interested in preserving religious freedoms, but also addressing the complaints of those living near the church. When he spotted Rufus in the back the courtroom, he asked him to come forward.

Rufus, with the judge's permission, asked both sides how many of them were Christians or hoped to be. All raised their hands. He reminded them of Paul's admonition against believers taking each other to court. He then asked the church if it would not be Christ-like to take into consideration their neighbor's concern, and likewise asked of the neighbors if they could

---

24. Moseley, "Victory Right Now!"
25. Moseley, "Victory Right Now!"; Moseley, *Manifest Victory*, 235–37.

come to an understanding of the church's desire to worship as they saw fit. The case ended then and there, with both sides coming to an understanding that met with the best interests of all concerned. Instead of being combative, Moseley urged compromise and a willingness to turn the other cheek.

Another courtroom incident involved a young man, a boy really, who had fallen in with the wrong crowd and began stealing. He apparently also tried to pass a couple of bad checks for a small amount of money. When Moseley became aware that the boy had an aunt and uncle living in the state, he contacted them and explained the difficulty and asked their help. The aunt and uncle quickly came to Macon and explained to the court that the boy had been orphaned, and was still young enough to make good in his life. Moseley voiced his support as well, and suggested that the aunt and uncle take the boy in to live with them. To this they gladly agreed and the judge, possessing loving judgment, suspended the sentence and allowed the boy to live with his relatives. Rufus later wrote that the boy did indeed make good, finding employment and making himself useful to those who knew him.[26]

There were many such stories that Moseley shared about how the court system, in using good judgment and exercising mercy, were able to save the lives of young people who might otherwise have gone into a life of crime. In today's throwaway society, where human beings are discarded as easily as yesterday's newspaper, this is something of a novel approach. It is sad to admit that it is also just as novel among too many Christians who will toss fellow believers aside for any number of reasons, usually moral shortcomings. I once heard it said that American Christianity is the only army in the world that kills its own wounded. Just as God has rendered unto every one of his children grace and mercy that is almost too good to be true, he likewise expects us to do the same with those who offend us.

Speaking the truth in love, even uncomfortable things, is at the center of utter sincerity. The Pharisees and Sadducees also spoke truth on a regular basis, but Christ reserved his most pointed reprimands for these self-righteous religious leaders. What I especially like is that the two groups represent conservative and liberal points of view respectively, and both were in grievous error as to the letter versus the spirit of the law. Yet when Christ spoke his criticisms, harsh as they were, they were meant as curatives for those to whom he spoke. Let us not forget that at least two Pharisees, Joseph of Arimathea and Nicodemus, heard truth from Jesus, and also recognized the Truth.

Rufus also believed that cutting remarks or sarcasm spoken outside of love were destructive. While in modern times, some charismatics quote

26. Moseley, *Manifest Victory*, 237–38.

the "life and death are in the power of the tongue" Scripture with regard to things they are claiming in petition or avoid saying on the premise that what is spoken will happen, Moseley meant that it was even more immediately true with regard to our words to those around us, especially family, friends, and Christian brethren. If we cannot speak in gentleness and mercy to these, how do we imagine that we will do so among those who do not know him? Or that our petitions will hold any power? Moseley sometimes said that it was his experience that those who are the hardest on others are too easy on themselves, that there is a tendency to mete out one form of truth for others, and a separate one for ourselves. Speak to each other as if you are speaking to Christ himself, for in truth you doing just that. Moreover, Moseley, like Francis of Assisi, was convinced of the need for being of few words, honoring silence, and allowing the Holy Spirit to thereby speak within.

There were times when Rufus Moseley was called upon to act as a peacemaker in especially difficult conditions. Moseley once encountered a man who exhibited the best of character when given over to the Holy Spirit, but was a danger to lash out violently in word and deed when he gave in to his lower nature. Apparently, some time earlier there had been an altercation between this man and another in a church that had festered to the point where a vituperative confrontation seemed inevitable. While at a meeting at this church, where Rufus was the guest speaker, the man who thought himself wronged entered the sanctuary and loudly demanded his say. He was intent on taking over the meeting, and apparently had a physique such that he probably would have been successful in doing so. Several people took the man to the lobby and tried to reason with him, but to no avail.[27]

Rufus described how this particular person, or any given to anger, was not unlike Shakespeare's King Lear, who in his rage rushes out into a thunderstorm, a suitable setting for his anger and descent into madness. The fool accompanying Lear speaks wisdom and suggests seeking shelter, but Lear's anger and pride was such that it was unthinkable. So, too, is it with the individual given over to anger and strife. Moseley himself then went in a back room to speak to the man, who by this time even dared them to call the police. Moseley offered to give the man the podium, but only if he was in the right spirit. To get there, Moseley told him he had to repent of the rage he had worked himself into, peacefully seek out the person whom he thought had wronged him, and together pray for the guidance of the Holy Spirit. The man's attitude began to soften, and as Moseley prayed for him, he began to confess his shortcomings. After a few minutes of this, the angry man said words to the effect that he was probably most at fault in the issue.

---

27. Moseley, *Manifest Victory*, 273–74.

Moseley heartily commended him for the change. Within a few minutes, Moseley and the man returned to the sanctuary where the now-humbled individual publicly confessed his wrongdoing and asked the forgiveness of the church in general and the other person in particular. What ensued was a time of healing and forgiveness on all sides, with a brother/brothers being restored to each other.[28]

Confession of our faults to others frees us from their harmful effects. Wrong attitudes or opinions, anything based on less than a loving spirit, produces emotional and spiritual venom that poisons and harms the person engaging in it. Hatred comes from this, and it is spiritually tantamount to murder. This is a malady of heart that affects the entirety of the human race, and is at the root of a great many evils in the world. It is small wonder that the enemy encourages things like racism, religious bigotry, misogyny, or any other foolish and destructive attitudes. I once heard it said that holding anger or hatred against another is like drinking poison and expecting it to affect the other person. Yet wrongs, real or perceived, are constantly knocking at the door to our hearts, demanding entrance and to be entertained. For the believer especially, it is something that absolutely cannot be tolerated. Because of the intense power of things like anger and strife, it can quickly escalate into harsh words or far worse. Prisons are filled with people who let their anger and hatred get the best of them.

In an effort to always act in utter sincerity towards all, there were times when, in spiritual matters, Moseley found that he had to be more direct than other times. Given his natural temperament, this was not always something easy for him to do. One such incident requiring this approach occurred in the summer of 1935. He had just returned from visiting his boyhood home near Elkin, North Carolina when he stopped at a religious camp in North Georgia, an outdoor Pentecostal gathering. A central tabernacle was surrounded with what Moseley described as booths, or cabins, with all manner of ministry, prayer, and testimonies going on at any given time. Rufus spoke with great delight at the openness to the Spirit he encountered as he went from meeting site to meeting site. Moseley thereafter referred to the campsites as a whole as "Glory Hill."[29]

The men and women broke company and had their own meetings, and to his considerable happiness, Moseley found that the children also had their own gatherings where the baptism of the Holy Spirit was discussed and prayed for. A little girl walked up to Moseley and began telling him of her own experience:

28. Moseley, *Manifest Victory*, 273–74.
29. Moseley, "Glory Hill."

> The afternoon that I arrived, Friday, August 2[, 1935], a little girl, looking to be about six, came in and reported that a neighbor little girl had received the baptism of the Holy Spirit at the children's prayer meeting that afternoon. The men have their prayer meeting out in the woods and the women have theirs, and the little girls have theirs. I am not sure about the little boys, whether they have a separate one or not. At almost any of the day or night Glory is likely to break out, anywhere on the Hill.[30]

While Moseley was listening this little girl's happy story, some distraught people rushed up to him and asked that he please hurry to a particular cabin where a lady was in great pain, some of them fearing she was near death.[31]

When he arrived at the cabin, he found it crowded with friends of the woman in question, all of them loudly bemoaning the illness and even stating in the hearing of the afflicted woman their belief that nothing could be done about it. Rufus quickly cleared the cabin of what he called "the observers of the body rather than lookers to the Lord." It upset him that these well-meaning Christian friends would take such a position, and even told them if Jesus were there in the flesh he would likewise clear them out. He then knelt beside the woman in pain and prayed for her, asking her to look away from her condition and receive Christ's healing promised to her. Within a few minutes, the woman began feeling better, and was quickly up and about. As Rufus found, it is not always pleasant to rebuke fellow believers, but sometimes it is the needful thing to do.[32] The unbelief dissipated and was replaced with laughter as the woman's friends returned. As Moseley often pointed out, when we are receptive to what he wants to give us, and ourselves pass it out to each and all and all of creation, we find a joy in the Holy Spirit that no circumstances can dim. Indeed, sometimes they produce a laughter born of that joy.

MINISTRY OF LAUGHTER

Rufus liked to refer to the story about Mark Twain, the noted author and agnostic, about laughter's healing balm. When told he was thought of as a humorist, Twain was reported to have said that he was not so much a humorist as simply honest. Truth was such a rare commodity that when people heard it, they had a tendency to laugh. Laughter was a constant in the life of Rufus Moseley, as this master raconteur peppered his lectures and

30. Moseley, "Glory Hill."
31. Moseley, *Manifest Victory*, 273–74.
32. Moseley, *Manifest Victory*, 273–74.

articles with stories that were sure to produce at least a smile. He made fun of doctrinal differences, too, such as the controversy over sanctification as a distinct, second experience of the Holy Spirit as opposed to the view of the baptism of the Holy Spirit and sanctification being an ongoing work. Rufus told the story of a humble mountain man who, along with his neighbor, had received the baptism of the Holy Spirit. These two mountaineers heard of a third man, who lived on the other side of the same mountain, who had received the sanctification experience. Not sure what this was, yet wanting it if it would further their Christian walk, the two hitched up a wagon and traveled to their neighbor to see what this sanctification was all about. When they arrived, they saw the sanctified man asleep in a porch hammock, his wife laboriously chopping wood off to the side. The two men looked at each other in silence for a moment until one of them remarked, "Well, so help me, I have been sanctified all my life and didn't know it!"[33]

E. Stanley Jones, one of Rufus's closest friends, wrote in the foreword to Moseley's book *Perfect Everything* that people often misunderstood Moseley's laughter, his habit of shaking his hands when he spoke, and the unmitigated joy he exuded. "Many are put off by his delivery," Jones wrote, "but you must understand that if his hands jiggle in spiritual rapture it is because it is the outer expression of his brain cells dancing in delight at the sheer joy of being. He is inwardly laughing at the rhythm of life and his outer expressions are the attempt to express that inner laughter."[34] Others stated that these outward manifestations repelled them, that they didn't like Rufus's delivery. One minister responded to this criticism by using a baseball analogy of a dominant major league baseball pitcher of the era: "Well, batters didn't like Walter Johnson's delivery either!"[35] Some who heard Moseley were even angered at his light-hearted approach. Wayne McLain spoke of seeing a few listeners upset to the point of walking out of some of his talks. "If I wanted a Vaudeville act, I would go to see one!" an offended attendee said as he left. It seems to be the case across the span of his life that people either "get" Moseley or they do not. Some who did understand him were part of a remarkable annual gathering in the western mountains of North Carolina.

---

33. McLain, *Resurrection Encounter*, 213.
34. Jones, Introduction to *Perfect Everything*, 9–10.
35. Jones, Introduction to *Perfect Everything*, 9–10.

MARS HILL

Sometime in the early 1930s, thought to be 1932, Rufus Moseley began attending annual summer meetings at Mars Hill College in Mars Hill, North Carolina. Initially established as something of a retreat center for the state's Baptist ministers and workers, over the course of just a few years it attracted many outside of that denomination and acted as a center for reconciliation between Evangelicals and Pentecostals. This happened a decade before Evangelicals and Pentecostals sat down together under the National Association of Evangelicals umbrella, and may have, in a small way, helped that process of unity.

By the mid-1930s, Mars Hill was regularly attracting Holiness groups, Pentecostals, and some mainline denominational visitors, making for a spirit of interaction seldom seen among these believers. Rufus Moseley was one of the earliest Pentecostals to attend. Invited by his friends, Mars Hill leaders Edwin Poteat and Walt Johnson, the three men made it a point to never miss the meetings and attend as many as the sessions as possible. It resulted in a deep and lasting friendship between especially Moseley and Poteat, even more so than they had enjoyed during the 1920s. Walt Johnson, a North Carolina Baptist preacher, served as the conference's primary organizer. Moseley was fond of calling him the "Sage of Mars Hill." Over the course of the 1930s, the two spoke at the same conferences around the South. E. Stanley Jones also began attending, and it helped create a model for his later Christian Ashrams. Indeed, in time, some of these ashrams were held in North Carolina.

Of the Mars Hill gatherings, Rufus said that the attendees "co-worked with God unusually well."[36] If the reader has never paid a visit to western North Carolina, in and around the Asheville area, they owe it to themselves to do so. The physical surroundings, at least to Moseley, added to the high quality of spiritual fellowship. In the immediate area, there are dozens of mountains that rise more than four thousand feet above sea level. One of these, apparently one of Rufus's favorites, was Mount Pisgah, from which one can see a great distance in several directions and view sublime vistas. Even into his late sixties, Moseley was an avid climber, and he loved to hike all over the area and spend time in nature. During these ventures on the trails, he was to recall a West Virginia friend who enjoyed hunting squirrels in the mountains. After this man had become a Christian, he would still walk the hills with his gun, stopping every so often to pray or just enjoy the beauty around him. On one such occasion, when he knelt in the woods for

---

36. Moseley, "First in the Kingdom."

a time of prayer, he found that several squirrels had joined him, apparently sensing that he was no threat. Suddenly realizing that shooting the squirrels would kill members of his prayer meeting, he never again walked in the woods with a gun.[37]

What was apparently special to all who attended the Mars Hill forums was the high spiritual refreshment and healing it provided. There are many stories, but one that typifies this spiritual rejuvenation involved a elderly pastor who suggested that it was his time to step down, for his congregation to find a new minister. Rufus overheard this, and suggested to the fatigued man that he become that new pastor himself. Over the course of ten days, Rufus and others spoke to this man, encouraged him, and set such a fire in him that he returned to his beloved country church with a new spiritual zeal. A year later, Moseley heard from some members of this man's church that they "had a new pastor" in the old one, and were highly pleased about it.[38]

There were other Pentecostal practices that began to come to the fore at the Mars Hill Baptist retreat. One of these involved prayers for physical healing. This provided the North Carolina Baptists with something of a quandary, as they did not accept divine healings as practiced among Pentecostals in the modern era. To their credit, however, they did not seek to quell the practice of praying for and expecting healing that occurred at those convocations. So understanding were Johnson and Poteat that they drove Moseley to evening Pentecostal meetings in and around Mars Hill, even inviting him to speak in a number of Baptist churches on any topic he wished. Speaking about baptism in the Holy Spirit was not frowned upon in these places, much to Moseley's surprise and delight.

There is no question that the Mars Hill events were a highlight of Rufus's year during the 1930s and early 1940s. A little further to the north of this retreat center was Elkin, North Carolina, where the Moseley family homestead was located, and would also be a regular place of visitation for him. Rufus looked up the old home, sometimes with family members, and made the rounds, seeing old haunts and neighbors. His ties to Mars Hill were often intertwined with his experiences with his beloved family, friends, and fellow Christians, but none more so than Edwin Poteat.

---

37. Moseley, "Good Things."
38. Moseley, "Something Brewing"; Moseley, *Manifest Victory*, 241–42.

SPIRITUAL GIANT AND HUMBLE FRIEND

As mentioned earlier, Poteat had been a professor at Mercer University until he, like Moseley many years earlier, had run afoul of the conservative Baptist administration. There were few people in Rufus's life that meant more to him that Poteat. He was a political and religious liberal, believing (for instance) that science and religion need not be adversaries. His support for evolution cost him many friends in the Baptist church, as well as other places, and this gentle soul found himself the target of sometimes vicious calumny from fundamentalists. Moseley understood him completely, having himself been targeted by conservatives in both the Baptist and Pentecostal worlds. He never neatly fit into any proscribed tradition, and like Poteat, this made him a perceived threat. Rufus's stepping out and publicly offering friendship and support to his colleague meant much to the man, and was one of the reasons he believed Moseley would be an asset to the Mars Hill forums.

In 1937, however, Edwin Poteat fell seriously ill with a cancer that forced his stay at Duke University Hospital and his first absence from the Mars Hill gathering that summer. Moseley visited his friend both before and after the North Carolina meeting, returning to report to Poteat all he could remember. The doctors had warned Moseley that Poteat was too fragile to speak, but could listen to what Rufus had to say. He reported that whenever he finished one story, Poteat would whisper, "Tell me more of Mars Hill!" On his last visit to his hospitalized friend, and again repeating all he could remember of Mars Hill, Poteat stopped him, and in a barely audible voice said, "Moseley, I love you." Rufus said that Poteat's words meant more to him than any other ever spoken to him, with the exception of his father's words as Moseley left for college, "I know nothing of the world you are to be in. I trust you."[39] Edwin Poteat, Christian, scholar, and humanitarian, may not have outlived the insults thrown his way by conservatives, but his spirit of love and forgiveness surely did.

After the death of Edwin Poteat, a remarkable young man was brought into the Mars Hill community as a regular speaker and facilitator. Olin T. Binkley, who served as professor and later president at Wake Forest University and professor at the University of North Carolina at Chapel Hill, impressed everyone with the quality of his walk with Christ and the depth of his teachings. He was in many regards a younger version of Poteat. He and Rufus spent many days together each year, and the bond between Moseley and the Binkley family grew as the years passed. Binkley saw in Rufus Moseley a unique combination of faith and intellectual ability that placed him in a position to have profound influence in many areas at once.

---

39. Moseley, *Manifest Victory*, 178.

Decades after Moseley's death, Wayne McLain interviewed Binkley about Moseley and asked him to give a short description of the man, of what stood out about him. Binkley responded by saying that Rufus was a very complex individual. When McLain asked him for clarification, he responded by saying, "He could one day be speaking to religious leaders in New York City, and a few days later be meeting the most basic needs of the poor and destitute in central Georgia."[40] True to his calling to those on the top of human privilege in economics, industry, and government, he would then combine it with work among those on the very bottom in prisons, poverty, or illness. He was ever active in trying to get the "up and outs" to work towards alleviating the suffering of the less fortunate. Besides coming to know Binkley, Rufus would make another acquaintance during this period who would have far-reaching influence on later spiritual movements in the United States.

AGNES SANFORD

Sometime during the latter half of 1939, Rufus Moseley received an invitation for a picnic lunch from a family of out-of-town strangers. This might strike some as odd, but in Rufus's world, he was constantly on the lookout for God bringing someone along with whom he might share and/or from whom he might learn. One of the members of this small entourage was Agnes Sanford, who went to Macon at the behest of her brother, then living in Augusta, Georgia. He had heard about Moseley, most likely from reading his newspaper columns or perhaps having heard him speak. For Agnes's part, she was to come to something of an understanding of Rufus Moseley's teachings on "Life as Love," and see him as something of an occasional mentor.

Agnes Mary White was born in China in 1887, the daughter of Presbyterian missionaries. Apparently she held a view of God in those early years as a rather strict disciplinarian, or at the least a rather distant reality. She returned to the United States in 1912, living with relatives in Raleigh, North Carolina. Agnes completed her education and later returned to China to help her parents. It was during this time period that she began to ponder the reality of prayer for healing, having read a number of books, some of which took in aspects of Christian Science and New Thought, and later began an exploration of pryaer for healing with her husband. In this regard, she was like Rufus Moseley, who was active in Christian Science from 1900 to 1910,

---

40. McLain, *Resurrection Encounter*, 111.

before leaving it for Pentecostalism. When the two met, they doubtless found they had much in common.[41]

While in China, she met Ted Sanford, an Episcopal missionary, and after falling in love, they married when Agnes was twenty-six years old. Agnes apparently suffered from periodic bouts of depression, and this emotional malady was to cause her to take a time off from mission work. As children came into the picture, her depression worsened. In 1925, her husband was offered a church in Moorestown, New Jersey, but this did little to ease her deepening emotional turmoil. Around that time, she met a certain Hollis Colwell who had visited the Sanford home and successfully prayed for the healing of Agnes's son. Though initially reluctant for herself, she likewise asked for healing of her depression, which apparently showed marked improvement after Colwell's prayer. It was also Colwell who then encouraged her to write in an effort to forestall later depression. However, on this particular afternoon in Macon, she was to meet a man she had never heard of before, someone who would be a shining light to her for many years to come.

In Sanford's autobiography, *Sealed Orders*, she described the events that led her to come to Macon, Georgia and meet Rufus Moseley. In the late summer of 1939, she visited her brother, who was then living in Augusta, Georgia. Along with her brother's family, they loaded the car with picnic baskets and made the two-and-a-half hour drive. Upon arriving, they looked Rufus up, and he directed them to a city park where they could sit, relax, and talk. After handing out sandwiches, what followed proved to be a life-changing experience for Agnes, and established a lasting relationship with Moseley:

> Brother Rufus began to talk. Three hours later I came back to earth still sitting with the sandwich in my hand, listening to such as I had never heard before. For this old man had truly seen Jesus and had been filled with His Spirit . . .
>
> [H]ere was a person who had seen—here was a man who had experienced in some measure that which the disciples experienced on the Day of Pentecost, and whose face shone with the joy of it, so that when he talked of the Lord, years fell away from him, and he was no longer an old man, but a youth, flaming with joy and love.
>
> I cannot remember just what he said. But the man himself I will never forget.[42]

---

41. De Artega, *Agnes Sanford and Her Companions*, 176–78.
42. Sanford, *Sealed Orders*, 191–92.

In the years to come, Moseley would visit Agnes and her family in New Jersey when he was in the Philadelphia area. It was also an important meeting in that it would foreshadow his coming into contact with Glenn Clark a few years later, a man whom Moseley knew only through his writings. When those two met, a lasting and deep friendship was established that would have far-reaching consequences. But before that meeting, Rufus Moseley was to encounter one of the more interesting, if not controversial, religious movements of the day.

OXFORD GROUP

Around 1933, Rufus Moseley became aware of a new Christian organization that particularly interested and impressed him. Called the Oxford Group, it was the brainchild of Frank Buchman, an American Lutheran pastor. Buchman had visited England in the first decade of the twentieth century, where he attended one of the Keswick convention meetings, a Christian gathering that began in 1875, meant to provide Bible teaching for those seeking a deeper life in Christ. Although originally an Anglican event, it quickly evolved into an interdenominational affair and attracted believers from around the world. In 1908, Buchman attended one of these meetings, and there met and was influenced by Jessie Penn-Lewis. Buchman dated his conversion experience to this time. In 1921, Buchman organized a coterie called First Century Christian Fellowship; before ten years had passed, he renamed it the Oxford Group. It met with both criticism and praise throughout its history, but in the early years it was widely viewed as an important movement for those seeking a deeper walk through Christ by overcoming fear and selfishness.

One of the features of this group was the simplicity of the gospel presented in local homes the organization was fond of calling "House Parties." Attendees were told that the Oxford Group was not a religion in and of itself, but rather a system of beliefs meant to encourage the seeking soul to seek an intimate walk with Christ. Some observers reckoned it more of a spiritual revolution rather than an organization, as there was a very basic framework that was the very model of simplicity. This was done on purpose, as the underlying principle was to encourage people to find and walk in Christ for themselves. This aspect of the group, at least, certainly was attractive to Moseley.

In 1933, Moseley and his friend Edwin Poteat attended a local Macon meeting of the Oxford Group. Led by two individuals named Sherwood (who went by "Sherry") Day and George Hammond, Poteat and Moseley had heard stories about it from a number of quarters, both in the United

States and overseas. Representatives from this organization had, by the mid-1930s, influence with those in industry and government worldwide. In fact, one of the criticisms of the group was that it seemed to cater to the rich and powerful. This would become more of an issue as the 1930s wore on, but as far as the representatives visiting Macon were concerned, they set forth day-to-day Christian living that would include all.

Moseley and Poteat must have been impressed when they heard tell of Oxford Group emphasis on what they called "The Four Absolutes." Borrowed from other writers, Buchman and the visiting evangelists (for lack of a better word) stressed absolute honesty, absolute purity, absolute unselfishness, and absolute love. Added to these were the "Four Practices" participants were expected to embrace. These included total surrender to Christ, commitment to listening to the leading of the Holy Spirit, restitution for past wrongs where possible, and the public sharing of past sins and temptations with other believers. If some of this sounds familiar, it is because Buchman's ideas were incorporated into the newly founded Alcoholics Anonymous organization, its two founders having been participants in the Oxford Group.

It would be the last practice, the public airing of temptations and sins, that would raise the most eyebrows. Some participants found it tantamount to emotional nudity, leaving one's innermost secrets open to one or more individuals. Others felt that it was uncomfortably close to cultic behavior, where one then becomes potentially dependent on the group or a given leader. At least as far as Rufus Moseley reported, he did not see such abuses, but did indicate that, while the openness was good, true repentance must be made to God. Moseley continued to attend periodically, and between 1933 and 1938, he would offer reports or updates of what he had seen or trusted sources told him.

Although not itself Pentecostal, the Oxford Group teachings, while simple, could and did become doctrinaire, and disagreement could get one labeled contrary. For instance, Moseley recalled seeing and hearing an instance where a group leader sharply rebuked someone over his attitude in a certain matter. The person rebuked may have had a wrong attitude, but the manner in which it was corrected was rather startling. Oxford adherents also were known for their use of slogans or sayings to sum up their ideas or teachings.[43] Despite this, Moseley found in the Oxford Group friends a refreshing absence of the things that divide believers, as well as things that tended to draw Christians together. Attempting to live a live hid with Christ

---

43. Some of these slogans include "Constipated Christians," "Every man a force, not a field," and "Pray stands for Powerful Radiograms Always Yours," to mention a few. One of the more authoritative works from the organization itself is Russell's *For Sinners Only*.

in God by following principles or formulae was quite useless, Sherwood Day told Moseley, as the power one needs to truly live the redeemed life was found in a relationship with Christ alone. Following formulae—something Moseley had always found less than appealing and effective—simply results in confusion, frustration and eventually giving up.

The conditions for knowing God are simple enough, but they are demanding and require a heart wholly sold out to him. As Moseley summarized his first impressions of the group,

> Among the conditions of knowing God, as our Oxford Group friends are emphasizing and proving, are absolute surrender, continuous surrender, God-guidance, God-service, a rigid dealing with sin, sharing, expressional activity, team work, and loyalty. As the friends emphasize, there must be the ideal and effort to be wholly loving, unselfish, pure, sincere, and honest. These are principles of the group.[44]

As Moseley's travels increased in the second half of the 1930s, he would attend Oxford Group meetings in other cities as well. In Philadelphia in particular, he heard of and found "house parties" that proved to be events of worth. He even visited the national headquarters in New York City.[45] If one can gauge by his reporting on this organization, Rufus's attendance was spotty at best, and given that he hated any semblance to sectarianism or denominationalism, he attended only when he could or when so led. By the late 1930s, Frank Buchman and the Oxford Group had come under increased criticism from other quarters, some of it serious.

As stated earlier, one of the criticisms of the Oxford Group was the perceived tendency to approach and appeal to persons of wealth and power. In the United States, this included Harvey Firestone of the Firestone Tire company, as well as Henry Ford. When Ford published his anti-Semitic diatribe, *The International Jew*, many questioned any ties to the carmaker. Worse, Buchman himself made a comment in an interview with *New York World-Telegram* that would haunt him for years to come: "I thank heaven for a man like Adolf Hitler, who built a front line of defense against the anti-Christ of Communism."[46] Buchman was not oblivious to the dangers of National Socialism (Nazis), though as Dietrich Bonhoeffer, the great German spiritual resistance leader, suggested, Buchman's efforts to influence

---

44. Moseley, "More About the Oxford Group."
45. Moseley, "Triumphant Life."
46. Quoted in Metaxas, *Bonhoeffer*, 290. Mextaxas's tome is a brilliant and insightful look at the life and teachings of Dietrich Bonhoeffer.

the Nazi leadership was arrant insanity, the result of a total misunderstanding of the true level of its evil.[47]

To be fair, Buchman also believed that unless the Nazi government sought Christ and His way that another world war was inevitable. Though failing to meet Hitler personally, he did meet with SS leader Heinrich Himmler a few times. Himmler came to see the Oxford Group as a threat to National Socialism and once the war broke out sought to shut it down wherever it existed. When reports of Nazi atrocities came to greater light in the mid-1930s, the stories were so horrific that few believed them. It was not until Krystallnacht, the "Night of the Broken Glass" when Jewish synagogues, businesses, and homes were vandalized or destroyed on the nights of November 9-10, 1938, that the world began to take the measure of the true horror of Hitler's regime. There is no indication that Moseley ever thought the Oxford Group a questionable organization during his involvement with them in the 1930s. Indeed, he met with Frank Buchman a number of times during the latter half of the decade and discussed at length its goals and approaches. On one occasion, Moseley even ran into Buchman on a Miami, Florida street and then spent the afternoon in fellowship.[48]

As the latter half of the 1930s progressed, Rufus did write again about politics, this time in a more geopolitical framework. Rufus Moseley's statements against the atrocities in Germany, beginning in the early part of the 1930's, increased as well. He never had any illusions about the nature of fascism or Nazism, but nonetheless prayed that the aggressor nations might come to their senses. But as his writings became more pointed and looking to international affairs, he never forgot the poor and downtrodden at home, and would continually ask that citizens and government alike not forget them.

ELIM FRIENDS

In the late 1930s, Moseley would continue his contact with his St. Louis friendships established the decade before. By this time, some of them had moved to western New York, where they met with an Ivan Spencer, who founded the Elim Fellowship in the mid 1920s, and Rufus reacquainted himself with Seely Kinne, whom he had met in Missouri. The former was a foundering member of the camp meetings and a Bible college bearing the same name. Moseley visited an Elim camp in the summer of 1938 near Hornell, New York, where he reported that his friends there were seeking

47. Metaxes, *Bonhoeffer*, 199, 250, 289–91.
48. Moseley, "Essentially Heaven on Earth."

to worship in the Spirit and to bring forth the church in the apostolic gifts of the Spirit.

By the 1930s, perhaps earlier, Elim leaders had come to emphasize what they called "Brideship," the belief that a special group of believers would reach a higher level of spiritual attainment than most Christians. This in time came to be tied to "Manchild" teachings which held that this special group of believers would achieve complete identification with Christ and his work on the cross, eventually resulting in overcoming physical death. As time passed, and many of those teaching this doctrine themselves died, it lost its popularity—not to mention its adherents—although it would come back to a degree when Latter Rain teachings became popular in the late 1940s, Elim itself becoming something of a bastion of those doctrines. The reader will remember that in the 1920s Rufus had encountered some St. Louis friends, possibly known to and influenced by Kinne, who contended that they would not see physical death.

In a biography of Ivan Spencer, entitled *Ivan Spencer: Willow in the Wind*, Moseley's visits to the western New York gatherings were fondly remembered. In this 1974 book, author Marion Meloon shares how "Moseley's gentle-spirited visits added the fragrance of his ministry on union with Christ."[49] She describes him as an extremist on health foods (Rufus had been a vegetarian since very early in the twentieth century), but nonetheless a buoyant, joyful individual who had a message of the life in Christ that was ahead of its time. Meloon goes on to state that Moseley shared with Spencer a vision of the church that was for the future, the details of which were not provided. While Rufus encouraged all believers to be in a place of union with Christ, and to let him live his life through each of us as we make our way toward perfection or full stature, he nonetheless was a firm believer in the visible second coming of Christ. Some in Latter Rain would later speak of preparation of the body of Christ to facilitate the coming millennium, and Rufus agreed up to a point.

This was, of course, before Elim had become a center of Latter Rain teachings in the late 1940s, with an emphasis on the rise of a special class of overcomers, what some would term the "Manifestation of the Sons of God" doctrine that held that a sort of super-church remnant would arise. This remnant was said to involve the rise of apostles and prophets akin to those of the first-century church—or even likened to Old Testament prophets such as Isaiah, Jeremiah, or Ezekiel. The Elim group earlier called this "Restorationism" or "Forward Moving," ideas that would in time come to

---

49. Meloon, *Ivan Spencer*, 134–35.

fruition in Latter Rain.[50] Rufus had earlier in life been put off by the arrogance that sometimes attends those claiming these high spiritual positions. It was much the same as his view of the gifts of the Spirit; he operated in all of them, but believed their emphasis over the "Life as Love" was to put the cart before the horse. Or worse, to create a self-appointed leadership that becomes domineering over others in the body of Christ. There is no indication that Moseley thought his Elim friends were of this mindset, but he knew from experience the dangers of spiritual pride. Of the gifts (and also true of the offices and rise of overcomers), Moseley had this to say:

> Of course, before the gifts can be placed in the church in fullness there must be the life lived in the Spirit and rich in the fruit of the Spirit, such as holy love, joy, peace, goodness, purity, sincerity, temperance, long-suffering, and compassion. To be like Christ on the outside and to have a church rich in his gifts, we must first be like Christ on the inside and have a church in the love, unity and power of the Holy Spirit.[51]

Of self-appointed "Apostles" and "Prophets," Rufus said:

> I have nothing against an order of Apostles and Prophets continuing on the earth, providing we can have real ones, but as I understand God's way for me, it is to get away from all of the big names of authority and leadership that have caused so much division among the people of God, and come into the place that Jesus called his disciples into, namely where each is the servant and friends of each other and all and the friend of all men, and the friend of God, and where the greatest are the most humble and the best servants of all.[52]

In today's charismatic world, where self-identifying oneself "apostle" or "prophet" is increasingly common, Moseley's words bear hearing.

As the late 1930s came to a close, the world was to see the threat and then reality of war arise once more. Rufus had foreseen this, of course, and with increased alarm had written about the horrors being played out in Asia and Europe. To many of his time, it was almost impossible to fathom that within a single generation a second World War would erupt, this one completely eclipsing the one before it. World War I had been called "The War to End all Wars," yet it was painfully apparent that it failed in that regard. Indeed, given many of the causes for the second global conflagration, the First World War had not in fact ended.

50. Meloon, *Ivan Spencer*, 87.
51. Moseley, "City for God."
52. Moseley, "City for God."

6

Perfect Everything

1940–1949

Lord, help me to live this day, quietly, easily.
To lean upon Thy great strength, trustfully, restfully.
To await the unfolding of Thy great will, patiently, serenely
To meet others, peacefully, joyously
To face tomorrow, confidently, courageously.

—FRANCIS OF ASSISI

With the dawning of the 1940s, keeping up with the travels of Rufus Moseley is like trying to follow a moth in flight. His lifelong pursuit of Life as Love was more intense than ever, but now he was traveling widely and sharing to a greater degree than ever before. Already well-known across the American South, his influence and reach during this period would expand nationwide, and even into Europe. Some of this, of course, was a result of the publication of his autobiography, but also as word-of-mouth endorsements increased. He would also, by decade's end, publish something of a follow-up to *Manifest Victory* entitled *Perfect Everything*. It was a work on the ministry of the Holy Spirit in the believer's life, and although shorter than his first book, was acclaimed as a superlative piece of literature on the topic. The Kingdom Troubadour from Macon, whose ministry had largely been tied to the South, would grow to the point where he would be sought nationally by business, government, and of course, religious leadership. Ever true to his original calling to seek out the "down-and-outs," he never allowed his expanding work to take him from those society and even the church had forgotten.

MANIFEST VICTORY

At some point in the late 1930s, prompted by friends and the Holy Spirit, Rufus Moseley began to ponder putting his life story to paper. It was something that seemed inevitable. For years, he had been telling his story in a piecemeal fashion through his newspaper column and in front of live audiences, but many thought it was time that he tell his story to a wider audience. Sometime after the Macon revival in 1935, he began to consider this more deeply, and during one of his yearly winter trips to Florida, floated the idea among trusted friends there. One of these, Grace Munsey, had been taking dictation from Rufus for his *Macon Telegraph* column for several years during his visits, and would again repeat this work for portions of the book. The result was a slow but sure gathering of material, and often told stories and teachings in the larger attempt to provide something of a literary skeleton from which to build. Up to this time, the most he had done along these lines were a couple of short introductions in which he shared something of his background. He was uncomfortable doing this, feeling (as did Saint Paul) that to discuss his educational pedigree or previous work as a professor would call too much attention to himself. The editors at the *Telegraph* insisted, however, when incoming mail included many such requests.

By 1939, Rufus Moseley had decided upon *The Quest* as the title of his autobiography. He highlighted the very beginning of the book with the words, "Timid conformity is death; there is only life in the Quest," and believed it an apt introduction to his life story. The book's introduction, however, was a rather ponderous beginning to what followed, and a source of some concern for potential publishers and reviewers. Among other things, Moseley was a philosopher, and the introduction was top-heavy with the explanation of his quest from that perspective. Later editions, including the most recently available since just 2014, includes the editor's suggestion that the reader go directly to chapter one, read the rest of the book, and then return to read the introduction afterwards. It is actually sage advice, though the fact that the introduction is not at the end of the book as a summary is perhaps due to Moseley's refusal to do so. The introduction to any book should set the stage for what follows, and to a degree this is so with *The*

Quest, but this particular introduction is, as the editors suggested, best read as a conclusion.

The June 4, 1939 edition of the *Macon Telegraph* reproduced a near-complete rendition of the introduction. His friends and colleagues at the newspaper had been among his greatest advocates for writing his life story, and the publishers generously committed a sizable portion of that Sunday's paper to promoting it. The *Telegraph* prefaced the introduction with:

> The following article is the introduction and summary of a book, *The Quest*, now in preparation by J.R. Moseley, religion and philosophy scholar. The author expects to have the volume ready for publication in the late autumn. Mr. Moseley, who writes a weekly religion column for the *Telegraph and Evening News*, tells in *The Quest* his life-long observations in a quest for the truest understanding and expression of religion.[1]

In his weekly columns before and after this, one can sense Rufus's excitement at the soon-to-be-released autobiography. Apparently enough letters and calls came in to the *Telegraph* that Moseley had to give a near-weekly update on the status of the book, especially once it went to press.

Already well-known across the South, his writings were getting attention in other parts of the nation as well, and the publication of his life story would serve only to increase his influence. Advance orders for the book began to come in at a precipitous rate, causing him embarrassment that so much interest in his life was taking place. Those who had advance reading of the manuscript—some of them leading theologians of the day, others friends or acquaintances—were glowing in their praise for it.

Once HarperCollins sent out his manuscript to outside readers, the reviews were a mixed bag: on one hand, there was almost universal praise for it as a modern work of Christian mysticism that put it in the same genre as others from centuries past; but on the other, there were complaints about the writing style. Moseley had a story to tell, and the dictation method he utilized just wasn't going to cut it. All of his newspaper columns had been dictated, making for considerable grammatical problems of the run-on sentence variety, as well as passive voice usage and misplaced modifiers, to name just a few. When these were in turn submitted to the *Macon Telegraph*, there wasn't always time to properly edit them. In nearly every case, *Telegraph* editors did at least break his essays down into specific subtopics; the additional problem was that the column title Moseley chose did not always reflect what appeared in the column itself. Knowing this, Moseley began to

---

1. "Moseley Is Preparing New Book."

work with specific subjects but again, to the detriment of the telling, insisted on dictating his book to others.

The publishers wisely understood that his story must be told in the folksy manner that he presented it, but it needed considerable work to make it flow in a consistent manner. Although Rufus was pleased with the HarperCollins edits, he did not like the idea of changing the title as they had insisted. "*The Quest*" was close or identical to other book titles, so they asked him to come up with another. His emphasis on "Life as Love" was obvious, yet that title was a bit difficult too; another term he used to describe union with Christ was "manifest victory," and that was chosen for the final title: *Manifest Victory: A Quest and a Testimony*.

As positive reviews came in, Moseley in humility believed it necessary to state his own shortcomings. "Of course, the estimates of me personally are just reminders of what I should and must be. The best I can say of myself, knowing as much about myself as I do, is that upon the whole I have meant well, blundered much, and been greatly loved and blessed by the Great Companion, Friend, Lover, and Savior."[2] Because he was now considered a spiritual leader, he repeated something he had been saying from the time he received the baptism of the Holy Spirit: for true brotherhood within Christianity to be advocated, religious titles should be dropped. Over the years he would yield on this, but generally only to state that the person about whom he was writing was, say, a pastor or priest at this or that church or parish.

While Rufus Moseley moved in many gifts of the Spirit, he never referred to himself accordingly. To do so, in his way thinking, was to give reign to the self life. He instead called himself a reporter, and *Manifest Victory* was written as a report, one who shared the things that he believed the Holy Spirit had spoken in and through him. Nor did he necessarily utilize the Pentecostal shibboleth "Thus saith the Lord!" so as to inform the hearer that something special was about to be said. Instead, he would simply share in a humble fashion, not calling attention to himself by using archaic Elizabethan English or by insisting on being treated as a prophet.

Rufus was of the opinion that if someone truly moved in the gifts or offices, his life would reflect it, and no advertising would be needed or wanted. As pointed out earlier, to Moseley, advertising oneself as "Apostle" or "Prophet" was likely an indication that something was seriously amiss. At the very least, using such titles begs the question "By whose authority?" As the years passed and people increasingly recognized the Holy Spirit's work in and through him, he would be consistently offered leadership in one organization, church, or other. As with the St. Louis group in the 1920s,

---

2. Moseley, "Quest of Quests."

he always refused. The fact that he belonged to no denomination or church, a problem with some, was to him something he guarded carefully, as he realized it would open more doors than it closed.

One of the most immediately noticeable things about the release of *Manifest Victory* was that the length of Rufus's weekly columns began to shrink. They still appeared in the Sunday editions of the *Telegraph*, but instead of being in the neighborhood of one thousand five hundred to two thousand words or more, they were reduced to around seven hundred to one thousand words, and as the decade of the 1940s wore on, would shrink even further. One also notes that most of these smaller articles were written when he was on the road, another immediate effect of the book's release. He would still offer his encouragement for union with Christ, but now would include physical descriptions of where he was at, with whom he met, and what was discussed.

By the end of 1940, when *Manifest Victory* was about to be released, there was also considerable anticipation among Rufus's friends and co-workers at the *Telegraph*. Moseley thought back to the pre-World War I days and his street ministry when he was widely considered a nobody, a religious fool who had thrown away a promising career in higher education. Now, some thirty years later, he was getting national attention for his unique ministry, and was to have even more opportunities as a result, both one-on-one as well as advisory roles in government and industry. The book also opened the door for his meeting with others who were to become vital lights in the mid-century American Pentecostal world. He would prove the older, more seasoned teacher, and those he influenced would themselves become great lights for the future. But first, there was to be yet another conflict on the world stage, and this one would dwarf World War I in death, destruction, and horrors.

WAR IN EUROPE

Throughout the late 1930s, Rufus watched the events in Europe with a historian and political scientist's eye, but also that of a spiritual person. He knew that the Versailles Treaty that ended World War I by blaming Germany for the war was a mistake, and a breeding ground for trouble down the road. Of course, German anger and humiliation in the wake of the war was widespread, and something that Adolf Hitler and Nazi party tapped into. Along with deep-seated anti-Semitism across Europe, there was a social and military mix that had shown early signs of trouble in the mid-1930s. In 1939, when war was declared, it hardly took him by surprise, although the initial lack of fighting in Western Europe until the spring of 1940 gave many a false hope. By then, Hitler would unleash his war machine that quickly overwhelmed that region and even threatened Britain with invasion. Things looked dark indeed, but the hope of many Americans was that the nation would stay out of the conflict. There was a strong isolationist movement in the United States, along with a vocal pro-German voice in the German-American Bund that spoke to the sizable immigrant community. Memories of the last war and its horrors were still fresh in everyone's mind. Worse, technology had improved sufficiently over the past two decades that most everyone knew the death toll in the next war could well dwarf the previous conflagration. General American sentiments against involvement in the war were strong, so even offering help to the combatants proved difficult.

America did maintain its distance, albeit in a cagey way. President Roosevelt offered Great Britain aid in the form of Lend-Lease and a host of programs meant to prevent the United Kingdom from falling to the German menace. Germany understood that it was probably just a matter of time before the United States entered the war on the side of Britain, but sought to forestall it for the time being. When Japan attacked the United States fleet at Pearl Harbor, it meant the Americans would be heavily involved in the Pacific, and for a while a limited threat to Germany. What few accurately gauged in the early days of the war was the incredible industrial power of the American economy, which when mobilized for war proved an unstoppable juggernaut. Once attacked, any remaining American sentiment for isolationism dissipated and was replaced with shock, anger, and then a terrible resolve.

Such were the days leading up to the war, and in its midst, Rufus Moseley continued to offer opinions from a distinctively Christian perspective, opinions which sometimes seemed out of touch with reality. While the world was screaming for war, Rufus was calling for the Sermon on the Mount and the power of love to overcome any problem. While he never changed his opinion about the Life as Love as the means of informing personal or foreign policy, he did begin to allow for lesser possibilities in approach.

Rufus Moseley was also of the opinion that, short of the Life as Love—since it was apparent that especially the aggressor nations would not agree to it—something of an international police force had to be implemented. At the end of World War I, he favored Woodrow Wilson's plan for the League of Nations, an institution established to prevent, or if necessary, take up arms in a united fashion against any nation bent on conquest or trouble. The United States, of course, did not join the League, and because of this the institution failed to stand up to Italian, Japanese, and German aggression. The other member nations, already weakened by World War I, simply lacked the strength to do anything about it. Moseley thought it a tragic mistake, and believed that with the conclusion of World War II there should be a new effort in this regard. He was, therefore, in support of the United Nations. He realized its limitations, of course, but believed the world was better off with it than without it.

Moseley also possessed a supernatural ability, described earlier, to discern spirits in individuals, but also seemed to have this same gift when looking at larger groups, such as nations at war. When he exercised it, it was never with condemnation and always in love. There were times when he would dismiss an evil spirit with a wave of the hand and a word of command. It is for that reason that his view of the international scene is important. He realized that the way to overcome evil is not to see individuals or nations as our enemies, but the spiritual forces that prompt them to act as they do. The truest way to overcome evil is therefore not by fighting, but through our own living in union with Christ and the supernatural Life of Love that it produces. Only light overcomes darkness; if two monsters fight it out, the worst monster wins. Likewise, if we could overcome the devil with the devil's fire, we would have an even bigger problem: ourselves. The antichrist spirit is only overcome with love.[3]

Throughout World War II, when Rufus traveled across the nation to speak, he constantly encountered families who had loved ones in the armed forces, some of whom lost family members on the distant battlefields of Africa, Europe, or in the Pacific. He offered consolation to those suffering such tragic losses, and encouraged others to believe God for the quick end of the war. He was asked once how we should pray about this, as virtually all combatant nations claimed God was on their side in one fashion or other. His response was to pray for all nations, including the Germans, Italians, and Japanese, and that their leaders would come to see the insanity of their actions. He firmly believed that utilizing heavenly love and giving it out could change the minds of the most depraved of leaders. This offended some of those hearing him, but he insisted that it was the right way to pray, that Christ himself commanded that we treat our enemies with love. It did not mean passively submitting to hostilities, and did include defending the weak, but to before all ask for God's working on the hearts and minds of the enemy, and short of that, to remove them from power and bring a quick conclusion to the conflict. With the ending of the war, however, he believed the message of love was just beginning.

Moseley was a believer that the world had to avoid the mistakes at the end of World War I and do everything possible to feed, clothe, and rebuild

---

3. McLain, *Resurrection Encounter*, 157–58.

the nations ravaged by war. As such, he cheered the establishment of the Marshall Plan, an American rebuilding effort of the Western European nations. Thankfully, American leadership recognized that to leave Europe in shambles would provide a breeding ground for communism. It is no exaggeration to say that the Marshall Plan saved Western Europe from falling under the domination and control of the Soviet Union. Likewise, in Japan, the United States established a remarkably gentle rebuilding program that amazed the Japanese people, who had been told that Americans were devils, and that if Japan were to lose the war, they would face enslavement.

There were other areas were Moseley was actively engaged in support of peace in the post war years, and this included encouraging European powers to give up their overseas empires. Britain, France, and especially Germany were no longer in any real position to hang on to their overseas colonies, but at least with France and Britain there was resistance to this. Britain was the first to recognize this, as its ability to maintain order in Palestine alone was evaporating with the flood of Jewish refugees into what would become the State of Israel. When Britain surrendered its mandate, and Zionist leadership in Palestine prepared to declare independence, Moseley rightly perceived that there was sure to be conflict. In India, Britain's largest colony, the Gandhi-led nonviolent resistance for independence became irresistible. A correspondent of Gandhi's, Moseley cheered the manner in which independence was sought and that the British came to the conclusion that its empire, once the world's greatest power, had entered its twilight. Rufus expressed amazement that it took a Hindu conversant with Christ's teachings to force a Christian empire to give up. He thought the same technique could be used elsewhere with similar results.

SOUTHERN TROUBADOUR IN THE YANKEE NORTH

Rufus Moseley traveled widely in the post-war years. He might be in Macon for a few weeks, followed by weeks or even months on the road. Rufus continued to visit his neighboring southern states as he had always done, but by 1940 one finds him in Indiana, Pennsylvania, Illinois, Iowa, the New England states, and especially New York. During this period, he continued to teach and encourage in the Life as Love wherever he found himself.

In January 1940, one of these early visits involved meeting with and speaking at Ted and Agnes Sanford's church in Moorestown, New Jersey. On that visit, Rufus had agreed to speak twice at the Sanford's Trinity Church. He was scheduled for an hour, but with the enthusiastic support of Agnes and those in attendance, he spoke for well over that length of time. One can already see a growing affinity between Sanford and Moseley, as he reports, "when she prays for the sick, the Holy Spirit power and anointing is put upon her hands, and where there is receptivity, He heals the sick and transforms life."[4] He also spoke of Agnes's visit to Macon a few months earlier, when they first met. Rufus said, "Mrs. Sanford and her brother and family were the friends who visited me in Macon some months ago and who gave me some of the best hours I have ever had with any friends."[5] While praising her and experiencing joy at being in her presence, he felt it necessary to state that it was Glorified Jesus and the Holy Spirit that makes it possible for any healing to occur; and, stating of New Thought and Christian Science, "It is precisely the Holy Ghost revelation and ministry of this Superlative Reality that is the superlative need of the churches, of New Thought, Christian Science, and other groups."[6]

In March 1942, there was for Rufus Moseley a personal loss that was difficult for him to bear. His older brother Charles, a physician in Greensboro, North Carolina, passed away at age seventy-seven. The two had been especially close during Rufus's youth, and he looked up to his big brother with love and admiration. None of those sentiments lessened as the years passed. He announced Charles's death in a March 15, 1942 *Macon Telegraph* article, and saw through it the terrible losses that families worldwide endured as a result of the war. Calling Charles's death "one of the keenest losses of my whole life," it served for him as something of a drive to see that the entirety of his life, spirit, soul, and body be dedicated to the losses others would surely incur as a result of conflict in Europe and the Pacific. He ended the short article by saying, "This comes as great comfort as we see our loved ones and loved ones of all drafted into the services of states at war with each other, your work in God will be your life preserver, and everyone who gives himself to doing everything he is sent here to do can live until his work is finished."[7]

"PERFECT EVERYTHING"

In the late 1930s, Rufus Moseley began employing the term "Perfect Everything" to describe the revelation of Christ to each believer in that place of union with Christ. As noted, his second book carried the same title.

4. Moseley, "Glory of the Cross."
5. Moseley, "Glory of the Cross."
6. Moseley, "Glory of the Cross."
7. Moseley, "Until Jesus Comes."

Admittedly sounding rather odd, it nonetheless succinctly encompasses what each of us discovers is the personality and character of Jesus. "The highest self-disclosure that Jesus makes of Himself is that He is Perfect Everything, giving Perfect Everything, inspiring Perfect Everything, enabling Perfect Everything, and commanding Perfect Everything."[8] On every level, in every circumstance, and most certainly in ways we cannot imagine, He is our Everything. Christ and Christ alone makes it possible to live the Life as Love.

This is especially true when one considers the very nature of union with Christ, the command to give love and only love to each and all, including our enemies. We learn to love by allowing Him to love us first, in the same way an infant learns of love from his parents. When given love, the child responds with love; when we respond to Christ's love, we cannot help but fall ever deeper in love with him and his way of life. In this place we learn to love even the most unlovable, and in so doing make them friends and coworkers in bringing the kingdom of God in manifest victory.[9] Everything truly works together for our and everyone else's good. We are given opportunity upon opportunity to manifest this love, and if we fail to do so, we can rest assured that another opportunity will quickly present itself. What believers have to learn is that everything that comes our way is there for us to properly respond to, and in doing so, redeem the situation or person. No one is beyond redemption.

> Jesus redeems and makes the best uses of even the worst past. He more than forgives us; He turns our liabilities into assets and self-made hells into Heaven. No matter how badly we mess life when we turn the messer and the mess over to Him, He unmesses the messer, and makes an asset of the mess.[10]

Moseley was also of the opinion that when we are in union with Christ, the past does not determine the future—rather, the present reshapes the past. He liked to quote C. S. Lewis's *The Great Divorce* about this, where the Oxford don states that heaven reaches backwards, and as we choose to manifest heaven on earth, our entire existence becomes an adjunct to heaven: even our terrible pasts are merely preludes to our ongoing salvation, and our ongoing salvation part of a divine denouement and predestination.[11]

---

8. Moseley, *Perfect Everything*, 19–20.
9. Moseley, *Perfect Everything*, 19–20.
10. Moseley, *Perfect Everything*, 20.
11. Moseley, *Perfect Everything*, 20.

All of this, of course, is contingent on our place of union in Christ. But as stated before, when we live outside of this conscious, moment-by-moment union, we learn from negative experience that if we are not keen on receiving back the things we give out, we had best give out only the best. Here it must be emphasized again that this union is not something we whip up in our own ability; we cannot shout or otherwise bluster our way into God's presence. This is something we obtain by entering at his feet, in recognition that he is the omnipotent, omnipresent, omniscient, and sovereign God over all things. He has the means for our living and abiding in the vine. To try to do this ourselves, or demand something outside of his will, is to beat our heads against a divine wall. Sooner or later we tire of our foolishness, come out of the wilderness, and live the lives he always intended.

The Holy Spirit is more than aware of the struggles his children engage in when they try, out of their own strength, to live the Life as Love. It is impossible, and Rufus regularly warned against it. It is akin to carrying about a pack of rocks on our backs and then trying to run. We may make what looks like limited progress, but the truth is that we not only are carrying burdens we were not meant to bear, but we are also going the wrong direction.

THE WAY OF THE PEACEMAKER

From the time he was a young man, Rufus Moseley's ministry was that of peacemaker, of seeking to bring those in harsh conflict together in love. Just as Paul tells us that "faith worketh by love," so too does peace. In fact, all of the fruits of the Spirit hinge on the commandment that love be kind, considerate, complaisant, patient, forgiving, and know no jealousy. Without divine love, our ability to be peacemakers is at best managing conflicts and not resolving them.

Moseley taught that it is manifestly obvious that we as believers must likewise live in peace so as to become peacemakers ourselves. While all believers are positionally at peace with God, we cannot live and give out that peace until we have sufficiently yielded to Christ that he can bring it forth in our lives. To the degree that we are in union with Jesus is directly tied to the level of peace we enjoy. If we in the slightest still take secret pleasure when something goes amiss for others, or harbor ill feelings, or wish misfortune on anyone, it is impossible to become a peacemaker. We cannot be a peacemaker, of course, until we love with his love, for the way of Jesus is always that of peace and peacemaking. When we are in that place of union, we cannot help but manifest what we live in and give out.

Moreover, a peacemaker is never disputatious, nor does he complain or grouse about circumstances, regardless of their severity. In this union of peace that works by love, we remain optimistic to God's loving purposes towards us, and resolve in even the worst of times to give out nothing but love. The mystics and saints of old knew this, and the greatest of these were able to thank God for all things in the midst of all manner of evil. Rufus once said, "It would be tragic to have power beyond love, wisdom, and goodness," meaning, of course, that without the loving spirit of Jesus and his way of Life as Love, we would be dangerous wielding power outside of him. At best, we would become selfish and power-hungry; at worst, we would become antichrists.

By further showing oneself to be a friend to all, one is put in the position of seeming impartiality, though in truth we are advocates for the Jesus Way. By not making demands of others, by being willing to go the second mile, not fighting over money or other trivialities, and only confessing one's own shortcomings, true results can be expected. Moseley also spoke periodically of keeping an active spiritual gauge on where he was at any given time. He knew that when the Spirit was particularly upon him, his "spiritual thermometer" was quite high; if he gave in to strife or contention or any other evil that might take him out of the moment-by-moment conscious union, it was low. Like a spiritual weatherman, he was constantly gauging it, wanting and asking for it to be keep perpetually high.

Early on, this caused him some consternation, as he seemed to go in and out of union rather often. He finally came to the realization that it was not by his power, but it was the Holy Spirit who enabled. Thus he was able to weigh each thought, word, and deed in the sense of how it affected his closeness in experience. It taught and teaches all of us the importance of residing in that place all the time. Prayer comes to the fore in this desire to seek after God and stay in union: not as a formula or type, but what it means to live in the actual presence of God. For Moseley had realized that to be in union with Christ was to be praying effectively.

THE EFFICACY OF PRAYER

Moseley defined prayer using Jesus as his measuring stick. "Jesus prayed the prayer of petition, intercession, affirmation, and thanksgiving. He prayed all these kinds of prayer to the very end and taught his disciples to pray them. Christ never did reach the place where He stopped humbling himself before the Father and where he substituted affirmation or realization for petition and intercession."[12] Rufus quickly found that one of the first of his Holy Spirit-guided prayers was for the burning up of everything that diverted the mind from being on God and from Rufus's heart centering on him. I cannot overstate the importance of this revelation at this point in his life: He already had been saved, baptized in the Holy Spirit, and been given great wisdom, but what he saw was that there was still too much of himself in the way.

Too often there is the temptation to see our Christian walk as a series of spiritual events that we experience, things we check off our "to-do" lists, as it were, failing to see that union with Christ is so very much more. We become attached to the idea that yes, we have Christ in our lives, perhaps are Spirit-filled, but then fall into a rut of routine. Rufus's realization of this—something that he saw periodically in his life—was the draw ever forward for him. In point of fact, the Holy Spirit had been directing and informing his prayer life and desires all along. Like most of us, he just did not initially see it.

When Jesus taught his disciples how to pray with the Lord's Prayer, it was with the emphasis that the Holy Spirit is always present, eager, and willing to answer our prayers. He will not, however, give us what we are not ready to receive or in fact do not really need. Prayers that are unredeemed, selfish, and geared toward fulfilling the flesh are, in Moseley's words, "in for hard sledding." As he further relates, "If persistent enough, it succeeds up to a point, but because of competition and conflict with other selfish and unredeemed forces, and most of all because it is in conflict with its own good and the Supreme power of God and goodness, it can have only limited success."[13] Rufus understood that while God wants to give us "the desires of our heart," he first seeks to make himself our chief desire. When in that place, our prayers do get answered because they are in line with the will of God.

Evil must fail for the good of all concerned, and this includes the prayers that any of us may pray on any given occasion. We all must be in union with Christ and living the life of love for our prayers to be truly effective, for our desires to be purified to the point where his desires are ours, and his will is what we seek above all else. It is when we are in that place that we can "ask what we will" and find it answered. I believe I can with accuracy say that Moseley would view some modern prayer in certain portions of American Christianity as something akin to a wishing well, and the Bible reduced to a book of incantations which, if properly confessed and spoken

---

12. Moseley, "How to Pray."
13. Moseley, *Manifest Victory*, 307–8.

aloud, force God to act. Indeed, such an approach would be alien to the saints and mystics across the span of church history.

Guided prayer, according to Moseley, transcends petitioning and other types of communication with the Almighty. Moseley was emphatic about the need to first pray that one's desires and prayers be guided by God. For decades, the Holy Spirit had been trying to get Rufus into this spirit of utter dependence, to guide his prayers and form his desires, but Moseley had been slow in seeing it. After hearing a story of divine multiplication in which a woman was short of funds for a project she believed to be within the will of God, Rufus saw the truth: When faced with a financial shortfall, the woman in question first asked the Holy Spirit to direct her prayers and desires. For Moseley, it was as if a light were turned on, and he saw something so fundamental that he was in awe at how dull he had been not seen it before.[14] The wisdom and necessity of this simple approach was grounded in love and utter sincerity, and was one of many "Kingdom Keys" he was given.

Once, he attended a meeting in a Macon home, where he was asked to lead the group in opening prayer. He asked that they join in making the initial request of the Holy Spirit to guide their desire and prayers. After he had done so, Moseley felt the Holy Spirit move him to inwardly pray to enter into union with Christ to the point where he never came out again. While he had long desired this, he reported that he could not remember ever specifically praying for this until that evening. As he related, "Nothing is more clearly and gloriously his will than for us to enter into him and abide in him forever. If we ask anything according to his will, and everything is according to his will that is best for us and all others; he hears and answers in terms of manifest experience as soon as we are made ready for his answer."[15] As Moseley pointed out, God cannot and will not be forced to do anything that is contrary to his nature and not in the best interests of all.

We must first and without hesitation seek what he wills, what he desires, and be willing to lay down personal concerns in the interest of serving God and others. Jesus is so loving and has so much to give that he is careful to give us nothing that can result in harm to ourselves or to others. If one could have the power of God to do such things, without the corresponding union and love, that person would be a danger to all. Rufus would constantly remind all who would hear that Jesus never did anything that he did not see or hear the Father do or speak. His very life was a prayer. Perhaps this is the core of prayer, worship, or anything else: that our lives become prayers, praise, worship and Love realized in ineffable union with Christ. At

---

14. Moseley, *Manifest Victory*, 201.
15. Moseley, *Manifest Victory*, 180–81.

the bottom of it all, our obedience to the Holy Spirit likewise makes our own lives a living prayer.

Shortly after his baptism in the Holy Spirit in 1910, Moseley found himself increasingly drawn into a hunger for God's best, a desire and flame that burned within him to his dying day. He would not settle for anything less. Through ineffable union with Christ, moment-by-moment conscious walking in Love, he came through what he described as spiritual "marriage, fruit-bearing, and identification" that opened door upon door without his asking. When one is in that place where the Father truly is guiding one's steps, the way is made clear before us. Rufus found in his search for God's best, the best work for him, and the work he could perform better than anyone else because it had been chosen for him, that prayer became increasingly simple and fruitful. When we are in union, our surrendered thoughts are his and become walking instruments of thanksgiving. Too often we think of prayer and praise as something we do rather than something we are when in union with him. We reduce both worthy practices and states of being into a system of works, of seeking to drum up some sort of spiritual fire that he alone can set ablaze.

Moseley recognized that there were hindrances to prayer, and identifying them was simple enough: disobedience and the unbelief it produces. Rufus also mentioned that some are proud of being vocal prayer-givers too, one who is articulate in their prayers. As with anything in our Christian lives, unless we operate out of selflessness and humility, we will find even well-spoken prayers to be shallow and producing little. Again, hindrances to prayer are generally as simple as selfishness, holding unforgiveness, and seeking the honor of men. He has already accomplished our deliverance and only seeks to have us enter into it. But if we insist on playing with our toys, he will, with sadness, allow it. Christ asks for nothing less than the death of the self life, and the cross is the most effective and only means of accomplishing it.

Finally, Rufus spoke of rote prayers that others have offered up from any number of different traditions: Catholic, Protestant, philosophical, or from the cults. They may contain an article of truth in them, but until one comes to the place of Life as Love union with him, they will be limited and produce dull, dry, and ineffective prayers. We need his help at every turn in this, and like all of the Christian life, it hinges on living in and giving out his love. To claim we do not need his help is to deny him. His death becomes ours, his resurrection becomes ours, and his prayers and desires become ours as well. It's what Moseley called the prayer and life of Perfect Everything.[16]

GLENN CLARK AND CAMPS FARTHEST OUT

Sometime in early February, 1942, Rufus Moseley and Glenn Clark (1882-1956) finally met. I say "finally" because Moseley had been aware of Clark as far back as the early 1920s when he read his "The Soul's Sincere Desire" article in the *Atlantic Monthly*.[17] It had appeared as a counterpoint to another article in the same issue descrying the efficacy of prayer.[18] At the time, Clark was a professor of literature and athletic coach at Macalester College in St. Paul, Minnesota. Rufus was impressed with what he read and remembered Clark over the years. In the late 1920s, Moseley read Clark's book-length treatment of the topic, a work which would help catapult the Minnesotan to national fame. In time, Rufus's crossing paths with Glenn Clark would prove to be a watershed moment in the history of the later Charismatic Movement, in that both men were destined to help shape it in a profound way. Like Moseley, Glenn Clark came out of a Mind Science background. By the mid-1940s, he was being lead toward an orthodox Pentecostal understanding of the faith, in no small part as a result of Rufus Moseley. In retrospect, it appears inevitable that the two of these influential men of God should meet, much to the blessing of them both and succeeding generations.

Born the second of six children, Glenn Clark enjoyed a childhood that was not unlike that of Rufus Moseley: idyllic, based on biblical principles, and with loving parents and family members. Raised a Presbyterian and schooled at one of the denomination's schools, Grinnell College in Iowa, he majored in literature. He took his graduate education at Harvard, and there had some of the same professors Moseley had years earlier. Excelling in academics, he was to shine just as brightly in the area of sports. When he joined the Macalester College faculty in St. Paul, Minnesota, also a Presbyterian school at the time, he taught both literature and served as an athletic coach. But it would be his detailed study of prayer and metaphysical schools of thought, coupled with his formation of Camps Farthest Out (CFO) in 1930, for which he was known in those early years. CFO in particular would have a lasting impact that would provide one of the springboards and nurseries for the fledgling Charismatic Movement in the 1960s.

16. Moseley, *Manifest Victory*, 311–13.

17. Clark, "Soul's Sincere Desire," 167–72.

18. Moseley, "Secular and Religious"; De Arteaga, *Agnes Sanford and Her Companions*, 142–43. I would also like to recommend Clark's autobiography, *Man's Reach*.

The first CFO camp was held in 1930 at Lake Koronis, in the central lake region of Minnesota. The basic philosophy of this camp, one that would be repeated as they spread across the United States, was for a time of outdoor recreation, serious study of spiritual matters, and fellowship across denominational lines. In those early days, camp sessions were taught from a decidedly New Thought philosophy and point of view. As word spread of the unique nature of the group, it expanded to include over forty gatherings in different parts of the nation. By 1942, Clark resigned his chair at Macalester to give full time to the organization and perhaps his greatest gift: writing.

It would be Clark's interest in prayer, as typified by *The Soul's Sincere Desire*, that occupied much of his time and efforts. He wrote detailed studies of prayer using the Psalms and Proverbs, and how if properly utilized prayers could be answered in a "scientific" fashion—that is to say, just as there are physical laws governing the natural universe, so too did he believe there were spiritual laws which, if obeyed, would see results. He obtained some of these ideas from any number of New Thought and Christian Science sources, perhaps none more so than Frank Rawson and Walter Lanyon. Clark could well have gone off in the Gnostic interpretation common in New Thought at the time, but was, to the benefit of millions, shown a better way.

The decade of the 1930s was a time when Glenn Clark most reflected New Thought ideas and philosophies. During this period, he had some rather odd views of the blood of Christ and utilized the deceptive language of the Mind Sciences to frame his theology, such as the view that evil in the world was essentially a problem of spiritual ignorance and not a matter of the heart. He likewise taught that sickness and disease could be overcome through prayer and positive thinking. There was a sort of Pollyanna naiveté common in Mind Sciences in this mode of thought, that if people were simply positive and made proper confessions, the world would be transformed. By the late 1930s, Clark was a nationally recognized New Thought proponent and spoke at their conferences and published in their journals. As the 1930s wound down, Clark at least began to investigate a different path that would take him away from those origins to a solidly Pentecostal belief system. Instrumental in this move toward orthodoxy, he met Frank Laubach and Rufus Moseley, both of them beginning their considerable involvement in the CFO movement from that point forward.

It is interesting to note that, while Moseley had himself shed Christian Science belief, he was nonetheless supportive of those, such as Glenn Clark, who were still moving away from it. Pentecostals sometimes harshly criticized Moseley for his involvement with Camps Farthest Out, in part because Clark opened his camps to all seekers, regardless of religious or philosophical background. Because of his willingness to fellowship with those with whom he may have clear theological differences, Rufus was often misunderstood. Some thought he believed and practiced "Mind Science" himself, while the truth of the matter was that he was firmly Pentecostal and sought to guide those willing to listen to that same truth.

FRANK LAUBACH AND THE "TOGETHER" GROUP

Rufus Moseley met Frank Laubach in 1942, the same year that both of them met Glenn Clark. It proved to be portentous for all concerned. Just as Moseley immediately took a liking to Clark, so too did he find in Laubach an individual with whom he shared many similar interests and viewpoints. Laubach was a Princeton University graduate (1909), and thereafter attended and graduated from Union Theological Seminary (1913). He went on to earn his PhD at Columbia University. He is best remembered for his remarkable literacy program which followed a system he invented that made it possible to teach reading skills in virtually any language. "Each one, teach one" became its popular slogan, and resulted in teaching more people to read than any other method. By the time of his death in 1970, his picture method was used in over three hundred languages in 103 countries. This methodology was first formed during his work in the Philippines, and proved to be the venue where he, like Moseley in Georgia, also learned of the work of the Holy Spirit. Although his work in promoting literacy is the best known to the public at large, his intense spirituality acted as a guide for millions more.

Laubach's entry into Camps Farthest Out was important for the same reasons as Moseley. Laubach authored a number of remarkable books about an intimate relationship with the Holy Spirit. *Letters of a Christian Mystic*, *The Game with Minutes*, and *Prayer: the Mightiest Force in the World* are but three truly noteworthy Laubach works. As with Moseley, Laubach came to be a CFO favorite with his gentle approach and deep well of encouragement. He was to later be involved in an advising role to American presidents, and was instrumental in having Moseley, Clark, and others in a committee that met on or near the first of each year in Washington, DC. This group would also include the great Quaker mystic and Haverford College professor Rufus Jones, as well as Episcopal priest, one-time Oxford Group member, and Alcoholics Anonymous pioneer Sam Shoemaker, John Peters of World Neighbors, Elton Trueblood of Earlham College, and for a time Starr Daily. Daily, who had a remarkable transformation from career criminal to a life in Christ, was also among the growing stable of speakers Glenn Clark had gathered. In 1946, this august group published an anthology of their work and view of life entitled *Together*.

The exact date Rufus was asked to join this group is not known with certainty, but is thought to have been in January 1943. Along with Laubach, Stanley Jones invited him to join because he was "a cross-fertilization of all the rest." Moseley made reference to this group each January in his newspaper columns, usually detailing some of their work, who may have been present, and the ongoing purpose of the group. Moseley took great pleasure in attending this group, and enjoyed the friendships and spiritual ties formed there. But before those days would come, Rufus would be actively at work bringing a Pentecostal message to his New Thought friends, and being careful to do so with the greatest of love.

As discussed in an earlier chapter, Moseley had been involved with Christian Science for nearly ten years, between 1900 and early 1910. Over the course of that decade, he had become increasingly uncomfortable with not only the doctrines and emphasis of Christian Science in particular, but of the Mind Sciences in general. As he would periodically do over the years, Moseley described the shortcomings of these efforts. In a short 1923 article entitled "Thought Movements," he observed that the Mind Sciences were "trying to get a point of view that will bring out the best and quickest results." Having been there before, Moseley saw it as a forlorn exercise, at least when compared to the power of the Holy Spirit. Moreover, the Holy Spirit was not a "force" to be manipulated, but rather a Person to be obeyed.

I believe that Rufus Moseley saw in Glenn Clark and Agnes Sanford two honest souls who were seeking God with the light they had when they met. Given that Moseley had trod the same paths these two were on in the 1930s and early 1940s, he had an understanding and compassion for them. He did not reproach them in a condescending manner, but rather from a position of honest appreciation and love for them, and indeed, all who were involved in the different metaphysical schools of thought. Because of his firsthand experience with the Mind Sciences, whether Christian Science, New Thought, and—though not himself ever involved in it—Unity, he realized that they "held to things in thought they wanted to see come to pass rather than having a firm grip on everlasting realities."[19] He knew their highly limited understanding of prayer and the true nature of faith. Nonetheless, Moseley understood Clark as well as Sanford, and was willing in a very unobtrusive and loving manner to show them a better way.

---

19. Moseley, "Thought Movements."

EXPANDING TRAVEL

Beginning in 1940, Rufus Moseley's travels would expand not only in geographic terms, but in the amount of time he was away from Macon. The publication of *Manifest Victory* was certainly part of the reason for this, but he also found himself in demand as a speaker from any number of conferences, denominations, and home groups. Home meetings were especially dear to him, as it allowed for greater ministry and one-on-one contact with those he sought to reach. One finds repeated mention of the same names during this period of these home groups. A few of these were New Thought groups who were seeking information about the New Birth, as well as the baptism of the Holy Spirit. One of these, a Mrs. Carl Gerlach of western New York State, received that baptism of the Holy Spirit, and thereafter became increasingly active in her giving prophetic words. Like Moseley, it led her out of Mind Sciences.

If a guess is to be made of the amount of time Rufus spent on the road in the 1940s, it would be no exaggeration to postulate that he was away from Macon perhaps eighty-five percent of the time. His time was split between denominational churches, house churches, denominational conventions and conferences, and CFO camps, the latter two making up the majority of his time by decade's end. He also took a European tour with a CFO group in 1948, a time when he was beginning to find increased physical trouble in getting around. By 1950, a cane was his constant companion, and shortly thereafter, a wheelchair. His CFO travels from 1945 on seemed to have given him special delight, as it took him all over the continental United States and into Canada. Some of those camps were still more influenced by New Thought than others, such as in California, and his message there was not always as well received as in other parts of the nation. After his death in 1954, CFO camps were thoroughly Pentecostal.

Throughout the 1950s and 1960s, CFO became a spiritual juggernaut that provided one of the few places a Christian could hear about the baptism of the Holy Spirit outside of a Pentecostal church. Many Christians from denominations who did not believe or understand the experience may well have been fearful to go into a Pentecostal house of worship, whereas CFO camps provided a safe and friendly venue where they could ask questions and feel comfortable doing so. Attendees were from across denominational lines, making the CFO a true harbinger of the later Charismatic Movement. It is one of the tragedies of history and memory that such an organization is so little known today, and its early leaders largely forgotten.

MAHATMAS GANDHI

In 1948, Rufus and the world heard most tragic news: Mahatmas Gandhi had been assassinated. To Moseley, Gandhi was the one world leader who seemed to best embody the approach he advocated as "Life as Love" in the sphere of international relations. First standing up against the Japanese, then British colonial rule of the subcontinent, and finally seeking peace between Hindus and Muslims were tasks of titanic proportions, but Gandhi's nonviolent approach nearly won the day. He succeeded against the British, but sadly was unable to bring together his own people, largely over religious differences. Gandhi well understood that this could mean bloodshed on an epic scale and certainly doomed his hope of uniting the vast land on a platform of cooperation and toleration. Moseley called the assassination "the most unfortunate shot fired at any human"[20] and prayed that his successors continue in Gandhi's love way, as well as his admiration for the work of the cross in solving the many problems of the human race. The loss of Gandhi deeply affected Moseley.

As early as 1924, Moseley wrote about Gandhi and expressed admiration for his methods and commitment to peace. After Rufus met Stanley Jones, who had worked in India and personally knew Gandhi (as well as Sundar Singh), Moseley began a limited correspondence with Gandhi in which they briefly expressed hopes for world peace and nonviolence. He once mentioned that he was able to reach his friend with no more than a "M. Gandhi, India" as an address! Rufus found it interesting that, while Gandhi held Christ in such high regard, he had difficulty with Christians. Gandhi once said that if Christians truly lived the life they claimed to follow, they would convert India in a short time. But the truth was that they did not practice what they preached, and to Gandhi, the Christian British Empire's use of violence and cruelty belied the efforts of any missionaries in the land. Sundar Singh, the great Sikh Christian from the Punjab, likewise found Western efforts to convert India to be doomed to failure for their lack of sincerity and their insistence on the adoption of Western ways.

Nonetheless, Moseley did not find in Gandhi an anti-Western bias as such, but he was adamantly opposed to the rampant materialism across the Christian world. Much of this Western materialism, Gandhi rightly saw, resulted in the exploitation of the poor and weak, the establishment of empires, and the denigration of the peoples and nations subjugated. He is said to have once remarked, "We must live simply so others may simply live." Rufus would point out that Gandhi did not practice passive resistance, but

---

20. Moseley, "Thoughts for Today," February 8, 1948.

rather heroic nonviolent resistance. The difference is that the latter gladly suffers for a cause and remains kind and loving. His was a revolution the like of which the world had never seen, and that while the Christian world claimed to have spiritual truth, India found in this humble man one who put the Sermon on the Mount into practice. As Rufus said, "Wherever there are no miracles of love, grace, healing, divine Presence, Power, and Glory, you have formal religion that is cold and has in it little which appeals to the extremely needy."[21]

In a February 1927 article, Moseley stated that it was Gandhi, not the Christian missionaries in India, who provided the best Christ-like example of how to live kingdom principles. The East, particularly the Indian subcontinent, had a long spiritual history when compared to the West. The non-Christian East could easily see through the vapid shallowness of much of the Christian world. Moseley held out the hope that since Christianity itself came out of the East, perhaps at some point a worthy response in the Western world could be found in identification with it. To Gandhi as well as Moseley, much of Western Christianity was in fact tied to materialism, acquisition of wealth, prestige and titles, and bore little similarity to the teachings of the carpenter of Nazareth. In this vein, Moseley believed that the harshest judgment was reserved for those who loudly praised the vine while refusing to enter into union with it. The answer, as he spoke it his whole life, was ineffable union with Christ, where the Life as Love reigned supreme. Nothing less is worthy to those who go by the name of Christ.

A few weeks after Gandhi's assassination, Muriel Lester, a friend and confidant of Gandhi's, visited Macon, where she delivered a public program on the life of the recently deceased leader. Both Lester and Gandhi were kindred souls, Moseley observed, as both came from relative prosperity and instead choose to live lives of simplicity in the interest of the many souls who needed their help. Both could have lived in comfort, but chose to identify themselves with those who needed them most. Moseley sat transfixed during her presentation as she laid out Gandhi's threefold path: Turning enemies into friends through the liberating power of love and good will; the law of truth, which is telling the truth even when those hearing it are upset by it; and honesty, which included keeping anything for oneself when others were in need. This reflects the idea of Tolstoy, who also said, "My crust of bread is not really mine until every other child of God has a crust as good and as large as mine." The kingdom principles Rufus hoped to pass on, he realized, were seen at least in part in Lester and Gandhi.[22]

---

21. Moseley, "Thoughts for Today," October 26, 1952.
22. Moseley, "Thoughts for Today," February 22, 1948.

Shortly after the death of Gandhi, Rufus Moseley was asked to sit for an interview about him on a local Macon radio station. He gladly accepted the invitation and spoke at length about the man he admired so very much. Just before the interview, one of those with Moseley asked if he thought Gandhi knew Jesus. Rufus smiled broadly and said, "I don't know whether he accepted Jesus when he was in India, but I know he has now!"[23] Moseley must have considered it a high honor to discuss Gandhi, his life, and how readily he seemed to operate in portions of the kingdom.

BIRTH OF THE MODERN STATE OF ISRAEL

In 1948, when the modern State of Israel was created, Rufus Moseley expressed the utmost concern for the Jewish and Arab inhabitants of region. He was quite aware that since the 1917 Balfour Declaration many Christians believed it to be a sign that the world was fast approaching the "Last Days," and the 1948 creation of the Jewish state only heightened those views. For decades, Rufus had been engaged in fundraising for all peoples of Palestine, and recognized that there were deep-seated concerns and injustices inflicted upon all parties concerned.

Moseley and his "Together" friends were well aware of the problems facing the new nation, and they discussed options every so often. Frank Laubach in particular was active in this regard, and would eventually submit suggestions to President Truman about the best manner in which to proceed for peace in the post-war world. But for Rufus, it is my suspicion that he saw Middle East strife in a different light than other Evangelicals of the day in that he was interested in seeing both sides come to an agreement for peace. He doubtless recalled Francis of Assisi's experience with Sultan Malik al-Kamil in 1219 in Egypt, and how two radically different people and belief systems came to forge a friendship.

In 1219, Francis of Assisi, along with a Brother Illuminato, had a most remarkable encounter with a Muslim ruler. After first meeting with Brother Elias in Acre, the two travelled to the front lines in the ongoing efforts of Christian rulers to rid the Holy Land of Muslim influence. Into this insanity, Francis—who had always had a streak of the knight in him—was to see firsthand the utter futility of religious wars. He found the Christian crusaders more in need of salvation than their Muslim counterparts. Immediately after a battle against the Muslims, one in which Francis had accurately predicted defeat for the Christian forces (and was called a coward for it), he and Brother Illuminato walked to the Muslim city of Damietta, home of

---

23. McLain, *Resurrection Encounter*, 156.

the Sultan who had defeated invaders.[24] Francis and Illuminato were halted outside of the city by guards who thought them spies and were prepared to behead the two then and there. Francis began to cry aloud "Sultan! Sultan!" whereupon they were taken to see him, Malik-al Kamil of Egypt. A young relative of the great Saladin, al Kamil was a model of courtesy to the two strangers, as much curious as he was puzzled. Malik al-Kamil was trained in philosophy and rhetoric (in the West, we forget that Islam had a high Renaissance period centuries before Europe), and when Francis was given the opportunity to share about Christ and the brotherhood, he politely listened.

Malik al-Kamil was genuinely impressed with Francis: here was a man who actually lived the Christian values he espoused, without a sword or threat of violence. How different was this Umbrian coming in gentleness and love, clothed as a beggar, while the Christian clerics who came with the Crusaders lived in opulence and encouraged Christian soldiers to slaughter the infidels in the name of the Prince of Peace. The three of them talked at some length, perhaps a week, with al-Kamil telling Francis that while his faith was beautiful, he (the Sultan) could not convert. To the utter amazement of the Crusaders and the religious, political, and military leaders accompanying them, Francis and Illuminato were freed unharmed and walked back to the camp bearing the friendship of the Sultan. Here is a case where "Life as Love" wins implacable enemies, where when in the right spirit seemingly impossible odds can and are overcome. Moseley was of the opinion that a similar approach was needed.

At a time when many Christians behave like the Crusaders with their religious justifications to kill, we find in Francis a better way. So, too, did Moseley, who was concerned that Evangelical Christianity's zeal for end-times fulfillment could run roughshod over both Arabs and Jews. It was not unusual for Rufus to hear Christians speak with great zeal about Israel and her place in end-times prophecy, but miss the greater kingdom message of Love. To many Christians in Moseley's day—as well as today—the Palestinians and Arabs were merely chess pieces on the grand eschatological board, and believers often spoke of their destruction with either glee or indifference. What Moseley pointed out and needs to be remembered today is that all of these people are God's children, that there are sizable Christian minorities within the Arab world, and that all of them, whether Jew or Muslim, are loved and cherished by the God who created them.

---

24. Spoto, *Reluctant Saint*, 157–62; Green, *God's Fool*, 203–8.

LIFE AS LOVE IN FULL BLOSSOM

As the 1940s drew to a close and Rufus neared his eighties, he found his body beginning to give out long before his spirit, which to the end burned with love and good will. He also gave in to repeated requests from friends and readers of *Manifest Victory* to write a follow-up work, something that he initially resisted. One is reminded of his days at graduate school at the University of Chicago, when Professor John Dewey asked Rufus to elaborate on some profound point he had made. Moseley's response was, "I have said it." To the end, he disliked elaboration, whether to ideas or spiritual truth. Nonetheless, he gave in, and around 1948 began the process of again dictating the book to trusted friends. This is not to say that Moseley did not publish at all between 1941 and 1949 (when *Perfect Everything* came out). He wrote several short items—booklets, really—on such topics as "The Reverse Side of the Cross," "Spiritual and Physical Rejuvenation," and "Why Jesus?," to name but a few. Some of these would be reproduced in later editions of *Manifest Victory* under the Harper-Collins imprint, as well as the edition Logos put out in the early 1970s. The most recent edition of *Manifest Victory*, available since 2014, carries some of these shorter works. It is, in my opinion, the best version now available.

The very title of his second and last book, *Perfect Everything*, catches the eye if only because of the oddity of it. Moseley joked that it was the best title of any book, at any time. Macalester Park Press of St. Paul, Minnesota was the initial publisher of the manuscript. Macalester Park had become the publishing house for Glenn Clark's Camps Farthest Out, and Clark was delighted to release it. Later editions would be picked up by others (some in England), and this provided Moseley with a greater audience than ever before. Many of the earliest charismatic leaders thus became familiar with Rufus through his written works, and passed on his wisdom to many others. For him and for those blessed with having read it, the book presents a summary of Rufus's ministry and revelation to that point. His health in decline, he dictated the book from a mostly seated position, increasingly in a wheelchair, but nonetheless continued to proclaim the healing message. Nearly every chapter of this remarkable book begins with the word "Perfect" and goes into detail on such topics as Perfect Light, Birth, Baptism, Key and Keys, Praise, Prayer, Guidance, Peacemaker, Health and Healing, Marriage and Rejuvenation, Triumph, and Gift. The few chapters not headed with "Perfect" are "Why Jesus?," an earlier work mentioned above, and "Getting in Union." "Getting in Union" is in fact Moseley's 1946 chapter submission for the anthology of the "Together" group. Unfortunately, *Perfect Everything* is currently out of print.

Perfect Everything is a difficult book to describe to those who have not read it, in part because it deals with revelations given to one man that are once simple and yet profound. Not that these were some sort of deep kingdom secrets that only the privileged few were given—Moseley himself despised such elitism—but because their very simplicity and power are simply not believed. All his life, Rufus proclaimed the availability of kingdom life to all who would but seek, believe, submit, and obey. What is especially enduring to me about *Perfect Everything* is that it continues the spirit of encouragement begun in *Manifest Victory* and brought to fruition. No matter where we are, no matter the place we have gotten ourselves into, the Father ever scans the horizon for the return of his wayward children. *Perfect Everything* is something of a guidebook for that returning prodigal back to the Father. Not just in the sense of salvation or the return of a backslidden believer, but for any who long for a deeper, more intimate walk in Christ.

As the decade of the 1940s waned, and World War II gave way before the ideological struggle between East and West in the Cold War, the nation faced new challenges. For Rufus, the answer was the same: ineffable union with Christ.

7

"I Have Run My Race"

1950—1954

Be praised, my Lord, for our sister, bodily death,
Whom no living man can escape.
Woe to those who die in sin.
Blessed are those who discover Thy holy will
The second death will do them no harm.

—Francis of Assisi

During the early 1950s, the final years of Rufus Moseley's life, there was to be little in the way of his slowing down. He was on the road perhaps as much during this period as any other, speaking at Camps Farthest Out meetings, church gatherings, and house churches, as well as mainline denominational churches across the United States and Canada. This was not without challenge or cost, as his physical condition began to noticeably decline, and during his final years he was in near-constant debilitating pain. Judging from family and physician reports, he suffered from advanced arthritis and an aggressive cancer, a condition which eventually bound him to a wheelchair. Nonetheless, Rufus continued to spread the message of union with Christ, the utter simplicity of the Christian walk, and the "Faith that works by Love" message he received in Macon, Georgia so many years before. Though his physical body began to break down, there were in these final years a spiritual presence about him that was palpable. Those who knew him best often described him as more spirit than body at this time.

Even as his health rapidly declined, his 1950s CFO talks were all over the continental United States and in Canada. Between 1951 and his passing in September 1954, Moseley spoke at CFO camps on several occasions in British Columbia, Oregon, California, Colorado, New York, Arkansas, Texas, Tennessee, Florida, Arizona, Arkansas, and Oklahoma. Over the previous five years, Rufus had become a favorite speaker of attendees, especially with young people. One of the qualities of Rufus's life was his youthfulness, despite his years, and his willingness to speak with, hear, and advise young people who eagerly sought him out. Still, his physical limitations necessitated that he sometimes be carried to a chair in front of his audience and surrounded by support pillows.[1] He was not fated to simply fade away; rather, he went out doing what he loved best. He resisted family efforts for him to return to Georgia during this difficult time, and continued travel and ministry until his death in 1954.

DIET AND THE BELIEVER

One of many areas close to the heart of Rufus Moseley was in the area of proper eating, or a regimented diet. He was a firm believer that many healings Christians sought could be avoided if they had but used common sense in eating well and getting enough exercise. As mentioned in an earlier chapter, Rufus was a sickly child and young adult, especially plagued with stomach and digestive problems. In the early 1890s, when he was a student at the University of Chicago, he went to a noted physician who specialized in these areas. It was here that he was told that he needed to change his eating habits and engage in outdoor activities that would expose him to fresh air and rigorous physical engagement. He did not take that advice at first, but when he encountered a severe case of appendicitis in his early thirties, he took up a lifestyle along the lines of what the physician had suggested.

From approximately 1902 until the end of his life, Rufus Moseley would eat nothing he described as "denatured," or nonorganic foods. His diet was rigorous, even spartan, often involving only a raw Irish potato in the morning, a snack of raisins or grapes, a light lunch of raw vegetables or fruit, and a light evening meal. If he ate at lunchtime, he often would

---

1. Eyewitness account from an email communication from Joyce Carol Tyson Carter, daughter of Tommy Tyson, sometime in June 2014. Joyce is now deceased, but not before giving me great encouragement for this project and insights into the life of her father and Rufus Moseley.

forego the evening meal. This met with concern among his family, who were of the opinion that his diet was unhealthy and nutritionally lacking. For instance, Rufus went from rarely consuming meat of any kind in the first decade of the twentieth century, to total abstinence from it by perhaps 1925. He obtained his protein via raw milk, fresh eggs, and a variety of nuts. A nut grinder was one of his constant traveling companions so he could pulverize pecans, peanuts, walnuts, or whatever was available in the areas he visited. He liked to say that, generally, the cheaper a food item is, the better it is for you.

Rufus believed that being outside as much as possible, getting fresh air and sunshine, are the very tonics of health. Drinking plenty of water and fruit juices were also important to him. For some reason, Moseley considered drinking a quart of room-temperature water a half hour before breakfast to also be beneficial. Rufus was also convinced of the healthy results obtained from eating raw honey three times a day. Exercise was vital as well, and Moseley obtained his through his perpetual walking or working in the family pecan grove. He was also an avid walker well into his sixties and early seventies. When at conferences, such as Mars Hill, he would regularly hike mountain paths. When in a city, he walked great distances if for no other reason than the exercise it provided. In the 1920s and 1930s, Rufus was a regular sight on the highway between Macon and his home in Byron, Georgia as well. It is some eighteen miles between those two communities, and it was not unusual for him to walk part of the way until a friend or stranger offered him a ride.

A confirmed teetotaler, he never consumed alcohol or used tobacco products of any kind. He was of the view that if the body was the temple of the Holy Spirit, the believer needs to take the greatest care of him/herself so as to constantly being able to do his work. He stressed this often over the course of his life, sometimes to the annoyance of his listeners and family. He believed that if a person, including a Christian, engaged in behaviors that were harmful, the onset of disease was a very real possibility. There were common sense rules for taking care of the body, and throughout his life Rufus was amazed at how often those rules were ignored or violated. Christians were, of course, free to pray for healing from the diseases caused by carelessness and destructive habits, but to Moseley it was infinitely better to not engage in activities that promoted illness. This included overeating too. One would not think that a man like Rufus Moseley, who was of diminutive size and stature, would ever have a problem with overeating. The truth is that he loved his time at the table as much as anyone, and admitted that he had to ask God's help in overcoming the temptation to eat more than he needed. Another practice of his that brought him embarrassment and even rebuke was his tendency to wolf down his food. A rather unsightly practice in his youth and middle years, as he aged he does not mention it further.[2]

Joyce Carole Tyson Carter, Tommy Tyson's daughter, told me a story about Moseley's eating habits and his ubiquitous grinder. Upon arrival at Tommy's home, one of the first things he would do was attach the grinder to their steel-topped table, apparently something common in southern kitchens at the time. He would then produce whatever nuts he happened to have brought with him and grind them up. A joyful memory for Joyce, she related how Rufus would then place grapes in a bowl, cover them with raw honey, and top it off with a flood of crushed nuts. It was Joyce's first introduction to the treat, and thereafter would think of Rufus whenever she would eat them. She also shared that Moseley once observed that the foods often thrown away or fed to hogs, such as skins from vegetables and fruits, are the very things people should be consuming because of their high vitamin, mineral, and fiber content.[3] Not all Christians agreed with him on his by-then vegetarian diet, and he was challenged about the issue every so often. Once, when he was speaking on the topic of diet before a church group, he was asked if a Christian could eat pork and still get to heaven. Moseley replied, "Yes, and the more you eat the quicker you will get there!"[4]

Although he often wrote about the need for a healthy diet, his family (and, at the end of his life, his physicians) thought him malnourished. His brother Millard likewise expressed concern about his brother's dietary restrictions and their long-term effect, and shared his concerns with Rufus's physicians in Oklahoma City, where Moseley spent his final days. Despite Moseley's insistence on a strict diet for himself, he did not tell others that they must likewise follow it. He freely shared his views on the topic, but made sure his audiences understood it was something he undertook himself, that he did not have any word about it as being necessary for everyone else. To my knowledge, none of those closest to Rufus felt compelled to do so, though it is possible some at least gave it a try.

PRIVATE SETTINGS AND PUBLIC TALKS

Joyce Carol also added a few other observations of Rufus during his visits, and gave a sense of what he was like in a private setting. Joyce recalled that when Rufus visited, there was something of an aura around him, a spirit that as a child she did not understand but nonetheless found attractive. Though

---

2. Moseley, "His Great, Wonderful Love."
3. Joyce Carole Tyson Carter email to the author, June 2014.
4. Moseley CFO talk, "What Jesus Spoke About on His last Night."

he was soft-spoken, she never had difficulty hearing him. Her recollections about his visits were that, at least around her, he did not seem to engage in "chit-chat," or small talk, but when he did speak it was kindly and profound. It could have been his declining health and the pain he increasingly encountered that made him less talkative, for earlier in life he would actively engage in all manner of conversation. She also recalled late in Rufus's life that he was a frequent guest speaker at her father's Methodist convocations, and how over the course of a week his audiences became smaller. Again, it was a case of not understanding this gentle spiritual giant:

> The first couple of nights the church would be packed to capacity, but by the end of the week only a handful composed the congregation. Undoubtedly only a few had the capacity to accommodate Brother Rufus's presence, his unusual personality . . . and of course his message . . . I marvel how a man with such an impressive [education] pedigree . . . spent most of his time going around the country changing diapers, scrubbing floors, taking care of the infirmed and living out the Love of Jesus at the base of human need and the height of human privilege."[5]

Rufus continued to make it a point to seek out leading figures in the American Christian world, as well as himself being sought out. The young up-and-comers, such as Billy Graham and Oral Roberts, he hoped to meet and encourage. It is not known for certain if he met Mr. Graham, though he apparently made an effort to do so, but he did make contact with Oral Roberts on at least two occasions. As with his time in the early years of the Pentecostal movement when he personally knew many of its leaders, late in life Rufus also sought out those who were in established ministries. This was sometimes done as a result of being moved to do so, as he sometimes had prophetic words to share with them.

ELIM BIBLE INSTITUTE AND LATTER RAIN

I have already shared that Rufus had established friendships with the people at Elim Bible Institute. He continued his visitations with them into early 1950, and in November of that year covered a national Latter Rain conference held in St. Louis as a reporter for the *Macon Telegraph*. By that time, Elim in western New York had become one of the hubs of Latter Rain teachings in the United States. For Rufus, his attending this conference was icing on the cake in that he also was able to visit Elim friends who had been able

---

5. Joyce Carole Tyson Carter email to the author, June 2014.

to make the trip. In his short article of November 19, 1950, he expressed his pleasure in finding "real enthusiasm beyond anything else I have recently witnessed." He even stated that there was great joy expressed when offerings were taken. "A great achievement!" he humorously added.[6]

Judging from his coverage, there was a strong emphasis on mission activity, especially at a time when Soviet and Chinese communism was spreading. "These friends are constantly praising the Lord with uplifted hands!" Moseley noted, and also was impressed with the strong sense of unity he found there. "We have to go from glory to glory," one conference attendee told Rufus, who heartily agreed. Moseley was not in agreement with all of Latter Rain's teachings, but as with his early contacts with CFO, he did not break off fellowship because of it. There is no question that he dearly loved these people, and it prompted him to visit time and again. The feeling was apparently mutual, as his visits were anticipated and joyful. In the period between 1938 and 1941, he even published six articles for the *Elim Pentecostal Herald*, most of these reprints of his *Macon Telegraph* articles. In the early 1970s, soon after I had read *Manifest Victory* for the first time, I met other young people who had either visited or attended Elim Bible school. From them I heard stories they in turn had had related to them about Rufus's visits to Elim in the 1930s and 1940s. The laughter and joy with which they shared reflected, decades later, the blessing Rufus brought with him during his visits there.

WILLIAM BRANHAM

Moseley also met with the controversial faith healer, William Branham, a leading proponent of the new healing revival. Branham has also from time to time been identified with the Latter Rain movement, although insofar as I can tell he did not belong to it. While Branham doubtless knew Latter Rain people (and perhaps influenced some), he did not, to the best of my knowledge, espouse Latter Rain theology. He had come on the scene in the 1930s and was famed for his alleged precise words of knowledge, but mostly for a healing ministry. Although Branham held to some heretical positions, he nonetheless was someone whom Moseley wanted to meet. Rufus had heard news that the faith-healer had come to consider himself "Elijah" for the end times, held a strange "serpent seed"[7] doctrine pertaining to women,

---

6. Moseley, "Thoughts for Today," November 19, 1950.

7. Branham's "serpent seed" doctrine was one of many he held that increasingly put him outside of orthodox Christianity. This doctrine holds that Satan had sexual relations with Eve, producing Cain, and that women thereafter were special instruments of

and denied the Trinity, but the stories both at home and abroad were such that Rufus thought it worth his time to find out for himself.[8] This is one area where Moseley differed from many of his contemporaries: If there were reports of the miraculous, he would look into it to see whether or not the reports were true. He was well aware that from time to time exorbitant claims were made concerning any number of events. Giving false credit to a fraudulent claim was not something that interested him.

Moseley first heard Branham speak in 1948 at a Florida crusade. As was true of most people who witnessed his crusades, Rufus was rather impressed. A few years later during the first week of February 1953, Branham invited Rufus to meet for an interview. Again, Rufus spoke of the humility of the man in their one-on-one encounter, and noted his disregard for material acquisition. He spoke of Branham's claim that an angel had appeared to him and told him he was to be an end-time prophet (the "Elijah" referred to earlier), that his commission was tied to the creation of the new State of Israel in 1948, and that he was to operate in all of the gifts of the Spirit. Rufus, as was often the case, was polite, spoke well of the man he was interviewing, even praised him where he could, but on these controversial claims was silent. He doubtless knew of Branham's increasingly unorthodox beliefs, and whether or not he spoke of them to the healer directly, as he often would, is not recorded.[9]

TOMMY TYSON AND WAYNE MCLAIN

Tommy Tyson and Wayne McLain were young men when first they met Rufus Moseley. Tyson's father, Jack, introduced him to Moseley when Tommy was still in the Coast Guard during World War II, and McLain met Rufus during one of Rufus's many speaking engagements at universities, in this case at Duke. Tommy was immediately impressed with Moseley's childlike faith and took a liking to him. After the war, Tommy would accompany Rufus to some of his speaking engagements at various Camps Farthest Out meetings. In the early 1950s, he went on to Duke University, where he intended to major in English and social work, but due to his interest in Quaker classics on prayer, came to a point where he believed he was called to preach. Because of Glenn Clark's own interest in that topic and impressive publications on prayer, it seemed only a matter of time before these two men met. Tommy later met Oral Roberts in the early 1960s and traveled with

---

the devil for deceiving men, especially ministers of the gospel.
  8. Moseley, "Thoughts for Today," April 15, 1953.
  9. Moseley, "Thoughts for Today," March 8, 1953.

him, in time becoming part of the newly opened Oral Roberts University. In some cases, Tommy would transcribe the talks Rufus would give at CFO and other gatherings. It is likely that it was Tyson who transcribed what would become one of Moseley's best remembered writings, "The Reverse Side of the Cross."

In accompanying Moseley, Tommy met and became close friends with Glenn Clark, who at one early-1950s CFO gathering declared Tyson to be a "rising star" within the movement. This was quite the compliment, given the already-impressive stable of speakers who were regulars in Clark's organization. Tommy pastored at a number of Methodist churches at the same time as his increasing involvement with CFO. Sadly, like his mentor, Tommy Tyson seems to have been forgotten by a considerable part of the charismatic world he so much helped to shape. He stood astride the movement a gentle giant, his influence felt to this day. Of all the many people Rufus met over the years, the author would most have liked to have met Tommy Tyson.[10]

Wayne McLain described meeting Moseley while he was still a student at Duke University. A friend approached him on campus and told him he had to hear this unusual pecan farmer and journalist speak. Told that Moseley had published his autobiography with Harper-Collins, a first-rate publishing house, McLain's interest was piqued, prompting him to see and hear for himself. Often these gatherings were informal affairs, given in a graduate or seminary class setting, followed by a lunch or dinner in which students would ask him questions. Rufus had been attracting interested hearers for some years, especially the young, and McLain was no exception. McLain became friends with Moseley and in time, like Tommy Tyson a few years later, traveled with Moseley and got to know him during the last nine years of Rufus's life.[11]

McLain sometimes grew exasperated with Rufus, finding his "Life as Love" message to be quite impossible in the modern world. He had come from a learning background, by his own admission, where Christianity was lived in a state of somber piety, and some of the theologians he studied had themselves said that the Sermon on the Mount was simply an impossible standard. In Rufus Moseley, he found one who, like Brother Lawrence over three hundred years earlier, declared just the opposite. Worse to McLain, Rufus seemed to be constantly in a good mood, laughing often, encouraging others in the faith, and doing so in a manner that denoted not only joy, but outright fun. It was quite beyond McLain's ken, and he let Rufus know about

---

10. See the website in memory of Tommy Tyson: http://www.tommytyson.org/. This site also contains recorded messages by Tyson.

11. McLain, *Resurrection Encounter*, 5–6.

it. On one occasion, he challenged Moseley over a testimony he gave that he (McLain) had heard before, hadn't understood, and finally got the point. Rufus laughed at this and likened McLain to a duck with his feathers laid back and the water simply rolling off. Now, in McLain's exasperation, the feathers were up and the water got through.[12]

Both of these men were privileged fellow travelers with Rufus and learned from him firsthand, and was to have a huge impact on both their ministries. In one letter in the Moseley family's possession, written after Rufus had died, McLain was described as a brilliant young preacher whose ministry mirrored Moseley's.[13] In truth, the same could be said of both Tommy Tyson and Wayne McLain. Both were friends and spoke together at various and sundry meetings, especially CFO affairs, over the decades following Rufus's passing. In one video that I was privileged to see, recorded sometime in the late 1990s, Tommy and Wayne took turns speaking, often punctuating their talks with things Rufus had said. Camps Farthest Out recordings made after Moseley's death contain references to him wherein speakers who knew him spoke with great love and appreciation.[14]

REMINISCENCES OF A SAINT

In early 1951, Rufus Moseley found himself in a thoughtful mood as he considered all of the wonderful things that had happened to him during his time in and around Macon, Georgia. He recorded these musings in his first newspaper column, published on January 14, 1951. He related how, on December 20, 1950 he showed up at the downtown offices of the *Macon Telegraph*, gathered his mail, and then proceeded on a tour of places that were of special value and remembrance to him. To my knowledge, he never learned to drive an automobile, so an unnamed friend drove him around the city, visiting first one and then another site. As he did so, memories flooded back of the many friends and spiritual experiences he had in the city he loved so well.

He stopped at Coleman Hill Park, a place he often went for prayer in the outdoors earlier in life. Many of the insights he would later share were given to him at this location, a hilltop sanctuary overlooking downtown Macon. One of these precious revelations had to do with union with Christ:

---

12. McLain, *Resurrection Encounter*, 10.

13. Letter from Francis Jordan to Millard Moseley, dated October 15, 1954, in the possession of the Moseley family descendents, used with their kind permission.

14. For an impressive collection of online recordings from CFO's illustrious past, see https://www.cfoclassicslibrary.org/library.

"Union with me is the union of interchange, a union of interaction, and a union of integration."[15] Stopping at the park and gazing over the city, he recalled "some of the most precious things in my whole life experience that have been his gifts to me here, in and about Macon."[16] He also stopped by Rose Hill cemetery, where as a young man he walked during times of quiet reflection. None of the locales were more precious to him than the antebellum mansion where, in 1910, he received the baptism in the Holy Spirit. Of this stop, a two- or three-block walk from Coleman Hill Park, he said:

> As many of these places are in and around Macon, the most holy and precious of all is the old Dannenberg Place at the corner of Georgia and Orange Street, where on the morning of March 22, 1910, the Glorified Jesus, according to his promise in John 14:21–23, manifested himself and quickly breathed or infused himself within very much according to the manner He is reported to have done with the eleven the night after his resurrection. Some time before this and in the same room when I was reading John 14 verse 20, "In that day you shall know at I am in the Father and ye in me and I in you," the Holy Presence overshadowed me.[17]

Built in 1840, this old mansion still stands today, although it is but a shadow of the beauty it once possessed. Whenever I drive by, I like to look up at it, ponder what happened to this remarkable man that night in 1910, and rejoice that I came to know something of Rufus's life and ministry.

Despite periodic difficulties with some family members, Rufus's memories of Byron were fond as well. He recalled how, in 1910, he moved into a two-story wood-frame home with his brother and sister-in-law, of that house burning down in 1930, and the brick home that was built on the same lot and served as his home until his death in 1954. The railroad tracks run in the front of the house, and just down the street, the small depot that serviced Byron still stands. Although his stay with his brother was to have its problems, Rufus deeply loved the family, and was grateful for the privilege of living there. Millard and Effie's daughter, Helen, was apparently one with whom Rufus had a special relationship. Early in her life, he reported her quietly coming into his room from time to time, joining her uncle when he was in prayer.

His driver then took him out to Lakeside near Macon, the scene of many prayer meetings with friends. Two of these from the early days of

15. Moseley, "Thoughts for Today," January 14, 1951.
16. Moseley, "Thoughts for Today," January 14, 1951.
17. Moseley, "Thoughts for Today," January 14, 1951.

street ministry, twin sisters Carro and Suzie Davis, had once lived there, and each time he visited the area after their departure north reminded him of the heady and humorously strange meetings he held with the two of them in downtown Macon. He also recalled that it was at Lakeside where he met "Friend John" for the second time, the man who went on to become Father Divine in New York City years later. The story of his meeting and reintroduction with Friend John was to be the cause of prolonged laughter among his friends, though Rufus also treasured knowing the man, regardless of the spiritual error Divine had fallen into.

Moseley also recalled his many African American friends, attending services at their house meetings and churches, and how deeply he cared for them. He recalled one incident in the early 1930s when an elderly black friend of his, a former slave, stopped him on Cherry Street in Macon and spoke with great joy that Christ saw fit to save him as a child. When things looked down, he told Moseley, he just had to remember that the devil is always voting against him, Christ votes for him, and how he votes decided the election. Moseley was in awe that after an early life in slavery and all the degradation it implies, his friend was always smiling, always willing to encourage and forgive, and always spoke of his Savior to all who would listen.

As they drove down College Street towards Mercer University, he also recalled his time as a professor there, when he began to offer verbal opposition to segregation and the litany of dehumanizing effects it produced. Mercer, as was true of most all Southern institutions of higher education, refused blacks admission. Even more predominant was segregation in restaurants and most any public places, but also in an area Moseley found most objectionable: Christian churches. He remembered an incident in the summer of 1936, when a young black mother and daughter walked along College Street near Washington Park. The little girl stopped and exclaimed her delight at the park's beauty and of her desire to go in and play. The mother told her child the park was "for white children," whereupon the little girl looked up at her mother and said, "Mama, I wish I was a white child!"[18]

Rufus never forgot the incident. It was a story he would tell again and again about the injustices of racial bigotry and hate, and how such things caused emotional scars which, if not healed, could cause dangerous social unrest. Foreseeing the civil rights struggle and our own times, he said, "I hope when minorities have the numbers and influence over whites they do not remember how they were treated; or if they do, they have forgiveness in their hearts. We [whites] have much to be forgiven."[19] He did live long

---

18. Moseley, "For White Children," December 6, 1936.
19. Moseley, "Thoughts for Today," April 20, 1952.

enough to see segregation begin to crack in the 1950s, and two years before he died, Moseley visited a recently desegregated church in Richmond, Virginia:

> When I was at the First Baptist Church in Richmond, Virginia, I attended a meeting where the white and black congregants met together as real brethren. One white brother who was not enjoying the desegregation, said to me, "There are a whole lot of colored people around here!" I replied, "If we are fortunate enough to get to heaven, I feel sure the percentage will be even higher!" He then said, "I'm from the South!" To which I replied, "and I'm from Georgia!"[20]

As his tour in and around Macon continued, Rufus went on to record other thoughts he had that proved to be a fine summary of his experience and life, none more so than his statement about that very day, "again asking for the leading guidance and choosing to make Jesus God with us, and His way of Life as Love not just first, but all and only."[21] He regularly wrote about the importance of gratitude and thanksgiving, but as he waxed nostalgic, his deep love for the city of Macon and vicinity came forth like few other times: "During the whole day I took more time off than usual to remember how kind Macon, Mercer, Lakeside and Byron have been to me. I found nearly everywhere I went memories so precious that the city became precious in a new way. Home after home that I passed recalled what great kindness I had received there."[22]

Even today, as one walks the streets of old Macon, those with a knowledge of Rufus's life and times can find the streets he trod, and if they are still standing, the buildings where meetings he attended took place. Because he often recorded street addresses of gatherings, it is not always difficult to find the locales, although street addresses have changed more than once over the past century. When one walks along College Street, the brick-paved side streets, and sees the wonderful antebellum homes all around, it still conveys a feel for the Macon of well over a century ago. Mercer University, of course, still stands, as does the original building that housed the entirety of the school in the 1890s. The attractive campus, especially in the historic section, fairly drips with a charm that Moseley loved so well. His declining physical condition doubtless helped prompt some of his memories, as it was apparent that he would be leaving his home for good in the not too distant future.

20. Moseley, "Thoughts for Today," April 20, 1952.
21. Moseley, "Thoughts for Today," January 14, 1951.
22. Moseley, "Thoughts for Today," January 14, 1951.

To the end of his life, Rufus Moseley held out hope for the healing of his body, even as it was wracked with pain and greatly limited his ability to simply cross a room. Over the previous thirty years, he had shared the hope for the believer to be translated through rapture. While he readily admitted he knew of no one who had yet experienced it, this didn't prevent him from hoping and asking. He never stopped preaching and teaching healing. Whatever our experiences that come to us through the Holy Spirit, Rufus Moseley was of the opinion that everywhere we go, everyone we meet, and in everything we encounter we should "ultimately and quickly walk as if it were holy ground as we learn to walk gently, kindly, and lovingly." Still, Rufus's final years were not without his witnessing some of the darker things in American life and dealing with them in love. Given some of his public political stands earlier in life, Rufus was to find in the early 1950s that speaking one's mind could get a person targeted as an enemy of the state.

MCCARTHYISM AND THE SECOND RED SCARE

As briefly discussed in an earlier chapter, sometime around 1943 Rufus Moseley and other members of the informal advisory group I simply call "Together" had provided spiritual insight and unofficial advice to the administrations of Franklin Roosevelt, Harry Truman, and Dwight D. Eisenhower; some cabinet members were known to periodically attend, as well. By the early years of the 1950s, however, the specter of McCarthyism, with its false accusations and political witch hunts for Communists in government, had raised its ugly head. Named for the freshman Republican senator from Wisconsin, Joseph McCarthy, accusations of communist leanings and leftist sentiments were enough to get one smeared with the suspicion of "un-American activity" or even treason. Institutions such as the State Department, Department of Defense and its respective branches, newspapers, book publishers, and Hollywood were subject to all manner of vilification. This was a time of blacklisting and firings, of fear and loathing, and Moseley's group was not immune.

Because Rufus Moseley had, in the 1920s and 1930s, advocated some of the social gospel of the time and embraced what he called "Christian communism" or "Christian socialism" to refer to the economic system of the early church as described in the Book of Acts, he was considered suspect. At one point in the 1930s, Rufus had stated,

> The difference between Christian Communism, which is free, voluntary, self-sacrificing, and wholly loving, and that of atheistic, violent, and compulsory taking of other people's goods is

the difference between the Kingdom of Heaven on Earth, and at least a good deal of hell on earth! But the only way to answer false brands of communism is to yield to enough of the spirit and love and practice of Jesus to have the real. How happy it would be for the over-privileged if they could get, or receive enough of heavenly wisdom and heavenly love and happily share with, and serve and be real brothers to the underprivileged.[23]

While not controversial in the 1930s, during the political witch hunts of the McCarthy era, anything and everything was suspect, apparently even the Book of Acts.

Moseley championed government oversight and regulation of big business, especially once the Great Depression took hold, and thought it was nothing short of Christian responsibility for government and the wealthy to help society's poorest and most destitute. He wrote numerous articles lauding corporations and the wealthy who took a socially responsible role, and had harsh words for those who had so much, while so many went without even the necessities of life. In the 1920s and 1930s, socialism was widely popular in the United States, and as a trained political scientist, Rufus understood its possibilities. He was to say that if people were not so afraid of the word "socialism," they could enjoy the best portions of it while avoiding its negative aspects.[24] The horrors of the Soviet Union under Stalin were not yet widely known at the time, but people generally were aware that there was a great difference between a political ideology like communism and an economic system like socialism. By the 1950s, as well as now, communism and socialism were used interchangeably, as if they were one and the same thing. Communist nations might use socialism, but so, too, do some Western democracies.[25]

In the madness of the McCarthy era, no such differentiations were made, and countless people were persecuted at the hands of the Wisconsin senator, his attack dog Roy Cohn, as well as the House Committee on Un-American Activities. Because the "Together" group had advised past administrations who were now accused of treasonous activities, they came under some scrutiny as well. Frank Laubach, who had advised a gentle and generous international role for the United States in the post-war years, was one such person of interest. Some of his ideas were reflected in the Marshall Plan, which had saved western Europe from communism in the post-World War II years. Thankfully nothing much ever came of it, at least as regards

---

23. Moseley, "Increasingly Blessed Days."
24. Moseley, *Manifest Victory*, 157–58.
25. Moseley, "Christian Communism"; Moseley, "God in Industry."

to Moseley. He died before McCarthy was rightly censured for his reckless activities that ruined lives and ended careers. Rufus did briefly write clarifications of what he meant back in the 1930s, but generally did not respond to the accusations. To Moseley, extreme right- or left-wing politics were equally dangerous and to be avoided. The divisiveness and strife so terribly present in the world and among Christians, the spirit of antichrist, prompted Rufus to write:

> It was the same antichrist spirit and weapons that influenced the Puritans at Salem, Massachusetts; it was the same antichrist spirit that used such great names and instruments as Calvin and Luther when they played the role of persecutor in Europe, or of the Catholic Church in the Inquisition in Italy and Spain. I might add that this also includes political inquisitions, holy wars or racial attitudes in our own time, especially when it stems from a desire to strike back at enemies, real or perceived. Just because we have yielded to the enemy and to this harsh, vitriolic, sanctimonious, and condemning spirit does not mean we have to stay there. We can, as we repent and return, enjoy the full fellowship and benefits of the Kingdom.[26]

Despite his views that were sometimes contrary to those around him in the South and conservative Christianity nationwide, Moseley so much exemplified the Life as Love ethic that few cared what his political positions might be. He took the born-again message, along with the great need for the believer to have the baptism in the Holy Spirit, to all denominations. In this regard, he is rightly considered the first charismatic. But while the storm in Washington was blowing about during the early Cold War, Rufus's continued decline in health became a very real, tangible source of concern for his family and friends.

FINAL JOURNEY

On March 9, 1954, Rufus's niece, Frances (brother Winfield's daughter), wrote a letter to the Millard Moseley family in Byron, Georgia about the alarming and rapidly declining health of her visiting uncle. Over the years, Rufus would periodically visit Winfield in his Florida home, but by 1954 his condition so concerned his relatives that they sought help in getting Rufus to return home to Byron. She writes as follows:

---

26. Moseley, *Perfect Everything*, 100.

> Uncle Rufus came on the train last week, and while not confined to the bed, he might as well be. He stays on the couch in the living room and must be waited on hand and foot for everything. He can walk only with the aid of a cane, and then only in great pain in his feet and legs . . . his face is a complete expression of pain . . . it is perfectly awful.[27]

Moseley did report his visit to Tavares, Florida, where his brother Winfield lived, in his newspaper column. He gives no indication whatsoever of his physical condition, nor was he likely to do so. He does report that he planned on attending a service in Tampa Bay in mid-month, followed by travel to CFO camps in Texas and elsewhere, but expressly stated no intention of returning to Georgia anytime soon.[28]

Rufus's refusal to return to Byron, judging from his niece's letter, surely portended to him the end was near. Exactly why he did not return to Byron would be mere speculation on my part, although it is known that he felt compelled to meet privately with Oral Roberts. His niece Frances went on to say that Moseley fully intended to continue to travel, and mentioned possibly visiting Tommy Tyson and family in Goldsboro, North Carolina. His family worried about who would take care of him during his travels, for it was plainly a fact that he could no longer take care of himself. Incredibly, despite his excruciating physical condition, he continued to faithfully write his weekly columns for the *Macon Telegraph*, with that same month of March containing a full month's tally. The writing pace was kept up until his death in September of 1954.

One of Rufus Moseley's Texas friends, knowing of his condition, had been praying for his healing. When he was still in Texas, she prayed for Rufus and later shared a prophetic word to and about him she believed to be from the Holy Spirit:

> Behold how great and glorious a witness for me! Who can doubt my radiance expressed in a body so frail which could have no radiance, no glory, of its own. My servant has accomplished exceeding greatness! This is but for a moment; consider the power of the Light permeating such a body, already more spirit than mortal. The blacker the valley, the greater the glory!
>
> Behold, no wavering in the testing, and for the unhealed to proclaim my healing power. How great a testimony! This is suffering for righteousness sake . . . little do you know how my kingdom has been enlarged because of my servant.

---

27. Letter from Frances Moseley to Martin Moseley, March 9, 1954.
28. Moseley, "Thoughts for Today," March 21, 1954.

Behold the glory of sharing in the suffering of the beloved Son. Can you not see the enabling Spirit? It is not always possible, because of the highest good for all to release from all suffering. Few have known such a ministry in Spirit and in Truth! Can you pray my will to be done in perfect trust? Can you know my grace is sufficient? Can you not give Rufus to me unquestionably?

I have bestowed every gift of the Spirit upon Rufus. He bears the fruit. We have worked hand-in-hand for the kingdom . . . I have proved Rufus willing to suffer all for My sake. Behold Mary at the foot of the Cross! Blessed is he that suffered for you, blessed is Rufus. Greater is he in heaven than on earth. Rejoice that the victory has been won. For the manifestation be not anxious. Great, I say, is his reward. My peace I give unto you, not as the world giveth, give I unto you![29]

By the summer of 1954, even speaking appeared to be increasingly burdensome to Rufus, something which doubtless had to be the source of considerable frustration for him.

Sometime during the week of July 18, Moseley reported that he had a dream where he was attending his own funeral. With him was his friend, E. Stanley Jones. In the dream, the two of them were discussing their life on earth and how all needed to be prepared, to not become sidetracked, or otherwise engage in unworthy thoughts, words, or deeds. Most of all, the two of them discussed the great need in the world for kingdom consciousness, not just among the unsaved, but also for believers who fail to live in the richness of Spirit provided to them.[30] When Rufus reported this dream to Jones, his friend said, "Rufus, I will conduct your funeral." To which Moseley replied, "I'd rather you conducted my resurrection!" Moseley many times over the years stated that Jesus never conducted a funeral, but had the joyous habit of raising the dead instead. He held out hope, even as he was dying, that healing might be his. I have to believe after that dream, however, he had a sense that it was not to be.

As he desired, Rufus Moseley was again able to meet with Oral Roberts when he finally made the painful journey to Oklahoma City during the summer of 1954. When they did meet, Rufus apparently had something of a private nature to share with him. Across the span of his Christian ministry, Moseley had words of knowledge or wisdom, or prophetic words, for many people over the years, some of them in leadership roles in religion and politics, and Roberts was no exception. While that word is not known, Rufus felt strongly enough to request and receive a meeting with the young

---

29. Prophetic word to and about Moseley, *Moseley Private Papers*.
30. Moseley, "Thoughts for Today," July 25, 1954.

evangelist. Shortly thereafter, Rufus Moseley's physical condition worsened to the point where he was hospitalized. Despite seeing the seriousness of his situation, he wrote a positive letter to his brother Millard in Byron, Georgia, dated August 17, 1954. In it, he gives an optimistic report of his condition, his ongoing treatment for arthritis, and the names and addresses of people to contact in Oklahoma City to ascertain his whereabouts. Sadly, neither Millard nor any of his siblings would see Rufus before he died.

For two months prior to his hospitalization and death, Rufus was staying at the home of a "Mrs. Roberts," though it is not known whether or not it was a relative of the evangelist. Three weeks after his passing, a Mrs. Francis Jordan who, along with two unnamed nurses, provided hospice care to Rufus, wrote to Millard about his brother. Rufus's family had understandably been concerned that he was not receiving proper care, fearing that he was not taking the proper medication and of course, suffering inanition as a result of not eating properly. Francis Jordan's letter assured Millard that his brother had received the best of care, and from trained nurses, before being transferred to the hospital. His cancer and arthritis by then causing him excruciating pain, Rufus's friends assured the family that everything possible had been done for him, and that those who provided the care were close, loving friends.[31]

By July of 1954, Rufus was transferred to McBride Hospital in Oklahoma City. Millard Moseley wrote a letter to the attending physician agreeing with the doctor's diagnosis that Rufus had advanced cancer as well as debilitating arthritis. Millard had shown Rufus's attending physician's report to his doctor in Byron, and he had interpreted the situation as very grim. As expected, Rufus was not expected to live very long. It was the beginning of the end, and the Moseley family in Byron prepared themselves for the inevitable.[32] Millard did express frustration with some of Rufus's Oklahoma City friends, thinking that they were unrealistically optimistic about his recovery given the diagnosis. Still, Rufus refused to return to Georgia, and insisted on speaking with other believers, writing his newspaper column, and spending his time in ministry until he could no longer do so. Tommy Tyson, one of Rufus's dearest friends, was aware of the seriousness of the situation when he wrote Moseley in August, offering him a permanent room in his Goldsboro, North Carolina home.

> Brother Rufus, there is nothing that is so demanding on my time for the next two weeks or so. If I can be of any help to you

---

31. Francis Jordan to Millard Moseley, Moseley Family Papers, October 15, 1954.

32. Letter of Millard Moseley to a Dr. Ishmael (Rufus's primary care physician), Moseley Family Papers, July 8, 1954.

whatsoever by coming to Oklahoma City, just have someone call me collect or send a telegram. It will only take me a couple of days or so to drive out and you know it would be a high honor to serve you in any way.[33]

The great love between student and teacher was there to the end, though that end came sooner than Tommy or anyone else not in Oklahoma City expected. Glenn Clark, with whom Moseley had spent so much time at CFO camps around the United States, wrote as well, although the letter did not reach Rufus in time. Still another young friend, Don Bashan, who was to go on to a prominent role in the Charismatic Movement decades later, also stopped by the hospital for a final visit. Rufus was very weak, but nonetheless greeted Bashan and encouraged him in the faith.[34] The flame, which was already burning very low, flickered for only a short time longer.

In his last days and hours, I can only imagine that this great saint of God would again reminisce about the rich life he lived, of the many lives he touched and who touched him, and of the many places that held special memories for him. His yearly summer treks to the mountains of western North Carolina were especially dear to him, and the retreats at Mars Hill College a source of great delight. He likewise cherished his visits to the old Moseley homestead near Elkin, North Carolina, where there were still descendents of the people he so treasured as a child. His thoughts in all likelihood also went to the great Christian leaders of ages past, as well as the revivalists who had so comforted him throughout his life: Francis of Assisi, Charles Finney, Dwight Moody. I wonder if he realized, even then, that he could already be counted in their company?

His precious memories of his time at Peabody, University of Chicago, Harvard University, and Heidelberg University in Germany, and the great minds who taught him and who thought so very highly of him, came before his mind's eye: W. H. Payne, Sam Jones, A. P. Bourland, Wycliffe Rose, Henry Pratt Judson, John Dewey, George Burnham Foster, James H. Tufts, George Herbert Mead, James Breasted, Henry von Horst, George Santayana, William James, and Josiah Royce. This parade of intellectual giants had a profound impact on his life, in much the same way as his own spiritual life benefited others. He doubtless also recalled his time at Mercer, a place that would forever hold a special place in his heart and affections, with great affection. Despite his disagreements with his conservative colleagues there, he loved and cherished the school, and the feeling was reciprocated.

---

33. Letter by Tommy Tyson to Rufus Moseley, August 8, 1954, Moseley Family Papers.

34. Bashan, "Four Faithful Men," 6–7.

But probably the places he most valued were the countless house churches he graced over the course of the previous thirty years, as well as the death cells, prisons, courthouses, and hospitals he frequently visited, and where he brought comfort to the suffering and the words of salvation to those about to go to the death chair.

In his later years, Rufus also came to treasure his time at CFO camps. One of them in particular, Kanuga Lake near Henderson, North Carolina, was his favorite. The Old Inn, with its famed "Porch of Heaven" overlooking the lake, was the scene of many impromptu Moseley teachings and prayer meetings. The beauty of the surroundings, coupled with the high spiritual fellowship, made for a truly memorable visit every time he had the chance. His visits to Lake Kanuga and the one-on-one sharing opportunities perhaps more than anything else provide a microcosm of the life and ministry of Rufus Moseley. Wayne McLain reported continually seeing Moseley surrounded by the spiritually hungry at such venues, asking for advice, prayer, and general guidance. And Rufus would give it, all stemming from that place of union with Christ, what he called the Life as Love or manifest victory, which he perpetually encouraged others to seek, occupy, and abide in as a present, yet eternal possession.[35]

As testifying to his own understanding that his life was nearing its end, someone showed Rufus a copy of a letter written by the great Indian saint, Sadhu Sundar Singh (1889–1929), concerning growing weary in body, and what it was that sustained him:

> Although my body gets very tired, by the grace of God I have great joy and peace, so that I constantly forget the weariness. Thanks and praise to the Lord! Day by day, my body is growing weaker. I do not know when my spirit will leave my body, but this I do know, it will not be long until I go to him. This has been revealed to me that I will not be here in the body when he comes, but from heaven with a great company of holy ones, I am to come back to the world. You may be living on the earth when he comes. He is coming quickly. Then we shall sit as his feet forever, Amen![36]

A great admirer of the Sikh Christian, Moseley thought about his own time of leaving earth, now surely very near.

I like to think that Moseley also considered that other spiritual troubadour whose life was so much like his own. When Francis of Assisi lay dying, he said to those present, "I am not a coward who fears death." Both Moseley and Francis accepted "Sister Death" with joy and perhaps no small

---

35. McLain, *Resurrection Encounter*, 222–23.
36. Moseley, "Thoughts for Today," May 2, 1954.

amount of relief. One of those closest to Francis was a woman strangely called "Brother Jacqueline," and he expressed a desire to see her before he died. Francis was aware that it was impossible for her to make the trip in time before his passing, so when she suddenly appeared at the door she was welcomed with the utmost joy. She told those present that she had heard a Voice tell her to leave immediately, but not before preparing one of Francis few indulgences: almond and honey cakes. Francis also had dictated a letter to his beloved Clare, a short note which spoke of his devotion to her and his encouragement for her to continue to follow Christ. When Francis finally passed, it was at once with great sorrow and joy, for he was surrounded by friends, and they knew he went on to the heavenly Father. One of Moseley's closest associates and young friends, Wayne McLain, like "Brother Jacqueline," showed up in time to see his friend and mentor before he died. When McLain visited Rufus in the hospital, he asked if he was in pain, prompting Moseley to roll over and say, "Wayne, I am so happy I don't know what in the world to do!"[37] Others would have come from afar, but those with whom he was closest over the years did not know the seriousness of his condition, and Moseley himself did not indicate to others that he was near death. He died on September 26, 1954.

A funeral was held for Rufus in Oklahoma City and was attended by many of his friends and those grateful for his life and ministry. A nephew from Byron took a train to Oklahoma and returned with his body for church services and burial. The second funeral service in Byron was attended by only a few friends and family, as well as a few religious leaders. One of these was a young Baptist preacher named Don Van Hoozier, who had just a few years earlier founded High Point Church on Macon's south side. In time, "Brother Don's" church became a center of considerable revivals and outreach. I had the honor of meeting this remarkable man of God during his last nine months on earth. He expressed great admiration for Rufus Moseley, and noted that everyone who knew him felt this way, as well.

In a 2010 letter to a friend who asked Don's memories of Rufus's funeral, he responded with his regrets that he never heard Rufus speak in person, and wanted to attend the farewell of this great servant of God. Thinking it would be packed to standing room only, Van Hoozier was shocked to find the Baptist sanctuary not even half full. He spoke of the service as being dry, the hymns sung lacking conviction; in short, the sort of meeting Rufus himself would have found uncomfortable. However, a young woman arose to sing: Sally Allen, a one-time music professor at Wesleyan College in Macon and one whom Rufus years earlier had helped to gain entrance into

---

37. McLain, *Resurrection Encounter*, 222–23.

the music program at Columbia University. An immensely talented vocalist, Sally sang, unaccompanied, the old nineteenth century spiritual, "Wayfaring Stranger." At that, Don Van Hoozier reported, the Holy Spirit descended on the service. Miss Allen herself stopped and sobbed several times before she could finish the song. At that point, attendees arose unannounced to share stories of what Rufus Moseley's life meant to them. It provided Brother Don the reason for attending, as he summed up the experience with "I left that service a different man and so grateful for having been there and seen the wonderful way God changed that service from death to life. I'll never forget it."[38]

One of Moseley's oldest friends was Dr. William Heard Kilpatrick, the internationally famous educator from Columbia University and collaborator with John Dewey in the twentieth-century reshaping of American public education. He and Rufus met during their Mercer days in the late 1890s, and offered support to each other against Mercer's sometimes difficult conservative mission. While Kilpatrick never embraced Moseley's mysticism or branch of Christian belief, he did recognize in his friend one of the great mystics in the history of the faith, and certainly in the history of the United States. His letter of condolence to Millard Moseley recalled some of their adventures together, as well as Rufus's own unique contribution to Christianity.[39]

The recollections of Rufus and his time of ministry poured in from all over the nation. Some of these stories, such as the one quoted below, were retold decades after his passing:

> Our daughter, Anne, now a teacher in Raleigh, North Carolina, was fascinated by our friend, Rufus Moseley, when he would come for visits to our home. In her childish eyes she could not see the great Christian writer and speaker that he was; she saw only that he loved her and all children.
>
> "You are born of the qualities you habitually give out," Dr. Moseley said. "If you give out hate, you become hateful; if you give out criticism, you become critical. If you give out love, you become lovely. So give out only love." Someone asked him in our congregation, "But Dr. Moseley, suppose they don't return your love?" His answer: "Increase the dose!"[40]

---

38. Letter from Don Van Hoozier to a Doctor Reed, February 20, 2010, used with the kind permission of Don's widow, Charlotte Van Hoozier.

39. Letter from William Heard Kilpatrick to Millard Moseley, Moseley Family Papers, October 1, 1954.

40. Camp, *Ineffable Union*, xxxi.

Another source of great praise for Rufus was the North Carolina Methodist Church, which after his death passed a resolution officially stating:

> In a sense, Rufus Moseley was God's troubadour, a Francis of Assisi to our age. But there was also a courage and conviction that made him a tower of strength and a giant of courage in a time of need. He was a mystic, not in the seclusion of the cloister, but in the marketplace, on the crowded city street, in the little white church by the side of the road and in the stately cathedral. He came always like a ray of nature's beautiful sunlight to tell us of the love of God.[41]

Though largely forgotten by today's charismatics and Pentecostals, Rufus Moseley cut a wide swath across American Christianity in the first half of the twentieth century. He made a detailed study of the world's religions and cults, participated in some of the Mind Science groups, and in the spring of 1910 was baptized in the Holy Spirit. At a time when the Pentecostal movement was debating just how to define itself, and what the Holy Spirit baptism actually meant, Moseley had a front-row seat to all of it and interacted with the movers and shakers, himself providing influence as the years passed. He sparred over the insistence that speaking in tongues was "the" proof of the baptism, rejected Oneness Pentecostalism when it made insistent demands on him, and blazed a path that, while Pentecostal, was uniquely his own.

Rufus Moseley was an intellectual in a movement which earlier in its history had, to a considerable degree, rejected higher education and looked askance at any possessing it; he was a liberal in a world and culture that was rigidly conservative. He was also an active campaigner against Jim Crow laws and segregation at a time when it was written in proverbial stone. An ardent opponent of the death penalty, he felt just as strongly for the need to regulate big business to ensure that workers were not exploited, and boldly asked of materialist America, "How much is enough?" Such positions would sometimes make him an outsider to the conservative world of large portions of American Christianity, perhaps especially so today. But first and foremost, Rufus took the born-again message, along with teaching the great need for the believer to have the baptism in the Holy Spirit, to all denominations and to anyone who would listen.

Rufus Moseley's greatest legacy was in the area of simplifying Christianity to its most basic and powerful component: living in conscious, moment-by-moment union with Christ. He shredded clichés and lived in a place that all believers are encouraged to occupy, where as believers we

---

41. Resolution adopted by the North Carolina Annual Conference of the Methodist Church, E.G. Purcell, Jr., October 30, 1954.

are truly seated in heavenly places in the here and now. Rufus blazed a path, or perhaps more accurately rediscovered Christianity's first-century origins wherein living in the Love of God, giving this Love out to each and all and all of creation, and then receiving back the same from On High multiplied thirty-, sixty-, and a hundredfold was the expectation and reality.

I will grant you that trying to define Rufus Moseley is not an easy task. Yet the greatest revelations given to him (and by that I mean he actively lived and shared them) can be boiled down to "Your only responsibility is the responsibility of staying in union with Christ," and the key to staying in that place of ineffable union is to "leave on the outside everything that keeps you on the outside of union." When we willingly shed those burdens and attitudes, and blissfully surrender to Christ, all of the fruit of the Spirit cannot help but blossom in our lives. What he called the "Life as Love" is simply giving out the love we want and need ourselves, and being kind, humble, gentle, loving, and allowing his character and life to be lived through each of us.

J. Rufus Moseley was buried in the Byron Baptist cemetery, now surrounded by siblings, in-laws, nephews and nieces. His gravesite, as unassuming as the man himself, contains the words that succinctly yet powerfully sum up his life and ministry:

> He found Jesus
> and His way of life as love
> as the Supreme Good.
> He experienced manifest victory.

Few lives have shone as brightly as that of this kindly gentleman from the South; yet like his Savior, he still holds forth a way of life that is not widely lived, not widely understood, yet is the very essence of the kingdom of God. As the mists of eternity parted for him, as if those of Avalon, this troubadour of the Holy Spirit entered the joy of his Lord, and was there greeted by family and friends who had gone on before him. His greatest joy, however, was seeing the King of the universe greet him, the One who had appeared to him in Macon so long ago. He didn't care that he had not achieved the fame and accolades that some nationally known religious leaders had; what he hoped most of all was that his life was pleasing to the One to whom it mattered most. In that regard, he met his goal and finished his race and was, at last, home.

Recommended Reading

Camp, Gregory S. *Ineffable Union with Christ: Living in the Kingdom: Selected Writings of J. Rufus Moseley, 1927–1937.*

De Arteaga, William L. *Agnes Sanford and Her Companions: The Assault on Cessationism and the Coming of the Charismatic Renewal.*

Drummond, Henry. *The Greatest Thing in the World.*

Green, Julien. *God's Fool.*

Julian of Norwich. *Revelations of Divine Love.*

Lawrence, Brother. *The Practice of the Presence of God.*

Moseley, Rufus. *Manifest Victory.*

———. *Perfect Everything.*

Nouwen, Henri. *Spiritual Direction: Wisdom for the Long Walk of Faith.*

Synan, Vinson. *The Holiness-Pentecostal Tradition: Charismatic Movements of the Twentieth Century.*

Talbot, John Michael. *The Way of the Mystics.*

———. *The World is My Cloister: Living from the Hermit Within.*

Tozer, A. W. *Pursuit of God.*

———. *Knowledge of the Holy.*

Voskamp, Ann. *A Thousand Gifts: A Dare to Live Fully Right Where You Are.*

——— *The Broken Way: A Daring Path into the Abundant Life.*

Bibliography

á Kempis, Thomas. *The Imitation of Christ*. Techney, IL: Divine Word, 1954.
Balmer, R. H. *The Encyclopedia of Evangelism*. Louisville: Westminster John Knox, 2002.
Bashan, Don. "Four Faithful Men." *New Wine* 14 (1982)
Blumhofer, Edith. *Aimee Semple McPherson: Everybody's Sister*. Grand Rapids: Eerdmans, 1993.
Bonaventure, Saint. *The Life of St. Francis of Assisi: A Biography of St. Francis of Assisi and Stories of His Followers*. Charlotte: Tan Classics, 2012.
Boon, M. Bowen. *The Candler School of Theology: Sixty Years of Service*. Atlanta: Emory University Press, 1974.
Brooks, Van Wyck. *The Flowering of New England*. New York: Dutton, 1936.
Camp, Gregory S. *Ineffable Union with Christ: Living in the Kingdom: Selected Writings of J. Rufus Moseley, 1870–1954*. Bloomington: Westbow, 2016.
———. *Selling Fear: Conspiracy Theories and End-Times Paranoia*. Grand Rapids: Baker, 1997.
Chesterton, G. K. *Saint Francis of Assisi*. Peabody: Henrickson, 1982.
Clark, Glenn. *A Man's Reach*. St. Paul: Macalester Park, 1977.
———. "The Soul's Sincere Desire." *Atlantic Monthly*.
———. *The Soul's Sincere Desire*. Boston: Little, Brown, 1928.
Clark, Miles. *Glenn Clark: His Life and Teachings*. Nashville: Abingdon, 1998.
The Cloud of Unknowing. London: Penguin Classics, 2001.
De Arteaga, William L. *Agnes Sanford and Her Companions: The Assault on Cessationism and the Coming Charismatic Renewal*. Eugene, OR: Wipf & Stock, 2015.
Dennis, J. A. "The Texas Herald, V. 4, No. 2, February 1953." *The Texas Herald*, February 1953. https://digitalshowcase.oru.edu/txherald/43/.
Emerson, Ralph Waldo. *The Complete Works of Ralph Waldo Emerson, Vol. 11: Miscellanies*. Boston: Houghton Mifflin, 1904.
———. "Forbearance." https://www.poets.org/poetsorg/poem/forbearance.
Etheridge, James. "Aimee and Smith Heard by Small Macon Crowd." *Macon Telegraph*, February 23, 1934.
Graves, Dan. "Mordecai Ham, Outspoken Evangelist." https://www.christianity.com/church/church-history/timeline/1801-1900/mordecai-ham-outspoken-evangelist-11630588.html.
Green, Julian. *God's Fool: The Life and Times of Francis of Assisi*. San Francisco: HarpersSan Francisco, 1987.
Ibsen, Henrik. *Emperor and the Galilean: A World Historical Drama*. Translated by Brian Johnson Lyme. Hanover: Smith & Kraus, 1999.

Jacobsen, Douglas, ed. *A Reader in Pentecostal Theology: Voices from the First Generation*. Bloomington: University of Indiana Press, 2006.

Johnson, Malcom. "Admitted Slayer Is Indicted Here." *Macon Telegraph*, October 15, 1927.

———. "Negro Is Sent to Await Chair." *Macon Telegraph*, June 26, 1928.

———. "Robert Jones Awaits Death in Exalted Mood, He Loves even Executioner." *Macon Telegraph*, May 7, 1928.

———. "Robert Jones Stentenced to Die in Chair December 14." *Macon Telegraph*, May 25, 1927.

———. "Slayer of Short Is Electrocuted." *Macon Telegraph*, June 28, 1928.

———. "Trial of Negro Starts Monday." *Macon Telegraph*, October 25, 1927.

Jones, E. Stanley. *Christ of the Indian Road*. Nashville: Abingdon-Cokesbury, 1970.

"J. Rufus Moseley." *The Mercerian*, Spring 1899.

Julian of Norwich. *Revelations of Divine Love*. Translated by Elizabeth Spearing. Reprint, London: Penguin Classics, 1998.

Kennedy, G. A. Studdert. *The Wicket Gate*. London: Hodder & Stoughton, 1923.

Kilpatrick, William H. "Introduction." In *Perfect Everything*, by J. Rufus Moseley, 9–11. Greensburgh: Manna, 1949.

———. "Foreword." In *Manifest Victory*, by J. Rufus Moseley, xi–xiii. San Paedro, Belize: Eternally Blessed, 2014.

Larson, Edward. *Summer for the Gods: The Scopes Trial and America's Continuing Debate over Science and Religion*. Cambridge: Harvard University Press, 1997.

Lawrence, Brother. *The Practice of the Presence of God*. New Kennsington, PA: Whitaker, 1982.

Lewis, C. S. *God in the Dock: Essays on Theology*. Grand Rapids: Eerdmans, 1970.

Maeterlinck, Maurice. *The Double Garden*. New York: Dodd Mead, 1905.

Manis, Andrew. *Macon Black and White: An Unutterable Separation in the American Century*. Macon: Mercer University Press, 2004.

Marlowe, Phillip. "The Tragical History of Dr. Faustus by Christopher Marlowe." http://www.lem.seed.pr.gov.br/arquivos/File/livrosliteraturaingles/faustus.pdf.

McLain, Wayne. *A Heavenly View: The Best of Rufus Moseley*. St. Paul: Macalester Park, 1993.

———. *A Resurrection Encounter: The Rufus Moseley Story*. St. Paul: Macalester Park, 1997.

McPherson, Aimee Semple. *This and That: The Experiences, Sermons, and Writings of Aimee Semple McPherson*. Charleston: CreateSpace, 2016.

Meloon, Marion. *Ivan Spencer: Willow in the Wind*. Lima, NY: Elim Bible Institute, 1997.

Metaxas, Eric. *Bonhoeffer: Pastor, Martyr, Prophet, Spy*. Nashville: Nelson, 2010.

Middle Georgia Archives, Washington Memorial Library, Macon, Georgia. *J. Rufus Moseley Collection*, 'folder 4, untitled transcript of a 1950 speech, Middle Georgia Archives, Washington Memorial Library, Macon, Georgia.

Moon, Tony. *From Plowboy to Pentecostal Bishop: The Life of J. H. King*. Lexington: Emeth, 2017.

Morris, Robert. *The Blessed Life*. Raleigh: Regal, 2004.

"Moseley Is Preparing New Book." *Macon Telegraph*, June 4, 1939.

Moseley, J. Rufus. "All But Love Fails." *Macon Telegraph*, September 25, 1932.

———. "All Important Needs." *Macon Telegraph*, May 13, 1930.

———. "All Taught of the Lord." *Macon Telegraph*, December 12, 1937.

Bibliography 205

———. "All Things Possible." *Macon Telegraph*, June 15, 1930.
———. "Antidote for Suicide." *Macon Telegraph*, July 14, 1929.
———. "Baptism of Fire." *Macon Telegraph*, December 22, 1928.
———. "Be Entirely Loving." *Macon Telegraph*, April 14, 1935.
———. "The Best That Can Be." *Macon Telegraph*, December 13, 1936.
———. "Bless and Help Everybody." *Macon Telegraph*, June 19, 1932.
———. "Christ and Money." *Macon Telegraph*, November 21, 1937.
———. "Christ Delivers." *Macon Telegraph*, October 8, 1939.
———. "Christ in the Death Cell." *Macon Telegraph*, July 1, 1928.
———. "The Christ of All Roads." *Macon Telegraph*, February 27, 1927.
———. "Christian Communism." *Macon Telegraph*, July 26, 1931.
———. "Christianity and Politics." *Macon Telegraph*, July 29, 1928.
———. "Christmas Every Day." *Macon Telegraph*, December 27, 1931.
———. "A City for God." *Macon Telegraph*, September 20, 1931.
———. "Essentially Heaven on Earth." *Macon Telegraph*, February 9, 1936.
———. "Everything in Christ." *Macon Telegraph*, September 9, 1929.
———. "First in the Kingdom." *Macon Telegraph*, August 20, 1939.
———. "For White Children." *Macon Telegraph*, December 6, 1936.
———. "Give Thanks for Everything." *Macon Telegraph*, May 7, 1935.
———. "Glorify Jesus in Everything." *Macon Telegraph*, May 16, 1938.
———. "Gloriously, Radiantly Happy." *Macon Telegraph*, April 28, 1935.
———. "Glory Hill." *Macon Telegraph*, August 17, 1935.
———. "The Glory of the Cross." *Macon Telegraph*, January 21, 1940.
———. "Go the Second Mile." *Macon Telegraph*, March 10, 1935.
———. "God in Industry." *Macon Telegraph*, April 26, 1931.
———. "Good Things." *Macon Telegraph*, November 28, 1937.
———. "Gospel Then and Now." *Macon Telegraph*, May 19, 1929.
———. "Happy Days in the Kingdom." *Macon Telegraph*, October 4, 1932.
———. "Heavenly Hellfire." *Macon Telegraph*, February 24, 1929.
———. "Hide in Me." *Macon Telegraph*, September 20, 1936.
———. "His Great, Wonderful Love." *Macon Telegraph*, May 7, 1939.
———. "Holy Grail at Home." *Macon Telegraph*, September 10, 1939.
———. "The Holy Kingdom." *Macon Telegraph*, August 26, 1934.
———. "Holy Love." *Macon Telegraph*, March 24, 1935.
———. "How to Pray." *Macon Telegraph*, December 1, 1929.
———. "In Heaven on Earth." *Macon Telegraph*, January 27, 1935.
———. "Increasingly Blessed Days." *Macon Telegraph*, May 24, 1936.
———. "The Jesus Way." *Macon Telegraph*, August 13, 1939.
———. "The Joy of God." *Macon Telegraph*, July 12, 1931.
———. "Joint Heirs with Christ." *Macon Telegraph*, February 24, 1935.
———. "J.R. Moseley Writes Card Explaining His Principles." *Macon Telegraph*, December 27, 1911.
———. "The Judgment of Enlightenment." *Macon Telegraph*, May 21, 1939.
———. "Kingdom at Hand." *Macon Telegraph*, December 17, 1939.
———. "Kingdom of God Emphasis." *Macon Telegraph*, July 31, 1938.
———. "Love Your Enemies." Macon Telegraph, April 7, 1935.
———. *Manifest Victory*. San Paedro, Belize: Eternally Blessed, 2014.
———. "The Mark of the Beast." *Macon Telegraph*, September 10, 1933.
———. "Ministry of the Spirit." *Macon Telegraph*, March 17, 1940.

———. "More About the Oxford Group." *Macon Telegraph*, May 14, 1933.
———. "More Divine Laughter." *Macon Telegraph*, September 16, 1932.
———. "A New Testamentarian, not a Communist." *Macon Telegraph*, May 17, 1936.
———. "Our Divine Appointment." *Macon Telegraph*, November 27, 1937.
———. *Perfect Everything*. Greensburgh: Manna, 1949.
———. "Perpetuating Pentecost." *Macon Telegraph*, June 8, 1930.
———. "The Quest of Quests." *Macon Telegraph*, April 7, 1940.
———. "Refused Admittance to Church; Big Crowd Hears Holy Rollers in Street." *Macon Telegraph*, December 25, 1911.
———. "The Religious Quest." *Macon Telegraph*, November 9, 1930.
———. "The Reverse Side of the Cross." In *A Heavenly View*, by Wayne McLain, 235–52. St. Paul: Macalester Park, 1993.
———. "The Secret of Jesus." *Macon Telegraph*, June 7, 1936.
———. "Secular and Religious." *Macon Telegraph*, August 24, 1924.
———. "Something Brewing." *Macon Telegraph*, August 2, 1936.
———. "The Spirit of Jesus." *Macon Telegraph*, July 17, 1938.
———. "Spiritual Gifts." *Macon Telegraph*, March 19, 1922.
———. "St. Francis of Assisi." *Macon Telegraph*, December 4, 1927.
———. "Stop Strife and Strike." *Macon Telegraph*, September 23, 1934.
———. "Thought Movements." *Macon Telegraph*, January 6, 1923.
———. "Thoughts for Today." *Macon Telegraph*, February 8, 1948.
———. "Thoughts for Today." *Macon Telegraph*, February 22, 1948.
———. "Thoughts for Today." *Macon Telegraph*, November 19, 1950.
———. "Thoughts for Today." *Macon Telegraph*, January 14, 1951.
———. "Thoughts for Today." *Macon Telegraph*, April 20, 1952.
———. "Thoughts for Today." *Macon Telegraph*, October 26, 1952.
———. "Thoughts for Today." *Macon Telegraph*, March 8, 1953.
———. "Thoughts for Today." *Macon Telegraph*, March 21, 1953.
———. "Thoughts for Today." *Macon Telegraph*, April 15, 1953.
———. "Thoughts for Today." *Macon Telegraph*, May 2, 1954.
———. "Thoughts for Today." *Macon Telegraph*, July 25, 1954.
———. "The Triumphant Life." *Macon Telegraph*, August 5, 1934.
———. "Union with Jesus." *Macon Telegraph*, March 31, 1935.
———. "Until Jesus Comes." *Macon Telegraph*, March 15, 1942.
———. "Victory Right Now!" *Macon Telegraph*. December 10, 1939.
———. "Viewpoints on His Religion and the Result of His Quest." *Macon Telegraph*, March 27, 1921.
———. "Walk in Love, Victory, and Glory." *Macon Telegraph*, June 11, 1939.
———. "The Wedding Garment." *Macon Telegraph*, January 12, 1930.
———. "What Jesus Spoke About on His Last Night." https://www.cfoclassicslibrary.org/library?speaker_id=19.
———. "Wholly the Lord's." *Macon Telegraph*, May 10, 1936.
———. "The Wonders of Love." *Macon Telegraph*, November 22, 1936.
———. "Ye are Gods." *Macon Telegraph*, July 14, 1929.
Moseley, Modie Young. *The Search for West Mosely/Moseley and His Descendants*. Abilene: AAA Printing, 1989.
Nouwen, Henri. *Spiritual Direction*. New York: HarperCollins, 2006.
Odo, Murray. *The Journey and the Dream*. Cincinnati: Franciscan Media, 2012.
Parker, Rebecca. *Sadhu Sundar Singh: Called of God*. Lawton, OK: Trumpet, 2013.

Bibliography

Pascal, Blaise. *Pensees*. Reprint, London: Penguin, 1995.
Pickard, Patricia. *The Davis Sisters*. Bangor, ME: Self-published, 2009.
Russell, Arthur James. *For Sinners Only*. London: Hoddar & Stoughton, 1932.
Sabatier, Paul. *The Life of Francis of Assisi*. New York: Scribner & Sons, 1894.
———. *The Road to Assisi: The Essential Biography of St. Francis*. Edited with introduction and annotations by Jon M. Sweeney. Brewster, MA: Paraclete, 2014.
Sanford, Agnes. *Sealed Orders*. Gainesville: Bridge-Logos, 1972.
Segraves, Daniel. *Andrew Urshan: A Theological Biography*. Lexington: Emeth, 2017.
Singh, Sadhu Sundar. *At the Master's Feet*. New York City: Wilder, 2014.
Spoto, Donald. *Reluctant Saint: The Life of Francis of Assisi*. New York: Penguin Compass, 2003.
Stewart, Dennis. "The Real Homer Simpson: Was an Innocent Man Executed for a Crime He Did Not Commit?" *Cleveland (Tennessee) Daily Banner*, September 13, 2017. http://clevelandbanner.com/stories/the-real-homer-simpson,65820.
Sutton, Matthew. *Sister Aimee: the Life of Aimee Semple McPherson*. Wilmington: Mariner, 2014.
Synan, Vinson. *The Century of the Holy Spirit: 100 Years of Pentecostal and Charismatic Renewal: How God Used a Handful of Christians to Spark a Worldwide Movement*. Nashville: Nelson, 2001.
———. *The Holiness-Pentecostal Tradition: Charismatic Movements of the Twentieth Century*. Grand Rapids: Eerdmans, 1997.
Talbot, John Michael. *Simplicity*. Ann Arbor: Charis, 1989.
Thompson, Augustine. *Francis of Assisi: A New Biography*. Ithica: Cornell University Press, 2112.
Thompson, Phyllis. *Sadhu Sundar Singh: A Biography of the Remarkable Indian Disciple of Jesus Christ*. London: Armour, 2005.
Tozer, A. W. *The Christian Book of Mystical Verse*. Reprint, Harrison: Christian, 1964.
———. *The Pursuit of God*. Minneapolis: Bethany, 2013.
Tyson, James L. *The Early Pentecostal Revival: History of Twentieth-century Pentecostals and the Pentecostal Assemblies of the World, 1901–30*. Hazelwood, MO: Word Aflame, 1995.
Vauchez, Andre. *Francis of Assisi: The Life and Afterlife of a Medieval Saint*. New Haven: Yale University Press, 2112.
Voskamp, Ann. *One Thousand Gifts: A Dare to Life Fully Right Where You Are*. Grand Rapids: Zondervan, 2010.
———. *The Way of Abundance: A 60-Day Journey into a Meaningful Life*. Grand Rapids: Zondervan, 2018.
———. *The Way of Brokenness: A Daring Path into the Abundant Life*. Grand Rapids: Zondervan, 2016.
Walters, Kerry. *Perfect Joy: Thirty Days with Francis of Assisi*. Cincinnati: Franciscan Media, 2016.
Warner, Wayne. "Mother Mary Moise of St. Louis: A Pioneer in Pentecostal Social Ministry." *Assemblies of God Heritage* 6.1 (Spring 1985–86) 6–7, 12–14.

Index

ACLU (American Civil Liberties Union), 78, 111
activism, 66–67, 68–93
African Americans, 63, 187. *see also* racism/racial segregation
Aimee Semple McPherson (Blumhofer), 112n35
Ainsworth, William, 76–77
al-Kamil, Malik, 173
Allen, Dr., 53–54
Allen, Sally, 197–98
American Civil Liberties Union (ACLU), 78, 111
American Presbyterian Training College, 59–60
Anderson, William, 69
Angelus Temple, 111–12
Anthony, Walter, 76–77
anti-evolution statutes, 78
anti-Semitism, 147–48, 155. *see also* Jews
Apostles, self-appointed, 150
Atkins, E. C., 84, 86
Azusa Street Pentecostalism, 38–39

Balfour Declaration, 103–4, 173
baptism of the Holy Spirit
 defined, 42
 as a gateway, 55
 of Moseley, 2, 38, 40–41, 43–50, 186, 199
Baptist Mercer University, 78–79
Bascom, Anthony, 77
Bashan, Don, 195

Bellevue Church of God, 112, 113, 115, 117
Beth Israel synagogue, 120
Binkley, Olin T., 142–43
Blackburn Avenue Pentecostal Tabernacle, 112, 113
Blessed Life (Morris), 107n29
Blumhofer, Edith
 Aimee Semple McPherson, 112n35
Bonhoeffer, Dietrich, 147–48
"Book of Ham," 119
Bourland, A. P., 21, 195
Branham, William, 182–83, 182–83n7
Breasted, James, 21, 195
"Brideship," 149
Brooks, Phillip, 108
Brother Illuminato, 173–74
"Brother Jacqueline," 197
Brotherhood Economics (Kagawa), 92
Bryan, William Jennings, 78
Buchman, Frank, 145, 146, 147, 148
Buglo, Frank, 134
Byron Baptist cemetery, 200

Callahan, Patrick Henry, 96–97
Camp, Gregory S.
 Ineffable Union with Christ: Living in the Kingdom, 10, 114–15
Camp Wheeler, 66
Camps Farthest Out (CFO), 106, 166–68, 170, 175, 182, 183, 184, 185, 196
"Canticle of the Creatures" (Francis of Assisi), 6–7
capital punishment, 82–87, 93, 98–99

Carter, Joyce Carol Tyson, 178n1, 180–81
Cashwell, Gaston, 42
Catholic Church
    Coughlin and, 101
    Moseley on, 70
CCC (Civilian Conservation Corps), 95–96
CFO (Camps Farthest Out), 106, 166–68, 170, 175, 182, 183, 184, 185, 196
Chadwick, Samuel, 43, 44
Charismatic Movement, 124, 166, 170, 195
Cherokee, 52
Chicago, University of, 21, 195
China famine, 109
Christ of the Indian Road (Jones), 90–91
Christian Ashram movement, 91
Christian Book of Mystical Verse (Tozer), 4
Christian communism, 189–90
Christian Science
    exploring, 28–33
    Holy Spirit vs., 31–32
    Moseley and, 2, 23, 25–27, 30, 40, 51–52, 169
    Sanford and, 143–44
Christian socialism, 189–90
Christian Taliban, 88
Christianity
    about, 88–90
    American, 199
    Ham on conspiracy against, 119
    Moseley on, 14
circuit walkers, 41–42
Civilian Conservation Corps (CCC), 95–96
Clark, Glenn, 106, 145, 166–68, 169, 175, 183–84, 195
    The Soul's Sincere Desire, 166, 167
Clarke, George Herbert, 59
"Cloud of Unknowing," 55–56
Cohn, Roy, 190
Coleman Hill Park, 185–86
Columbia University, 168
Colwell, Hollis, 144
communism, Christian, 189–90

Copeland, J.B., 61
"cosmic consciousness," 46
Coughlin, Charles, 100–101, 119
courtroom incidents, 134–35
covetousness, 109
creeping socialism, 101
Crockett, 61

Daily, Starr, 168–69
Darrow, Clarence, 78
Darwinism, growing threat of, 111
Davis, Carro, 58–60, 187
Davis, Suzie, 58–60, 187
Day, Sherwood "Sherry," 145–46, 146–47
death penalty, 82–87, 93, 98–99
Dewey, John, 21, 22–23, 175, 195, 198
discernment of spirits, 76–77
dishonesty, 36–37. *see also* honesty
"Dixie Flyer" passenger train, 72–73
Door of Hope, 73–74
Dorothy Phillips Mission, 73–74
Dr. Faustus (Marlow), 127–28
Drummond, Henry
    The Greatest Thing in the World, 21
Dryden, Mr. and Mrs. Ben, 71
Duke University, 183
Dunaway, B. H., 98
Durham, Plato, 63–64
Durham, William, 58

economic justice, Moseley's advocacy of, 93
economics, Moseley's views on, 97–98
Eddy, Mary Baker, 26, 29, 31, 32, 51–52, 67
education, 10, 14–15
Edwards, Harry Stillwell, 33
Eisenhower, Dwight D., 11, 189
Elim Bible Institute, 181–82
Elim Fellowship, 148–50
Elim Pentecostal Herald, 182
Emerson, Ralph Waldo, 16, 22, 65, 126–27, 126n5
Emory University, 63
Emperor and the Galilean (Ibsen), 56
end-times prognostication, from Moseley, 100–104

Episcopal church, 74
Etheridge, James, Jr., 112
Europe, war in, 155–58
existence, four empires of, 55–56
externals of the kingdom, internals of the kingdom *vs.*, 80

faith, of Theresa Moseley, 13
family, 9, 12, 15–16, 56–58
Far East, suffering in the, 109–11
Father Divine. *See* "Friend John"
Finney, Charles, 195
Fire-Baptized Holiness Church, 41–42
Firestone, Harvey, 147
Firestone Tire Company, 147
First Century Christian Fellowship. *see* Oxford Group
First Presbyterian Church, 58, 59
"first-hander," 4
Ford, Henry
    The International Jew, 147
Foster, George Burnham, 21, 195
four empires of existence, 55–56
"Four Practices," 146
"The Four Absolutes," 146
Fox, George, 77
Francis of Assisi
    "Canticle of the Creatures," 6–7
    death of, 196–97
    differences between Moseley and, 7
    encounter with Muslim ruler, 173–74
    influence of, 4–6, 195
    "Lady Poverty," 104
    ministry of, 48
    similarities between Moseley and, 5–7, 107
"Friend John," 61–62, 187

The Game with Minutes (Laubach), 168
Gandhi, Mahatmas, 11, 70, 158, 171–73
Gay, 98–99
geopolitical realities, Moseley on, 94
Georgia, University of, 27
Gerlach, Carl, 170
gifts of the Spirit, 52–54
Glennon, John, 79
"Glory Hill," 137

God in the Dock (Lewis), 89
Good News Church, 115
Graham, Billy, 181
gratitude
    as a gift of Moseley, 54
    primacy of, 128–31
Great Depression, 95–98
The Greatest Thing in the World (Drummond), 21
The Great Divorce (Lewis), 160–61
Grinnell College, 166
guided prayer, 164
Gum Orchard School, 17

Ham, Mordecai Fowler, 118–21
Hammond, George, 145–46
Hampton, Ed, 16–17
Hanna, Judge, 26
happiness, 8–9
Harvard University, 23, 166, 195
Hays, Anthony Garfield, 78
healings, 30–31, 113–14, 141
Heidelberg University, 23, 195
High Point Church, 197–98
Hill, A. P., 75
Hill, Walter B., 27
Himmler, Heinrich, 148
history, of Moseley family, 15–16
Hitler, Adolf, 147, 155, 156
Holiness movement, 38
Holy Spirit
    baptism of the, 2, 38, 40–41, 42, 43–50, 55, 186, 199
    Christian Science *vs.*, 30, 31–32
    Moseley on, 23
honesty, 13, 98–99. *see also* dishonesty
Hoover, Herbert, 88, 119
House Committee on Un-American Activities, 190
Human-Divine, 55

Ibsen, Henrik, 19
    Emperor and the Galilean, 56
"Ineffable Union." *See* Life as Love
Ineffable Union with Christ: Living in the Kingdom (Camp), 10, 114–15
internals of the kingdom, externals of the kingdom *vs.*, 80

The International Jew (Ford), 147
Israel, 104, 173–74
Ivan Spencer: Willow in the Wind (Spencer), 149

Jackson, Stonewall, 75
jailhouse conversions, 83–84
James, William, 25–26, 28, 195
    The Variety of Religious Experience, 23
"Jawhawk Nazis," 101
"Jesus Only" teachings, 60
Jews, 120–21, 147–48, 155
Jim Crow laws, 93, 199
Johnson, Malcolm, 83–84
Johnson, Walter, 109, 139, 140
Jones, E. Stanley, 139, 140, 169, 171, 193
    Christ of the Indian Road, 90–91
Jones, Robert, 83–87
Jones, Sam, 21, 195
Jordan, Francis, 194
joy, 125–27
Judd, Matt, 115
Judd, Suzie Kennedy, 115
Judson, Henry Pratt, 21, 195

Kagawa, Toyokiko, 90, 111
    Brotherhood Economics, 92
    Research in the Psychology of the Poor, 92
Kanuga Lake, 196
Kelly, O., 113–14
Kennedy, G. A. Studdert, 97
Kennedy, Gladys (Perkins), 115–18
Kennedy, William Chester, 115
Keswick convention meetings, 145
"Keys of the Kingdom," 74
Kilpatrick, William Heard, 27, 80, 198
King, Joseph Hillary, 41–43, 45–46, 59
Kingdom response, 94–121
The Kingdom Troubador, 151–52
Kinne, Seeley D., 75, 148, 149
Kobe Theological Seminary, 92
Krystallnacht, the "Night of the Broken Glass," 148

"Lady Poverty" (Francis of Assisi), 104
Lanyon, Walter, 167

Larson, Edward
    Summer for the Gods, 78n21
Latter Rain movement, 75, 149–50, 181–82
Laubach, Frank, 168–69, 173, 190–91
    The Game with Minutes, 168
    Letters of a Christian Mystic, 168
    Prayer: the Mightiest Force in the World, 168
laughter, ministry of, 138–39
League of Nations, 65, 156–57
Lend-Lease, 156
Lester, Muriel, 172
Letters of a Christian Mystic (Laubach), 168
Lewis, C. S.
    God in the Dock, 89
    The Great Divorce, 160–61
Life as Love, 1, 2, 9, 24, 53, 55, 70–71, 102–3, 131, 150, 156, 160–61, 165–66, 171, 174–76, 188, 191, 196, 200
Lloyd George, David, 88
love ethic, 109
Love Mandate, 104
"Love never fails," 64
Love Way, 64
loving judgment, 131–38
lynching, 63

Macalester College, 166, 167
Macalester Park Press, 175
Macon Christian Science forum, 43–44
Macon "debate," 112
Macon Pentecostal Revival (1935), 112–18
Maeterlinck, Maurice, 34
Malone, Dudley F., 78
"Manchild" teachings, 149
Manifest Victory (Moseley), 1, 9, 11, 91, 95, 124, 133, 151, 152–55, 175
"manifest victory." *see* Life as Love
"Manifestation of the Sons of God" doctrine, 149
Marcusson, Isaac, 120
"Mark of the Beast" (Moseley), 101–2
Marlow, Christopher
    Dr. Faustus, 127–28

Index

Mars Hill College, 140–41
Mars Hill conference, 91
Marshall Plan, 158
Martin, Edward, 45
McBride Hospital, 194
McCarthy, Joseph, 189
McCarthyism, 189–91
McClellan, Archibald, 32
McLain, Wayne
    asked for stories about Moseley, 106–7
    interview with Binkley, 143
    on Life as Love, 28
    on Moseley at a retreat, 24
    on Moseley at Kanuga Lake, 196
    on Moseley's appearance, 105–6
    at Moseley's death, 197
    on Moseley's encounter with the Living Jesus, 48
    on Moseley's gifts of discernment, 77
    on Moseley's quest, 38
    relationship with Moseley, 11, 183–85
    A Resurrection Encounter, 3
McPherson, Aimee Semple, 93
Mead, George Herbert, 21, 195
Mencken, H. L., 78, 93, 111–12
Mercer University, 23, 24–27, 187, 188–89, 195–96
mercy, 131–38
midwest ministry, 79–83
Mind Sciences, 2, 166, 167, 169, 199
ministry
    of laughter, 138–39
    midwest, 79–83
    of reconciliation, 75–76
    St. Louis, 72–75
    street, 58–60
Moise, Mary G., 73–74, 80
Moody, Dwight, 195
Morgan, Campbell, 127
Morris, Robert
    Blessed Life, 107n29
Morrow, Bascom, 87
Moselely, Maude, 18
Moseley, Charles
    death of, 159
    education of, 18
    influencers of, 16–17
    relationship with Moseley, 15
Moseley, Effie, 53, 56, 186
Moseley, Frances, 191, 192
Moseley, Helen, 186
Moseley, James "Cubby"
    military career of, 12, 17
    Moseley on honesty of, 13
    youth and family life of, 12–13
Moseley, Joel Rufus
    as an activist, 66–67, 68–93
    baptism in the Holy Spirit of, 2, 38, 40–41, 43–50, 186, 199
    beliefs and teachings of, 3, 11, 22, 71
    birth of, 12
    on capital punishment, 82–87, 93, 98–99
    Carter's observations of, 180–81
    on the Catholic Church, 70
    Christian Science and, 23, 25–27, 30, 40
    Christian walk of, 2–3, 19–20, 40, 54, 105, 106
    on Christianity, 14, 90, 96
    coined the word "Totalist," 22
    as a cotton picker, 57
    death and burial of, 193, 197–98, 200
    declining health of, 31, 177–78, 178n1, 191, 194
    on diet and exercise, 178–80
    on discernment of spirits, 52–54, 76–77, 150, 157
    on "Dixie Flyer" passenger train, 72–73
    early life of, 1–2
    on economics, 93, 97–98
    education of, 10, 14–15, 17–24
    on efficacy of prayer, 162–66
    Elim Fellowship and, 148–50
    on Emerson, 126–27, 126n5
    end-times prognostication of, 100–104
    family of, 9, 12, 15–16, 56–58, 186
    final days of, 191–200
    on four empires of existence, 55–56
    on geopolitical realities, 94

Moseley, Joel Rufus (*continued*)
  on "Glory Hill," 137
  on gratitude, 54, 128–31
  as a guest speaker at churches, 57, 59
  on Ham, 120
  happiness of, 8–9
  on healings, 30–31, 141
  on Holy Spirit, 23
  on Human-Divine, 55
  influencers of, 2–6, 10–11, 16–19, 21–23, 90–92, 126, 181, 195
  on Jews, 120–21, 147–48
  on Jim Crow laws, 93, 199
  "Keys of the Kingdom," 74, 81
  Life as Love, 1, 2, 9, 24, 53, 55, 70–71, 102–3, 131, 150, 156, 160–61, 165–66, 171, 174–76, 188, 191, 196, 200
  on love ethic, 109
  love of nature of, 6–7
  on loving judgment, 131–38
  on making enemies into friends, 133
  Manifest Victory, 1, 9, 11, 91, 95, 124, 133, 151, 152–55, 175
  "Mark of the Beast," 101–2
  at Mars Hill College, 140–41
  on mercy, 131–38
  ministries of, 9, 66, 68–69, 72–76, 79–84, 134
  on misuse of money, 108–9
  New Thought and, 23, 25–26, 30
  on Oneness Pentecostalism, 199
  opposition to America's entry into World War I, 64–66
  Oxford Group and, 145–47
  as a pariah, 60–61
  Peabody College and, 33
  as peacemaker, 75–76, 161–62
  on Pentecostalism, 41–43
  Perfect Everything, 9, 11, 91, 139, 151–76, 175–76
  physical appearance and characteristics of, 3–4, 105–6, 137–38, 179
  on politics, 88–89, 90
  as presidential advisor, 11
  on Protestant and Catholic churches, 70
  The Quest, 1, 124, 152–53
  on racism/racial segregation, 9–10, 82–83, 93, 187–88, 199
  relationship with brother Charles, 15
  relationship with Elim Bible Institute, 181–82
  relationship with McLain, 183–85
  relationship with Poteat, 142–43
  relationship with Urshan, 59–60
  on relief efforts, 95–96
  as a reporter, 66–93
  as a saint, 185–89
  at sanitarium, 53–54
  on Satan, 127–28
  "second blessing," 48
  on self-appointed Apostles and Prophets, 150
  sense of calling for, 20–21
  similarities/differences between Francis of Assisi and, 5–7, 107
  simplicity of, 7–8
  on sins, 36–37, 109, 135–36
  as a social commentator, 66–67
  as a southern troubador in the North, 158–59
  support of separation of church and state by, 88
  as a teacher/professor, 17, 23, 24–27
  on thanksgiving, 54, 128–31
  on tithing, 107–8
  travel of, 82, 170–71
  on union with Christ, 9, 81, 103, 125–26, 160–61, 165
  views on wanting to keep his giving a secret, 69, 106, 114–15, 117–18
  water baptism of, 20
  "Woman in the Wilderness," 50–51
  working in family pecan grove, 57
  writings of, 1, 9, 10, 66–67, 69–70, 87, 124, 182
Moseley, Maude, 87
Moseley, Millard, 18, 53, 56, 180, 186, 191, 194, 198
Moseley, Theresa, 12, 13, 44, 53

Index

Moseley, (James) Winfield, 18, 191, 192
Mulberry Street Methodist Church, 43, 76–77
Munsey, Grace, 152

National Recovery Act (NRA), 95–96, 101
Nazism, 147–48, 155
New Deal programs, 95–96, 100–101
New Thought, 23, 25–26, 30, 167
North Carolina Methodist Church, 199
Nouwen, Henri
    Spiritual Direction, 104–5
NRA (National Recovery Act), 95–96, 101

One Thousand Gifts (Voskamp), 128–29
Oneness, 75
Oneness Pentecostalism, 60, 72, 74, 199
Oral Roberts University, 117, 184
Oxford Group, 145–48, 146n43

Palmer Raids, 69
Park, John, 17
Pascal, Blaise
    Pensees, 89–90
Payne, W. H., 21, 195
Peabody College, 18, 19, 21, 33–34, 195
peach growers, Moseley as an agent for, 67
Pearl Harbor, 156
Penn, W. E., 19–20
Penn-Lewis, Jessie, 145
Pensees (Pascal), 89–90
Pentecostal Rescue Center, 73–74
Pentecostalism
    Azusa Street, 38–39
    Mary Moise and, 74
    Moseley exploring claims of, 41–43
    Oneness, 60, 72, 74, 199
Perfect Everything (Moseley), 9, 11, 91, 139, 151–76, 175–76
"Perfect Everything." *see* Life as Love
Persian Pentecostal Mission, 59–60
Peters, John, 168
Plato, 18–19, 126
politics, 88–90, 101
Pollock, Daniel, 27
"positive affirmations," 28–29

Poteat, Edwin M., 78–79, 140, 141, 142–43, 145–46
prayer, efficacy of, 162–66
Prayer: the Mightiest Force in the World (Laubach), 168
presidential advisor, Moseley as, 11
Princeton University, 168
prison ministry, 9, 83–84. *see also* capital punishment
Prophets, Moseley on self-appointed, 150
Protestant church, 70

Quakerism, 77
The Quest (Moseley), 1, 124, 152–53
Quimby, Phineas, 26

racism/racial segregation, 9–10, 63, 82–83, 93, 187–88, 199
Ragsdale, B. D., 24–25
Rawson, Frank, 167
Red Scare, 189–90
relief efforts, Moseley on, 67, 95–96
religion, combined with politics, 101
reporter, Moseley as a, 68–93
Research in the Psychology of the Poor (Kagawa), 92
resurrection story, 115–18
A Resurrection Encounter (McLain), 3
"The Reverse Side of the Cross," 46, 184
revival services, 19–20
right-wing conspiracy theories, 101
Roberts, Oral, 181, 184, 192, 193–94
Roosevelt, Eleanor, 101
Roosevelt, Franklin, 11, 33, 95–96, 100, 101, 156, 189
Rose, Wycliffe, 21, 33–34, 195
Rose Hill cemetery, 186
Rosenwald, Julius, 119
rote prayers, 165–66
Royce, Josiah, 23, 195
Russell, Bertrand, 93
Russell, Richard, 99
Russia famine, 109

Sage of Concord, 65
Sanford, Agnes, 143–45, 159, 169
    Sealed Orders, 144
Sanford, Ted, 144, 159

Santayana, George, 23, 195
Satan, 127–28
Scopes, John, 78–79
Scopes Monkey Trial, 22, 78–79
Sealed Orders (Sanford), 144
"second blessing," 48
Second Great Awakening, 38
Semple McPherson, Aimee, 111–12, 112n35
    This and That, 112n35
separation of church and state, 88–90
"serpent seed" doctrine, 182–83n7
serpent spirit, 77
Seymour, William, 41
Shoemaker, Sam, 168
Short, Wesley, 83, 86
Silver Shirts, 101
Simpson, Homer, 87
Singh, Sadhu Sundar, 90, 91–92, 171, 196
Sister Aimee (Sutton), 112n35
Smith, Al, 88, 119
Smith, Charles Lee, 111, 112
social commentator, Moseley as a, 66–67
socialism
    Christian, 189–90
    creeping, 101
Socrates, 19
The Soul's Sincere Desire (Clark), 166, 167
speaking in tongues, 41, 42, 47, 52, 114
Spencer, Ivan, 75, 148
    Ivan Spencer: Willow in the Wind, 149
spirit
    discernment of, 76–77
    gifts of the, 52–54
Spiritual Direction (Nouwen), 104–5
spiritual gifts, 150
spiritual leaders, 68–93
spiritual reporters, 69–71
St. Louis ministry, 72–75
Stalin, Joseph, 190
State Prison Farm, 98
Stetson, Augusta, 67
stock market crash, 94
street ministry, 58–60

suicide, Moseley's writings on, 87
Summer for the Gods (Larson), 78n21
Sutton, Matthew
    Sister Aimee, 112n35
Swing, David, 21–22

teacher, Moseley as a, 17
Tennessee Valley Authority (TVA), 95–96
Tennyson, Alfred Lord, 19
thanksgiving
    as a gift of Moseley, 54
    primacy of, 128–31
theology, of Moseley, 11
This and That (Semple McPherson), 112n35
Thoreau, Henry David, 22
tithing, 107–8
"Together" group, 168–69, 190–91
Tokyo Presbyterian College, 92
tongues, speaking in, 41, 42, 47, 52, 114
Tozer, A. W., 132
    Christian Book of Mystical Verse, 4
"Transcendental Club," 25
Transcendentalism, 22
troubadors, of thirteenth century, 6
Trueblood, Elton, 168
Truman, Harry, 11, 173, 189
Tsu Fok, 110
Tufts, James H., 21, 195
TVA (Tennessee Valley Authority), 95–96
Twain, Mark, 138
Tyson, Tommy, 11, 105–6, 178n1, 180, 183–85, 192, 194–95

unemployment, 95
Union Theological Seminary, 168
union with Christ, 160–61
University of Chicago, 21, 195
University of Georgia, 27
Urshan, Andrew D., 58, 59–60

Van Hoozier, Don, 197–98
Vanderbilt University, 18
The Variety of Religious Experience (James), 23
voluntary downward mobility, 104–5

von Horst, Henry, 21, 195
Voskamp, Ann
   One Thousand Gifts, 128–29
   The Way of Abundance, 131
   The Way of Brokenness, 130–31

war
   approach of, 124–50
   atrocities of, 109–11
   in Europe, 155–58
water baptism, 20
The Way of Abundance (Voskamp), 131
The Way of Brokenness (Voskamp), 130–31
Wesley, John, 38
Westminster Presbyterian Church, 21–22

White, Agnes Mary. *see* Sanford, Agnes
Wilson, Woodrow, 65, 66–67, 156–57
Winrod, Gerald, 101
"Woman in the Wilderness," 45–46, 50–51
women preachers, 111–12
Works Progress Administration (WPA), 95–96
World War I, 60–61, 64–66
World War II, 157
WPA (Works Progress Administration), 95–96
writings, of Moseley, 10. *see also specific titles*

xenolalia, 52

www.ingramcontent.com/pod-product-compliance
Lightning Source LLC
Chambersburg PA
CBHW070253230426
43664CB00014B/2514